Recasting Folk in the Himalayas

FOLKLORE STUDIES
IN A MULTICULTURAL
WORLD

The Folklore Studies in a Multicultural World series is a collaborative venture of the University of Illinois Press, the University Press of Mississippi, the University of Wisconsin Press, and the American Folklore Society, made possible by a generous grant from the Andrew W. Mellon Foundation. The series emphasizes the interdisciplinary and international nature of current folklore scholarship, documenting connections between communities and their cultural production. Series volumes highlight aspects of folklore studies such as world folk cultures, folk art and music, foodways, dance, African American and ethnic studies, gender and queer studies, and popular culture.

Recasting Folk in the Himalayas

Indian Music, Media, and Social Mobility

STEFAN FIOL

UNIVERSITY OF
ILLINOIS PRESS
Urbana, Chicago, and Springfield

Publication of this book is supported by grants from the Andrew W. Mellon Foundation, the AMS 75 PAYS Endowment of the American Musicological Society, funded in part by the National Endowment for the Humanities and the Andrew W. Mellon Foundation, and from the L. J. and Mary C. Skaggs Folklore Fund.

Library of Congress Control Number: 2017944757
ISBN 978-0-252-04120-4 (hardcover)
ISBN 978-0-252-08275-7 (paperback)
ISBN 978-0-252-09978-6 (e-book)

For Meera

Contents

Illustrations

Music examples

Acknowledgments

My first visit to the Indian Himalayas in 1999 was a journey to understand the country where my father had been raised and where my grandparents had spent more than fifty years of their lives. I could not have guessed that I would be dedicating much of the next fifteen years of my life to the region, but I am indebted to my grandparents and my father for planting the seeds. I have returned to Uttarakhand for five fieldwork trips that were generously supported by fellowships and grants from the Wenner-Gren Foundation, the Fulbright-Hays Program, the American Institute of Indian Studies, and the University of Cincinnati Faculty Development Council. I also want to acknowledge the American Musicological Society for a generous publication subvention.

This book is the result of the generosity and goodwill of many people in Uttarakhand. First and foremost, my deepest gratitude goes to Dr. Datta Ram Purohit and his family, who opened their home, their library, and their hearts to me as they have to many before and after me. Doctor Purohit's enthusiasm for sharing his encyclopedic knowledge of the region's cultural practices offered me more insights and opportunities than I can count. I thank Gokaran Bamrara for patiently sitting with me day after day and teaching me Garhwali songs and phrases. I am indebted to Sohan Lal, Sukaru Das, Shiv Charan, Bachan Dei, and their families for welcoming me to their villages, for revealing to me the depths of their artistry, and for trusting me and my research agenda. I thank Pritam Bhartwan for his enthusiastic encouragement of my research and for his willingness to blindly follow me on a tour of the American heartland. I am grateful to Narendra Singh Negi for generously sharing his wisdom with me. Among the many people in Delhi who have helped me, very special thanks go to Dhirendra Singh Rawat and his family for inviting my family into their home and spearheading my research efforts in innumerable ways.

My Dehradun-based relatives—Uncle David, Aunt Eleanor, Phil, and Amina—were a constant source of support to me during my time there. I am also grateful to Swami S. Chandra and his organization Shail Kala Sangam for supporting my work and for introducing me to many wonderful artists in the early stages of my research. I also thank Himanshu Ahuja and Shah Alam for their companionship and support on many motorcycle adventures.

Among the many musicians and scholars from Uttarakhand who have encouraged this research and opened up new avenues of inquiry, I want to acknowledge Jeet Singh Negi, Heera Singh Rana, Giriraj, Chandra Singh Rahi, Virendra Negi, Shekhar Pathak, Girish Tiwari ("Girda"), Maheshwar P. Joshi, Govind Chatak, Uma Shankar ("Satish"), Ratan Singh ("Jaunsari"), Meena Rana, Sanjay Kumola, Kalpana Chauhan, Anand Lal Shah, H. Soni ("Pumpum"), Anuradha Nirala, Mehindra Singh Chauhan, Sangeeta Daundiyal, Suwarn Rawat, Deewan Kandwal, Bhagwat Upreti, Himanshu Joshi, Subash Pande, Chandan Basora, Mayur Nichani, Vikas Rajput, and Dinesh Rai. All of these individuals shared insights about music and social identity in Uttarakhand with candor and openness; I have attempted to accurately represent their perspectives in these pages.

I am grateful for the unconditional support of many friends and colleagues—and their abstaining from rolling their eyes each time I told them how close I was to finishing this book. I especially thank Tony Perman, Carol Babiracki, and an anonymous reviewer for reading this manuscript and offering feedback. Many friends and colleagues invited me to colloquia and symposia and contributed to the ideas that appear in these pages; in particular, I acknowledge Andrew Alter, Fred Smith, Philip Lutgendorf, Anup Kumar, William "Bo" Sax, Karin Polit, Luke Whitmore, Kaley Mason, Anna Schultz, Jayson Beaster-Jones, Marty Hatch, Daniel Neuman, Shubha Chaudhury, Anna Morcom, Noe Dinnerstein, Ratnakar Tripathy, Aditi Deo, Florence Nowak, Jennifer Fraser, Katherine Schofield, Zoe Sherinian, Denise Nuttall, Dave McDonald, Eduardo Herrera, Fernando Rios, Shailaja Paik, Laura Jenkins, and Barbara Ramusack. I am grateful to Laurie Matheson, Julie Laut, Jane Zanichkowsky, and the entire editorial staff at the University of Illinois Press for their efforts to improve this book. My colleagues at the University of Cincinnati, the University of Rochester, and the University of Illinois at Urbana-Champaign have been a constant source of encouragement. Ellen Koskoff, Carol Babiracki, Charles Capwell, Daniel Neuman, and

Thomas Turino are enduring mentors who continue to shape my thinking. My mother, Marlena Fiol, was a pivotal reader and thought provocateur in the writing phase of this project. My grandfather, Bruno Nettl, introduced the field of ethnomusicology to me at an early age and cultivated my interest in things worldly and musical. In him I have a model for a successful academic and, more important, for a socially engaged, well-loved, and sensational human being. Finally, I offer my eternal gratitude to Meera, my companion through all of the ethereal highs and lows of living in Uttarakhand. Her support carried me through the fieldwork and writing stages, and her insights and intuition shaped and refined all of the ideas in the pages that follow.

Recasting Folk in the Himalayas

Introduction

In April 2005 I attended the video shoot for the singer Mehindra Chauhan's new album *Meenu Ai* in his village in the northwest corner of the Garhwal Himalayas. A production team of about fifteen individuals, including the producer, director, drivers, makeup artists, soundmen, lighting assistants, actors, and cameramen, assembled at Chauhan's home after a seven-hour drive up the Yamuna River valley from the regional capital city of Dehradun. At about ten o'clock at night the crew set up a generator to power their spotlights while the director enlisted the help of the village headman to bring local residents out of their homes and into the courtyard. As several women approached, the director advised them to return home, clean themselves up, and put on their finest festival clothes because he deemed them unsuitable to appear on camera as they were.

After long delays, approximately fifty men and women assembled in a circle in the courtyard. The director coached them on how to synchronize their stepping patterns with the barely audible playback of the cassette recording (commercially released several weeks earlier) through a small sound system (figure 0.1). The tempo of the audio recording was unnaturally slow for this type of dance-song (locally performed at festivals and referred to as *tandi*), and the dancers found it difficult to move together. In order to rectify this, they began singing along with Chauhan's recorded voice, but this made it difficult to hear the playback and gradually increased the tempo, to the director's consternation. Chauhan, meanwhile, was reminding the hereditary dhol drummers to mime the action of drumming without actually striking the drumheads because doing so again drowned out the playback device, making it difficult for the dancers to follow the correct tempo.

Watching this bizarre scene from a distance, I asked an elderly woman seated on the edge of the courtyard if she was excited to have her village represented on this commercial album. To my surprise, she replied that a number of video albums had previously been filmed in this village and that it was, in fact, becoming a nuisance because the production teams made demands without giving anything back.[1]

This anecdote raises a number of questions that I explore throughout this book. What are the motivations for and consequences of manufacturing folk culture and folk music (*lok sanskriti* and *lok geet* in North Indian languages) in this way? How are these terms used and understood by people living inside and outside Uttarakhand? How are the ideas and sounds of folk music mediated, on one hand, by market capitalism, the state, and the music industry, and on the other, by indigenous knowledge systems and values? Who is entitled to create folk music, and how do caste, class, gender, and other categories of social identity delimit who can and cannot be a "folk artist"? How and why have the meanings of *folk* or *lok* evolved in response to the social and political circumstances of late colonialism, cultural nationalism, intrastate regionalism, and neoliberalism? Finally, why has the idea of folk music come to simultaneously signify the exalted, timeless, and celebrated

Fig. 0.1. On-site production of Mehindra Chauhan's VCD *Meenu Ai*, 2005 (courtesy S. Fiol)

aspects of national, regional, or ethnolinguistic heritage and the backward, primitive, and shameful aspects of cultural practice?

As a study of musical life in the regional state of Uttarakhand in the Indian Himalayas, this book examines the production of folk music by the use of academic texts, cultural performances, and vernacular commercial recordings.[2] In contrast to existing ethnographies of folk music in South Asia, I do not approach folk music as a stable analytical category or as one end of a continuum of musical life opposite classical music or popular music; rather, I understand folk music to be a multidimensional concept that has been discursively produced and connected to a wide-ranging and evolving set of expressive practices.

Blending historical and ethnographic approaches, this book traces the influence of colonialist, nationalist, and regionalist ideologies on current conceptualizations of folk music and on various approaches to "folklorizing" musical practice. Although many valences of the concept of folk music in Uttarakhand—such as village provenance, anonymous composition, historical continuity, and communal variation—are consistent with its meanings elsewhere in India and beyond, the folk concept has also acquired a distinctive set of associations in the central Himalayas owing to the region's distinctive caste and gender relations, regionalist political dynamics, social migratory patterns, and sacred landscape.

Building on recent ethnographies,[3] I understand folklorization as the recontextualized composition or performance of local artistic practices as a means to express cultural identity to oneself and to others. I follow Rios (2012) and Turino (2000) in thinking about folklorization as a process driven by cosmopolitan values for refining and improving local traditions. Throughout this book I examine folklorization as a dual process of modernist reform involving *turning dying folk into living folk*, that is, seeking to revive particular traditions that are imagined to be on the verge of extinction, and *separating the folk sound from the folk performer's body*, that is, identifying folkness as an intrinsic but detachable quality of particular bodies and musical elements. I trace these two intertwined processes across a variety of temporal settings, showing how and why folkness has been indexically connected to notions of historical and cultural loss, as well as to the bodies of subaltern peoples.

Recasting Folk in the Himalayas explores a paradox at the heart of the folk concept whereby it can signify either a universal quality (or stage) of humanity or a marker of alterity and subordination. At what point does the connotation of *folk* shift from a descriptive feature of cultural expression that is attributed more or less equally to all members of society to something that is the birthright of specific communities of people? Who assumes the privilege (or curse) of being called a folk artist, and how does the body lay claim to folk identity in particular ways? The inverse questions are equally important: After the concept of folk has been coupled with specific (kinds of) bodies, how does it become decoupled from those bodies? How are understandings of the folk artist as a specific other (who they are) converted into understandings of a generic folk heritage accessible to anyone in the society (who we are), or vice versa?

Karl Miller's study of race and musical performance in the United States explores similar lines of inquiry (2010). Miller illuminates a transition from what he calls the "minstrelsy paradigm" of the late nineteenth and early twentieth centuries, when folk authenticity was performative (for example, whites could employ and imitate black forms), to the "folklore paradigm" of the mid-twentieth century, when folk authenticity became part of an essentializing discourse through which racialized bodies were attached to distinct white and black performance styles and genres. I am describing a similar discursive shift in the Indian context, but in reverse order and with caste substituting for race. In early-twentieth-century India, low-caste, rural hereditary artisans were often identified as "the folk" in a pejorative sense, particularly in contrast to the colonial (Indian and non-Indian) elite. As the folklore industry grew into an important arm of cultural nationalism in the mid-twentieth century, however, upper-caste and upper-class individuals began to appropriate folk forms and the title of folk artist. By the late twentieth century, neoliberal market forces encouraged the widespread diffusion of the folk brand across India and the diaspora, and yet only those with adequate economic means could benefit from it.

In the central Himalayas, as in many other parts of South Asia, the development of music and dance as a specialized professional activity has historically taken place within a relatively small group of low-status hereditary communities locally referred to as *Shilpkar* (artisans).[4] In recent decades, Shilpkar performers have been directly implicated in the efforts of high-status artists and politicians to appropriate or reform their embodied knowledge and practices. Although many Shilpkar performers continue to fulfill traditional obligations through music and dance, all have been affected by strategies of reform. As a new breed of high-status folk artists has emerged, some Shilpkar performers have willingly or unwillingly stopped performing, while others continue to assert the relevance of their hereditary knowledge and social occupation.

Reformist efforts carried out in the name of folk have also impacted the ways Shilpkar musicians self-identify. During my first visits to Garhwali villages in 1999 and 2003, Shilpkar musicians almost always identified themselves by their personal names or occupational caste (*jati*) names; the term *folk artist* (*lok kalakar*) had little meaning or relevance to their lives. In most places in Uttarakhand, if one were to ask to meet a lok kalakar, one would likely be directed to the home of a high-status musician, frequently someone who has recorded an album in the city.[5] Over the course of the past decade, however, a range of Shilpkar performers including bards, female wedding singers, drummers, and healers have appropriated the title of folk artist. For some, this title is a point of pride and accomplishment; it also serves as a marker of status and style, conveying a sense of authenticity and rootedness in village-based traditions. Yet the decision to use this title or to label one's performance as tradition or heritage—ideas that Michael Herzfeld describes as part of a "global hierarchy of value" (2004: 25)—can also prevent them from being viewed as fully modern. Academics, NGOs, and such state agencies as Sangeet Natak Akademi only designate someone a folk artist if he or she is understood to be maintaining a "vanishing folk art"; following this, they may be granted a pension or, in rare cases, free accommodation in government housing (Naithani 2006a). The label "folk" is thus a double-edged sword: although it has become a potent marketing genre and a marker of status, it also signifies a lack of relevance in contemporary India, and it has become a lifeline to the shrinking number of patronage opportunities for Shilpkar performers.

This book focuses on a variety of individuals from the central Himalayas who have been instrumental in producing folk music as a discursive idea and a set of expressive practices in strikingly different historical and cultural settings. Juxtaposing performance contexts in Himalayan villages with urban recording studios and staged performances in Delhi, I demonstrate how particular discursive and musical practices have emerged within and between sites of contrasting values and expectations. I allow the varied perspectives of the largely upper-caste, upper-class male reformers, who have spearheaded processes of folklorization, to resonate with and collide against the diverse perspectives of women and hereditary musicians who have been most directly impacted by these processes, even as they may have contributed to them. In this way, I tread a middle ground between a post-structural critique of folk discourse in India and an assessment of the ways this discourse has generated a space of recognition and agency for many musicians at the margins of society. This theoretical position is in dialogue with some of the most insightful recent scholarship to emerge from postcolonial, feminist, and subaltern studies (Chakrabarty 2000; Mahmood 2000; Nicholls 2000; A. Rao 2009).

Although this ethnography focuses on only one region, it illuminates issues facing vernacular recording artists across the subcontinent. Most of the chapters in the book focus on individuals who have participated in the production of "Uttarakhandi *geet*," a marketing label for songs in the Garhwali, Kumaoni, and Jaunsari languages that are commercially produced in urban centers (primarily Delhi). The majority of mass-mediated music in South Asia is recorded in vernacular languages and is marketed to and consumed by people belonging to a specific region. Hindi film music (colloquially known as Bollywood) has near nationwide diffusion because Hindi serves as a lingua franca for much of the subcontinent; nonetheless, in almost every region of India popular music in the vernacular outsells Hindi film music, international pop, and Indi-pop. I have met few non-Uttarakhandis who listen to Uttarakhandi geet with any regularity, yet throughout Uttarakhand this genre easily outsells any other, including Hindi film music.

Hindi film music and vernacular music cannot be understood in isolation, however, because their histories of style have been mutual and symbiotic. For nearly a century, the interaction of artists from various parts of South Asia, many of whom circulated freely between Mumbai's film music industry and smaller-scale vernacular industries, has resulted in a distilled pop-folk aesthetic that can be heard on Hindi film soundtracks as well as vernacular recordings through much of the subcontinent (Fiol 2016). Aspects of this pervasive aesthetic include the preference for high vocal range, free-rhythm cadenzas on the bamboo flute (*bansuri*), pentatonic modes, rhythmical cycles in six (*dadra* and *khemta*) or eight (*kaherva*), binary melodic phrases (*asthai-antara*) separated by instrumental breaks, and a predictable core instrumentation consisting of dholak, tabla, guitar, mandolin, octopad, flute, and electronic samples and vocals, supplemented by one or two indigenous instruments. Of course, each vernacular musical style also has its own diverse range of local (folk) elements that make it uniquely meaningful to cultural insiders; I discuss these aspects of Uttarakhandi geet in the pages that follow.

Recordings of Uttarakhandi geet have circulated via gramophone recordings and radio broadcasts since the 1940s, via regional films and cassette recordings since the 1980s, via television programs and video compact disc recordings since 2000, and via mobile phone downloads and online sharing and streaming sites since 2007. Musical production has been concentrated in Delhi and to a lesser extent in the regional capital, Dehradun. The music is consumed wherever vernacular speakers have settled: in Himalayan villages and towns, in the urban plains of North India, and in the international diaspora (in particular, Oman, the United Arab Emirates, Australia, New Zealand, the United States, and Canada).

As with other genres of vernacular recorded music across India, the production of Uttarakhandi geet mushroomed between the early 1980s and the early years of the twenty-first century as a result of large-scale urban migration, financial deregulation, trade liberalization, and the dissemination of inexpensive sound reproduction technologies (Manuel 1993). Producing and consuming vernacular recordings became a particularly significant (and marketable) modality of expressing regionalist sentiment after 2000, when the separate regional state of Uttarakhand was formed following a protracted populist movement fueled by decades of political corruption, ecological degradation, and economic underdevelopment. Successive coalition governments in Delhi between 1998 and 2014 encouraged a resurgence of regionalism in many parts of India as the central government became increasingly reliant on fulfilling the demands of regional political factions in order to maintain a majority.

Uttarakhand's music industry so far lacks the kind of polished folkloric compilation recordings that are easily found in Nepal and in Indian regions with established tourist economies such as Rajasthan, Himachal Pradesh, and Kerala. To the consternation of some local producers and government officials, Uttarakhand also lacks an identifiable folk style or folk community that is well known outside the region and corresponds to, for instance, *ras-garba* in Gujarat, *bhangra* in Punjab, Baul *gan* in Bengal, and Langa-Manganiya music in Rajasthan. One could try to explain this absence in a variety of ways (for example, by looking at Uttarakhand's relatively recent statehood, its geographic and economic position on the periphery of the national and global economies, or the subordinated social position of Shilpkar artists), but I find the premise itself curious. What are the conditions that have led to the expectation that each Indian region have a single marketable folk genre? How have particular groups of folk musicians and folk genres been converted into brands that are used to promote regional political and economic ventures?

According to a newspaper article, "the [Uttarakhandi] government is all set to forge a cultural identity by designating a folk song, folk instrument, fairs and cultural practices specific to the state" (Sharma 2015). That the government was still trying to forge this cultural identity more than fifteen years after the creation of the state is surprising and reflects a recent investment in regional tourism as well as a desire to cultivate new cultural allegiances that supersede the longstanding ethnolinguistic differences and tensions between Garhwal and Kumaon, the eastern and western halves of the region.

Albums that were once marketed as Garhwali geet or Kumaoni geet are now usually marketed as Uttarakhandi geet, reflecting this rather new political and cultural reality. The vast majority of albums feature at least one or two tracks labeled folk song (lok geet) or traditional song (*paramparik geet*), such as the song by Chauhan described above, though their relation to autochthonous village-based musical practices is not always clear. Even as some debate the authenticity of commercial folk songs, however, these recordings provide an important way for local residents and Uttarakhandi migrants to articulate regional identities. While it is not surprising that productions of Uttarakhandi geet have become increasingly linked to discourses of folk, these connections are all the more fascinating because the spaces of musical and cultural evocation (village life in Uttarakhand) are culturally and geographically removed from the spaces of production (recording studios in Delhi and other urban centers in North India) and consumption (predominantly the migrant and diasporic communities outside Uttarakhand). The distance that separates many recording artists and consumers from their mountain villages intensifies the outpourings of longing, nostalgia, frustration, and spirituality found in many songs. Moreover, the regional singers' experiences of traveling between Uttarakhand and Delhi allow them to act as cultural intermediaries, choosing the sounds and themes that may be understood as authentically folk while articulating the desire for regional and national belonging.

Measuring Social Rank and Social Mobility

In Uttarakhand, as in many other parts of India, a relatively small number of hereditary caste communities provide nearly all of the music and dance required for social gatherings and for life-cycle and calendrical rituals. Drawing on my own research and the work of other ethnomusicologists and anthropologists of South Asia, I propose four overlapping domains of social life that interface with caste ranking and provide general indications of social status among hereditary musicians in the state.

- *Gender*: In Uttarakhand, as in many other regions, male musicians may become specialists in performance of percussion instruments, ballads, long ritual songs, and many genres of urban popular song. There is a patriarchal order in South Asia that restrains women from performing in public; performance traditions that involve public dancing by women have suffered a dramatic loss of status during the past century (Morcom 2013). Women's performance is generally confined to private or all-female spaces. Women in Uttarakhand have distinct song repertoires to accompany such activities as cutting grass, hauling wood from forests, and sowing rice paddies, and they maintain unique song repertoires for calendrical festivals and such important life-cycle rituals as marriage and childbirth.
- *Patronage*: It is common for professional musicians, who must depend on payment for their livelihood, to be ascribed a lower rank than amateur or semi-professional musicians (Thompson 1993; Neuman, Chaudhuri,

and Kothari 2006; Jairazbhoy 1977). The primary mode of patronage—for example, whether a musician is remunerated in cash or kind—correlates differently with social rank depending on location, but historically, long-standing patron-client exchanges (*jajmani*) in rural areas are conducted in kind. They confer less status than do the more recent cash-based forms of patronage in urbanized areas.

- *Place*: The social rank of hereditary musicians is intimately connected with the place where they maintain their primary residence. In Uttarakhand, Shilpkar musicians live in segregated parts of towns or villages. Musicians who live in Delhi or other urban centers may also live in segregated areas, and may experience considerable discrimination, but they are understood to have attained, respectively, a higher social standing than their village kin. Just as mobility bestowed prestige on medieval court musicians (Bakhle 2005), urban migration allows hereditary musicians to access more diverse employment opportunities. Claims to indigeneity and authenticity are also linked to land rights and state privileges, however, making the issue of residence more ambiguous.

- *Repertory*: The function of a hereditary musician's repertory often is indicative of social rank; for example, performers of ritual music may have a (temporarily) higher status than performers of secular music or music for entertainment, although there are exceptions to this rule. Instrumentation is also pivotal to social status because performers of aerophones and membranophones (instruments that require contact with saliva or animal skins) tend to occupy a lower rank in South Asian contexts than do string players or vocalists. In recent decades it has become common for brass bands from the North Indian urban plains to perform for weddings in the mountains; often these bands are hired instead of local Shilpkar drummers, or the two ensembles are asked to share performance duties, producing a predictably cacophonous result. Despite the higher cost of transporting and hosting brass bands, they confer higher status on their hosts as a result of their professional attire, diverse instrumentation, non-local provenance, and versatile repertory.

These four domains provide starting points for understanding the relative social position of the three Shilpkar communities that I explore in this book: Jagariya, Bajgi, and Baddi. Jagariya, also called Gurus or Hurkiyas (in reference to the hourglass-shaped pressure drum, the *hurka*), are male healers who lead possession rituals (*jagar*). Jagariya is a caste-like designation in the sense that it is an occupational title, but it does not denote an endogamous group and is thus a more fluid social identity than Bajgi or Baddi. There is considerable flexibility in social rank among Jagariya (Sax 2009); most healers, including Pritam Bhartwan (see chapter 6), come from Shilpkar backgrounds, but some come from upper-caste (Brahmin or Rajput) back-grounds. Typically, the knowledge of and aptitude for healing and drumming are passed down through the male line within a family, but it is unusual for more than one or two male members of a single family to become healers. Healing rituals are a supplemental form of income for many Jagariya, and it is common for them to be offered a fee, rather than having to request it up front. Finally, successful Jagariya travel widely within Uttarakhand and migrant communities in North India in order to fulfill the requests of devotees. Their spatial mobility, semi-professional status, and indirect mode of patronage, as well as the sacred function of their musical performance and the looseness of their caste affiliation all help explain why Jagariya have the highest status of the three groups under consideration.

Bajgi, also called Auji, are the most ubiquitous group of musicians in Uttarakhand; like the Damai of Nepal (Tingey 1994), they are predominantly drummers and tailors (see chapter 4). The relative rank of Bajgi communities varies across this region, but they typically fall at the lower middle to the lower end of the caste hierarchy. In most villages in Uttarakhand, male Bajgi are required to play the dhol and damaun drums at the local temple or at the homes of high-caste patrons during calendrical and life-cycle rituals. One result of this hereditary duty is that Bajgi musicians are geographically dispersed across the region. Nonetheless, their spatial mobility is mostly confined to particular seasons in which they lead processions of local deities or wedding parties. Historically, Bajgi drummers were collectively remunerated by all of their patrons in kind in the form of provisions, clothing, and some token cash payment; with the dominance of the monetary economy, this traditional system has deteriorated, leading many drummers to negotiate cash payments after completing their ritual obligations.

The third and lowest-ranking community is an "untouchable" caste known the Baddi (also referred to as Beda; see chapter 5). Similar to the Gaine musicians of Nepal, the Baddi are itinerant entertainers; historically they performed as husband-wife duos, with the husband singing and playing a small cylindrical two-headed drum (the *dholki*) and the wife singing while dancing. Like a number of other peripatetic hereditary communities across South Asia, the Baddi are considered ritually auspicious and socially polluted (Fiol 2012a). They trace their origins to the divine consort of Shiva and Parvati and are not merely devotees but are part of this divine consort's flesh and literally embody its divine qualities. Once celebrated for performing life-endangering rope-sliding (*bedwart*) and rope-swinging (*lang*) fertility rituals (banned by the British colonial administration in the late nineteenth century), the Baddi are among the lowest-ranked social groups in Uttarakhand, and their survival as a community of public entertainers remains very much in doubt. Their itinerant lifestyle was supported by a patronage system known as *dadwar* (itself a form of reciprocal exchange between caste groups more commonly referred to as *jajmani* in South Asia), according to which they would be entitled to a fixed remuneration in kind for performing in a prescribed number of villages within a certain region (*birti*) annually or biannually. As shown in chapter 5, the decay of this patronage system, the stigmatization of public performance by women, and the denial of land rights have resulted in the devaluation of their music, the depreciation of their status, and the progressive decline in the livelihood of this community.

If it appears straightforward to establish the relative social rank of communities such as the Jagariya, Bajgi, and Baddi, the issue of social mobility is more challenging. Among anthropologists and ethnomusicologists, the term *social mobility* has commonly been used to refer to shifts in the social rank or status of an individual or group within a stratified society (Osella and Osella 2000: 10). In the 1960s and 1970s, scholars documented the myriad ways in which particular South Asian communities aspired to a higher social position through the adoption of new or modified external attributes (such as surname, caste label, dress, instrumentation, residence, or object of devotion).[6] Yet the main challenge of using the term *social mobility* is apparent in this body of scholarship; everyone's social position is constantly in flux, and so, in order for the term to have any precise meaning, scholars must construct a stable set of reference points against which a change in social position can be assessed. Thus, scholars such as Singer, Marriott, and Srinivas interpreted rich ethnographic data with broad explanatory concepts such as modernization and Sanskritization—concepts that, while elegant in their simplicity and useful for outlining broad historical processes across and between social groups, also tend to simplify social life.[7] Missing in much of this literature is a sense of the complexity of an individual's actions and motivations for aspiring to a higher social position. Also missing from this less-reflexive period in so-called pre-crisis anthropology is an awareness of the subjective nature of perceiving social mobility, both in terms of who is observing (usually an ambiguously positioned, economically privileged scholar) and in terms of who is being observed (in this case, low-status artisans).

A related issue in much of this literature is the idea of the assumption that an Indian sense of self is collectivist in orientation and thus fundamentally at odds with the individualist-oriented Western sense of self. Wedded to the idea that the caste system is the sociologically defining attribute of Indian civilization is this idea that Indian selfhood is, at its core, a collection of attributes and dispositions acquired through more or less regulated interactions with socially ranked groups (see Marriott 1976). Within this paradigm, the behavior of the individual was significant mainly insofar as it represented a type of interaction between two (or more) differently positioned groups, and the individual's social position was significant mainly insofar as it could be plotted in relation to a monolithic caste system.

In recent decades, scholars have advanced other approaches to social mobility and caste in South Asia: demonstrating the fluidity of caste labels in different social and historical settings (for example, Brown 2006; Lybarger 2011); deconstructing official narratives of caste hierarchy by exposing one or more subaltern, localized narratives (for example, Soneji 2012; Walker 2014; Morcom 2013); foregrounding the ambiguous social standing of individuals operating in competing or contradictory social milieus (for example, Maciszewski 2001; Babiracki 2004); and foregrounding the importance of age group, residence, gender, and class as social variables that may account for social status to an equal or greater degree than caste (for example, Liechty 2003). These approaches caution against the overdetermination of caste, while opening up more nuanced ways of thinking about caste as a constraining or enabling factor in social mobility.

If asked, most residents of Uttarakhand would rank individuals from Jagariya, Bajgi, and Baddi backgrounds from high to low in that order, regardless of discrepancies in residence, age, or socioeconomic class. Yet the relative ranking of each of these communities within any locality is contingent on other factors. For example, Bajgi drummers have higher status in western Garhwal than they do in eastern Garhwal; this is at least in part a result of the higher proportion of upper-caste Rajputs and Brahmins living in the eastern hills. In the 1920s and 1930s the activities of Arya Samaj reformers in Almora and other areas of Uttarakhand also contributed to the so-called Brahmanization of many Shilpkar artisans, which led to an elevation or at least a blurring of status (Sebring 1972). Moreover, the ways in which caste delimits a social role as opposed to a (more temporary) social identity varies greatly from case to case; in other words, the extent to which labels may be cast off is contextually variable (see Babiracki 2008). For instance, in recent years larger numbers of hereditary specialists have been represented on regional recordings, but this representation does not necessarily translate into equal access or agency (democratization), nor does participation necessarily lead to upward social mobility. Indeed, although participating in commercial recordings may still hold allure for some hereditary musicians and may bring certain advantages, it also carries considerable risks that can undermine positions of status in rural performance contexts. All this is to say that any assessment of social mobility needs to be understood as multifaceted and contingent on local categories and circumstances.

Positions and Limitations of the Ethnographer

My interest in the music, society, and landscapes of the central Himalayas was stoked by childhood stories that my father related about his upbringing in North India. The son of Presbyterian missionaries, my father went to an international boarding school in the hill station of Mussoorie, where he developed a fascination with trekking in Garhwal. My first opportunity to visit the region came in 1999, when I spent the better part of a year exploring Garhwal and Kumaon on foot and motorbike and by bus. I returned to the region for research, conducting twenty-two months' worth of fieldwork there between 2003 and 2007, followed by several shorter visits during the summers of 2010, 2011, and 2014. During my fieldwork I traveled frequently between Delhi, urbanized areas in Uttarakhand (Dehradun, Pauri, Srinagar, Haldwani, Almora, and Nainital), and a number of villages in the Pauri, Tehri, Rudraprayag, Chamoli, and Almora Districts, often accompanying musicians in transit (see figure 0.2).

A multi-sited approach to fieldwork was pivotal to my understanding how small-scale and large-scale mobility impacted the social lives of contemporary musicians, their recordings, and their audiences. Yet my own mobility created limitations. I was not able to study the creative practices of a single

Fig. 0.2. Uttarakhand (courtesy Natalie Fiol)

community or locality over a long period of time. Moreover, because of the fluctuations in language between one river valley and another, I learned to speak and understand only a very generic form of the Garhwali language, one that, not surprisingly, is also used in much of the commercial music of the region. I am fluent in Hindi and was able to converse with almost everyone in this language, with the exception of older women in more remote parts of the region.

I have made a point of including the perspectives of diverse people involved in the production and consumption of Uttarakhandi geet, such as village entrepreneurs, regional folklorists and politicians, hereditary and non-hereditary musicians, music directors, and producers. As I interacted with individuals in these various roles and settings, I found extremely variable positions and perspectives with regard to efforts at folklorization.

My own position as a white male North American scholar opened many doors that I came to realize were closed to many of my Indian colleagues. I was fortunate to spend time with many of Uttarakhand's best-known recording artists and studio professionals, including Narendra Singh Negi, Meena Rana, Hira Singh Rana, Chander Singh Rahi, Pritam Bhartwan, Gajender Rana, Sangita Daundiyal, Sohan Lal, Sukaru Das, Jeet Singh Negi, Deewan Kandwal, Santosh Khetwal, Kalpana Chauhan, Subhash Pande, Sanjay Kumola, Virendra Negi, and H. Soni ("Pumpum"). In an attempt to balance the exceptional with the everyday, I also sought out lesser-known performers, many of whom are exceptional in all but the commercial sense. I conducted all interviews in Hindi and translated them into English, unless otherwise noted. With their consent, I have chosen to use the real names of many of the individuals profiled in this book; however, because of the sensitive nature of some of the content discussed, I have hidden the identity of some of my interlocutors.

In Uttarakhand, much music making happens in women's spaces, often as accompaniment to work. As a male outsider it was challenging to interact with women or ask them questions about music-making. Women in rural areas generally have far less leisure time than do men. Everyday life is strictly segregated by gender, and I was able to access predominantly male-dominated activities, such as commercial music production and reception more easily than women's activities. As I discuss in chapter 5, however, male professional singers frequently present village songs and commercially recorded songs that express the emotional life of women. Public performances of *laman, khuder geet, ghasiyari geet, nyoli,* and a wide range of dance-song styles frequently involve a cross-gender identification wherein male performers articulate pain and longing through female subjectivities.

My position as an outsider studying folklorization from a distance began to change as performance became more integrated into my fieldwork and my professional life as an ethnomusicologist. In 2010 I was asked by the College-Conservatory of Music at the University of Cincinnati to direct a world music ensemble. I spent a summer in Garhwal studying with Sohan Lal and Sukaru Das (see chapter 4) to gain a rudimentary knowledge of drumming patterns, and I was an apprentice in the making of six sets of various drums that I shipped to Cincinnati. I had little in the way of formal pedagogical models. Almost all learning within hereditary families in Uttarakhand is accomplished informally as young people imitate elders. And although a number of folkloric ensembles have been created in Uttarakhand, currently no institutions train people to dance, sing, or perform on any of the indigenous instruments that are at the core of village-based expressive life such as the *dhol* (a double-headed barrel drum), the *damaun* (a small kettledrum), the *naggara* (a large kettledrum), the hurka (an hourglass-shaped pressure drum), the *thali* (a brass plate), the *mashakbaja* (bagpipes), the *muruli* (a bamboo flute), the *ransingha* (an S-shaped natural horn), the *turi* or *bhankora* (a straight natural horn), and the *binai* (a mouth harp).

As the first Uttarakhandi music ensemble to be formed outside India, this effort attracted a great deal of positive attention within the Uttarakhandi diaspora on this continent. I received numerous emails of encouragement, such as this one from a Garhwali businessman in California: "Being an Uttarakhandi I appreciate your work because even [the] new generation of Uttarakhand is not finding any interest in our folk music but you guys took it to international platform." During a trip to Garhwal in 2014, I learned that a friend and local businessman had been organizing nightly screenings in his village of a downloaded video of my ensemble.[8] After reading about my student ensemble in a local Garhwali newspaper, a village primary school teacher submitted a letter of protest to her administration, writing that if someone from North America can teach Uttarakhandi music in a foreign university, this music ought to be included in the school curriculum in Uttarakhand. It has been rewarding to hear of such overwhelmingly positive responses. I believe that my students have benefited from the experience of studying this music, and I have attempted to simulate the learning process in Garhwal by emphasizing rote learning, the vocalization of drum syllables before playing, the expansion of interlocking figures around core patterns, and walking while playing.

At the same time, I have been forced to confront the challenges of teaching this music in a North American conservatory. The expectation that the ensemble perform concerts after a semester of learning has led me to simplify and condense some areas of the repertory, introduce more melodic variety in other areas, expand the instrumentation, provide more structured introductions and cadences, and even dress the ensemble in traditional costumes. In Uttarakhand, drumming typically occurs in small ensembles of two or three performers; in my ensemble, I have arranged items to be played in groups of ten to twelve students, corresponding to the required class size. Like many of my colleagues in ethnomusicology who direct "world music" ensembles (see Solis 2004), I am directly engaging in the processes of folklorization that I seek to investigate throughout this book. As I attempt to create an ensemble that is representative of diverse dance and musical styles from Uttarakhand, I am also fashioning an idiosyncratic experience that caters to the needs of the conservatory and "the American *tabula rasa*" (ibid.: 9) and that is devoid of most extramusical aspects of performance in the central Himalayas. This awareness has made me more sympathetic to the efforts of some of the folklorists and producers I describe in this book, who similarly recontextualize the music of subaltern specialists, and who, like me, can be characterized as modernist cosmopolitans. At the same time, my experiences as an ensemble director have made me more critical of folklorization efforts that attempt to re-caste artistic traditions by silencing the Shilpkar performer.

The Tyranny of Folk

Romila Thapar has forcefully called attention to the "tyranny of labels," the way they intercede in historiography, "[forcing] interpretations into a single category so that the infinite shades of difference within them disappear" (1996: 3). This is undoubtedly the case with folk, a category with layers of historical and cultural significance that have become inseparably bound in contemporary discourse. The relatively recent diffusion of the term *folk* (and its cognates *Volk* and *lok*) in colloquial speech across much of the world has coincided with a growing skepticism and critique of the term in European and North American academia.[9] A significant body of scholarship details the ideological contradictions of the folk concept in various historical and cultural permutations.[10] The identification of folk almost always involves a combination of academic, state, and market interests that benefit from encountering Others. Modernist reformers generally value forms and practices that they deem at risk of disappearing and in need of protection or revival, which local populations may read as interference. While purportedly identifying pure folk forms, however, scholars tend to selectively choose cultural forms that have already been folklorized, that is, reworked and remediated through cosmopolitan values and aesthetics. Another common critique is that the folk music concept is frequently presented as a set of sonic and cultural practices that exist as timeless markers of tradition, locality, region, and nation. The discourse of folk tends to gloss over historical particularities encapsulating "that full range of indigenous modes of drama, theatre, and performance that emerged diachronically over two millennia but have assumed a synchronous existence in the present" (Dharwadker 2005: 310).

Some North American folklorists, motivated by disciplinary angst, have responded to these critiques by asserting the analytic usefulness of the term even as they have refuted some of the assumptions inherited from Enlightenment romanticism and scientific rationalism.[11] The ethnomusicologist Philip Bohlman (1988) has likewise advocated a dynamic and flexible concept of folk music that might facilitate cross-cultural comparison. Yet most North American scholars regularly sidestep the term *folk* altogether, substituting such terms as *traditional, vernacular, indigenous,* or *local.*

In South Asian studies, the complex historical and epistemological legacy of the term *folk music* (*lok geet* in North Indian languages) has rarely been questioned.[12] "Folk" remains a catch-all designation for a miscellany of relatively static sonic and cultural practices that mark local or regional identity. As a legacy of colonialism, cultural nationalism or regionalism, and neoliberalism, the term *folk* indexes the primordial adaptations of humans to their environment. It follows that all regions and communities in India are believed to have their own corresponding varieties of folk arts. Yet according to this modernist line of thinking, the more socially and geographically isolated a place is from cities, roads, and other forms of modern infrastructure, the more it is assumed to have a pure style of folk art untainted by modernity. Communities living in remote regions—the desert-dwelling hereditary musicians of Rajasthan, the tribal communities of central India and the Western Ghats, the fishermen and mendicant musicians of Bengal, and the mountain-dwelling residents of the Himalayas—are thus imbued with a unique folk authenticity. It is sometimes assumed that the inhabitants of mountainous regions including the Nilgiris, the Western Ghats, the Hindu Kush, and the central and eastern Himalayas retain unspoiled musical and cultural traditions because the mountains form a natural barrier against cultural influences from neighboring plains regions. Although a mountainous location is an important factor in understanding musical evolution, such assumptions are unhelpful. Contemporary village music in the central Himalayas has been shaped by instruments and musical practices brought by waves of migrants from western India for more than a millennium, as well as by British colonialists from the eighteenth to the mid-twentieth century and by Muslim, Sikh, Nepali, and Bihari migrants during the past century in particular. In the northeastern state of Nagaland, to take another example, European and American musical forms, first introduced by Western missionaries, have been popular for centuries. Many locals have embraced gospel, country, and rock in place of long-suppressed indigenous forms of music. Because of the modernist expectation that rural areas should have their own local forms of folk music, however, many local cosmopolitans have felt obliged to revive indigenous styles and instruments. The growth of the annual Hornbill Festival in Kohima, initiated in 2000, is a manifesta-tion of the value placed on folk music in recent years; despite the atrophy of traditional musical forms in most rural areas, youth don traditional dress to perform a variety of folk dances and songs before an audience of tourists and urban cosmopolitans (Naga n.d.).

This tendency to locate folk authenticity in particular subnational regions is common to many national contexts (for example, Appalachia in the United States, Pirin in Bulgaria, and Karelia in Finland). State patronage, through the influence of radio, cultural policy, and festivals, has long sustained the ideologies of folkloric purity in these regions, but increasingly this work is being carried out within networks of capital that connect local elites with migrant and diasporic populations. As Tim Oakes writes, "[G]lobal capital-ism has adopted the idea of 'regional culture' as an important criteri[on] for investment, and localities now endeavor to represent themselves in terms of cultural dynamism and uniqueness" (2000: 673–674).

Rather than trying to confine folk music only to local, village-based settings (thereby underlining its authenticity) or only urban cosmopolitan settings (thereby underlining its constructedness), I argue that the discourse of folk is produced in the sites of convergence between different systems of value and expectation. There is a problematic tendency among scholars to con-ceptualize folk as a space that belongs to subalterns and is appropriated by outsiders. In this book, I advocate the idea that scholars need to be attuned to the ways the discourse of folk animates a particular relationship between insiders and outsiders, as well as between geographic peripheries and cen-ters. My approach thus aligns with several recent ethnographic studies that critically examine the meanings of folk within a contested field of discourse and practice.[13]

Given the prevalence of the folk concept in everyday discourse, and the long history of folklore studies in South Asia, it is surprising that the concept of folklorization has not been rigorously applied to South Asian performance traditions. An advantage of the term *folklorization* is that it displaces any reified notion of the folk, compelling us to recognize the production of folk as a processual and performative undertaking. Folklorization is motivated by a range of economic, political, and cultural interests, as state actors seek to generate new signs of nationalist and regionalist identification, entrepreneurs seek to produce new cultural commodities, and migrants seek to revive or retain cultural traditions in new environments. When folklorization plays out across hierarchical social landscapes marked by differences in gender, class, caste, and race, there are predictable consequences. In Uttarakhand, as communities of Shilpkar musicians such as the Baddi have become romanticized through folkloric productions, some members of these communities have found it difficult to live up to these idealizations (compare Krakauer 2015). Others have been pushed to the margins of regional culture industry as high-caste musicians have assumed ownership of cultural production. At the very moment when Shilpkar musicians are discursively positioned as the true folk artists, they are also being positioned as repositories of dying oral traditions and divested of their contemporary relevance.

It is critical to foreground the real-life consequences of folklorization for low-status musician communities across South Asia. At the same time, it is important to point out that the motivations and effects of folklorization are not singular or straightforward. It would be facile to assume that folklorization is equivalent to cultural appropriation. Such claims need to be grounded in empirical studies that contextualize the actions and motivations of all people involved. In each case, it is necessary to ask what and whom *folk* stands for in a particular moment and who assumes cultural ownership of it. While Shilpkar musicians in Uttarakhand have been routinely misrepresented in efforts at folklorization, many have absorbed the essentialist terms of identity politics and used them to their own advantage, claiming that they are the authentic owners of folk arts (compare Mendoza 2008).

Many non-Shilpkar elites demonstrate a "possessive investment in indigenous practices," a phrase used by Joshua Tucker to "highlight the tight relation between acceptable public discourses of indigeneity and the market in indigenous authenticity" (2013: 40). Tucker articulates many of the problematic aspects of indigenous-nonindigenous collaborations in the Peruvian highlands but also demonstrates that "the success of such marketing often depends on the sincere and highly personal investment that nonindigenous subjects come to make in ethnic identities that they feel to be partially their own" (ibid.). Throughout my fieldwork I encountered high-caste interlocutors expressing a similar degree of emotional investment and personal meaning in folklorization efforts. Their personal connection does not obfuscate caste privilege or a responsibility to less-privileged Shilpkar performers, but it highlights the degree to which folkloric performance allows for multiple interpretations of cultural ownership and identity politics.

The Legacies of Folk and Classical

The resiliency of the folk concept in South Asian studies—and the lack of a critical apparatus to this point—has much to do with the way "folk" has been employed as an analytical category that is opposed to "classical".[14] I seek to interrogate these terms as subjects of analysis, asking how they have been discursively produced in relation to one another.[15] The contrast between folk and classical in South Asian studies is rooted in a legacy of binary structuralist models—for instance, Great Tradition/little tradition (Redfield 1955; Singer 1972), Sanskritization/vernacularization (Srinivas 1989)—that attempt to holistically account for all cultural production in India while implicitly privileging text-based, pan-regional traditions. In much of this literature, classical music stands for the pinnacle of musical development fostered by elite patrons and cultivated on a foundation of earlier, more primitive, stratum of folk music.[16]

Peter Manuel (2015) theorizes an "intermediary sphere" between classical music and folk music in India. He clearly distinguishes a number of intermediary genres using the well-worn markers of classical music (for example, textualization, elite patronage, explicit theorization, and codification), but he is unable to establish analytical markers of folk music to the same degree. Manuel insists that "folk music . . . remains a useful designation for a vast and diverse body of music" (85). Nonetheless, he repeatedly characterizes folk music "in negative terms" as "simple" or "unsophisticated" and as lacking an explicitly articulated theory. In an aside, Manuel notes that many of the "intermediate" genres he describes are "emically categorized, whether problematically or not, as folk music (*lok geet*)" (ibid.: 86), but this observation does not deter him from characterizing folk music as an essentially premodern phenomenon, remarking that "the realm of 'folk' itself diminishes as Indian society continues to modernize" (ibid.: 83).

Manuel's article is an example of a broader post-structural turn in South Asian ethnomusicology in which the idea of classical music has been deconstructed while folk music has been left as an unmarked and essentialized category. A number of studies in ethnomusicology document the efforts of early- and mid-twentieth-century reformers to elevate certain contemporary performance styles into emblems of Indian classical heritage (Bakhle 2005; Schofield 2010; Soneji 2012; Subramanian 2006; Walker 2014; Weidman 2006). This process necessarily entailed the silencing and purging of undesirable, polluting elements, notably subaltern communities of professional, female, lower-caste, and Muslim hereditary performers.

Recasting Folk documents the ways in which another set of reformers (often institutionally linked to the reformers of classical music) sought to create value for folk traditions by resorting to similar processes of codification, adaptation, and exclusion. A central goal of this book is to demonstrate that processes of classicization in South Asia need to be understood in conjunction with processes of folklorization, and vice versa. Folk music needs to be understood not as a mere byproduct of (or source for) classical music, nor as simply an outcome of classical traditions becoming "localized" (see Ramanujan 1993); rather, it must be conceptualized as part of a dialectic that has structured the imagination of India as a holistic cultural area. As Vasudha Dalmia writes in her historical study of Indian theater, "the two, the classicizing of tradition and the turn to the common 'folk', were then in a sense interdependent processes" (2006: 158).

If the folk label once circulated primarily through the academic discourse of Indologists describing timeless or vanishing village traditions, it has moved gradually and irreversibly into everyday discourse in North India. This book exposes an unspoken contradiction in the contemporary discourse of folk: as a quality of cultural forms and practices, folk identifies something belonging to everyone; as a quality of certain kinds of people, folk has been used to alternately identify or exclude the hereditary artisan.

Plan of the Book

Although the discourse of folk music could be studied at virtually any time in the past century, this work focuses on three distinct periods when ideas about folk music have acquired particular salience in Uttarakhand and in North India more broadly. Chapter 1 explores the late nineteenth and early twentieth centuries, a period when indigenous and British colonial elites gathered local knowledge from Shilpkar performers and inscribed this knowledge within the emerging discipline of folklore studies. Depending on the shifting ideological and political positions with respect to local caste hierarchies, Aryan migration theories, and colonial administrative agendas, scholars used folklore to call attention alternately to the exceptional character of central Himalayan society as a whole and to the backward and superstitious character of particular castes and communities within it. I illuminate the way the folk concept was a critical instrument of colonial domination even as it offered local Indian elites the opportunity to compare Himalayan societies favorably with European societies.

Beginning in the late 1940s, artists from a variety of backgrounds—urban and rural, upper-caste and lower-caste, professional and amateur, heredi-tary and non-hereditary—began to self-identify as folk artists in an effort to stimulate political change. Much as the term *folk* had subversive and leftist political associations in the United States during the 1950s and 1960s, folk arts in India emerged "from the popular appeal of village forms, their potential for subversive social meaning, and their connection with various forms of populist street theatre" (Dharwadker 2005: 312). In chapter 2 I examine the decades before and after Indian independence when leftist cultural orga-nizations such as the Indian People's Theatre Association began adopting rural cultural forms as part of an international effort to combat fascism by bringing class consciousness to the masses. These efforts were gradually coopted by state institutions of the Nehru administration that sought to codify regional folkloric (and classical) genres in order to promote diversity while suppressing antinationalist sentiment. I focus on the life and creative efforts of Mohan Upreti, an influential political activist and composer who cultivated folk theater in Delhi by fusing influences from the international Communist movement, Hindustani music, the Almora-based Ramlila, and the stories and performance styles of Kumaoni balladeers. Upreti and other reformers created a new context for understanding folk music in urban India, and in the process they fashioned themselves as a new kind of folk artist.

The remainder of the book (chapters 3–6) examines the period between 1980 and 2010, when folk music production experienced a boom in India not unlike that of the 1960s and 1970s in North America. In the words of one journalist, "[T]he audience for Indian ethnic folk music is getting fashionable, with performers moving from their open air venues in jungles and villages to perform in closed spaces across cities" (Chatterjee 2011). Evidence of this boom can be found in the emergence of recording labels dedicated to folk music (Amarass Records, Beat of India), television shows featuring folk music (Indian Idol introduced a "folk" category in 2008, requiring that all contestants sing songs from their respective regions), domestic and international folk festivals (Virasat, Blue Lotus Festival, Rajasthan International Folk Festival, Kolkata International Folk Music Festival), all-night urban spectacles called *jagran* that merge possession rituals with celebrations of regional heritage, and an increasing number of commercially successful, cosmopolitan performers who incorporate village-based styles of music and dance. Indian government agencies such as Sangeet Natak Akademi and the Indira Gandhi Centre for the Performing Arts and international funding agencies such as the Ford Foundation have continued to fund workshops and publications dedicated to the preservation of India's "vanishing folk cultures." Independent folk music archives such as Lokayan Sansthan in Rajasthan have emerged in physical as well as virtual spaces. This variety of commercial activities and interests—private and public, for-profit and not-for-profit, local and translocal—exposes a desire to capitalize on the folk music craze at all levels of the music and entertainment industry.

Chapter 3 examines the various factors that have precipitated the most recent phase of interest in Indian folk music, including the growing economic clout of regional migrants in Indian metropolises and in the diaspora, the growing economic and political significance of regional polities within the federalist democracy, and the broad neoliberal reforms of the 1990s, which resulted in the privatization of state-owned enterprises, the deregulation of the economy, and the liberalization of trade and industry. I focus in particular on the semi-professional musical activist and reformer Narendra Singh Negi, who has sustained a forty-year career as Uttarakhand's most commercially successful musician through a commitment to developing the "folk element" in his vernacular recordings.

Shilpkar musicians in Uttarakhand occupy a liminal social position; although they live in highly impoverished and stigmatized communities, they perform critical social roles by communicating with divinities through sacred rituals and facilitating social dancing at festivals. Chapter 4 focuses on the experiences of Sohan Lal, one of the few individuals from the Bajgi community of drummers to have established a professional career in both rural and urban contexts, for both lower- and upper-caste patrons. Being labeled a folk artist has benefited Sohan Lal in some respects, earning him both monetary and social capital, but it has led to significant compromises in terms of the presentation and interpretation of his music.

In chapter 5 I critique the assumption found in much South Asian scholarship (for example Ghosh 2004; Jassal 2012; Primdahl 1993) that women are the natural repositories of folk culture. Although this sentiment is often rooted in an important feminist motivation to challenge oppressive ideologies within patriarchal societies, I argue that it is ultimately unhelpful to think about folk culture or oral tradition as an inherently male or female domain of cultural production. I critique the gendering of the folk concept by comparing and contrasting the experiences of two professional female artists in Uttarakhand. Both women have established their professional identities through interpretations of village-based repertoires of song and dance, but each performer has experienced different degrees of acceptance and inclusion within the vernacular music industry as a result of her social position and caste background. I argue that gender identity plays a significant role in shaping the social and musical experiences of female professional artists, but that it needs to be considered in combination with class, caste, residence, and other social variables.

The Himalayan region of Uttarakhand is an intriguing context in which to critique ideas about folk music because it is located at the margins of the nation while being deeply integrated into its spiritual imaginaries and politico-economic foundations. Despite generating great spiritual wealth in the form of Hindu pilgrimage destinations and great monetary wealth in the form of hydroelectricity, Uttarakhand remains one of the most impoverished regions in India. By some estimates, nearly 40 percent of the total population of eleven million people now lives outside Uttarakhand in urban centers in India and abroad. A large percentage of these migrant and diasporic popula-tions are a generation or two removed from a village upbringing, yet remain emotionally connected to their region of origin. For these individuals, folk music has become a powerful sign of identification, even if there is often limited knowledge of the vernacular language (Garhwali, Kumaoni, Jaunsari) or of village-based musical styles. In chapter 6 I examine how participation in all-night possession rituals called *jagar* has become an important marker of regional belonging and devotional expression for many migrants living far from home. Although jagar rituals have a long history of being driven underground and stigmatized as "folk religion" (Sontheimer 1995), I show how they have more recently been rebranded as a positive element of regional folk, largely through the commercial recordings and stage performances of the hereditary drummer and healer Pritam Bhartwan.

1 Genealogies of the Folk Concept in Colonial Uttarakhand

This chapter offers evidence from the central Himalayas to support the claim that the contemporary concept of *lok* in South Asia—whether articulated as *lok sangeet* (folk arts), *lok dharm* (folk religion), or *lok sanskriti* (folk culture)—is rooted in the colonial encounter and in the colonial imposition of the folk concept and the methods of folkloristics.[1] Although there are important pre-colonial ideological precedents that I consider below, the concept of lok, or folk, emerged as a critical instrument of colonial rule in the nineteenth and early twentieth centuries. The word *folk* does not appear in colonial documents in India until the late nineteenth century. Nonetheless, terms such as *tribal, peasant, savage,* and *primitive* marked the Otherness of the Himalayan subject while also making that Otherness more familiar. These terms became the ideological precedents that enabled a concept of folk to take root in the late colonial period.[2] European interpretations of central Himalayan landscapes, social structure, and cultural practices evolved alongside new political and economic imperatives and new ways of theorizing human societies. Initially, Europeans used the folk concept as a tool with which they could measure their cultural distance from mountain populations (glossed as Paharis) and make comparisons with other "folk societies" with whom they were more familiar, in particular, Scots. Eventually, "folk" became an important category by means of which the colonial elite, both European and Indian, would designate ancient practices and distinguish "backward" from more "advanced" social groups within the Himalayas.

This chapter encompasses the broad historical time frame of the nineteenth and early twentieth centuries, tracing the routes and roots of the folk concept in the central Himalayas through various sources including colonial administrative documents, contemporary cultural histories in English and in Hindi, vernacular literature in Garhwali and Kumaoni, and contemporary performances of heroic ballads. Because my focus is the development of the folk concept and related ideas during the colonial period, I depart from a strictly chronological presentation at times, although I make an effort to ground the ideas in material and social history. Toward the end of the chapter I explore the methods of producing history and folklore in the central Himalayas, focusing on the collaborations between the scholar-missionary Ebenezer Sherman Oakley and the indigenous folklorists Tara Dutt Gairola and Ganga Datt Upreti.

Colonial perspectives on central Himalayan folklore, music, and society were always multiple and evolving. British attitudes about biological and social evolution and the economic prospects and spiritual ecstasy of Himalayan landscapes shifted over the course of the eighteenth and nineteenth centuries, shaping the discourse of folklore and folk society accordingly.[3] Moreover, the relative status of the performer vis-à-vis colonial theories of caste, race, gender, and social evolution became crucial to designations of folk. Wherever possible I have included first-hand descriptions of early musical practice, but one gets only a fragmented understanding of musical sound from these sources. As Babiracki notes (1991), textual content and performance context, rather than sound, were the basis of making distinctions between folk music and nonfolk music in colonial sources.

Genealogies of *Volk*, *Folk*, and *Lok*

The phonetic and semantic similarities between the Sanskrit-Hindi *lok-a*, the English folk, and the German *Volk* suggest a shared etymology, but the direction of influence is not at all clear. One possible etymology of *folk* posits that it is a non-Germanic cognate from the Latin *vulgus*, or "common people." According to the German substrate hypothesis, however, *Volk* and its Romance language analogues derive from a contact language or creole resulting from the synthesis of proto-Germanic–speaking and Indo-European–speaking populations.

Lacking clear etymological evidence, many scholars have scoured the historical record for the ideological roots of the "folk music" concept in Europe[4] and India.[5] The scholarly consensus for the past half-century has been that late-eighteenth-century German intellectuals such as Johann Gottfried Herder, Friedrich von Schiller, and their contemporaries were the first to articulate the Volk concept, which then spread to other parts of Europe and beyond. Nationalist sentiment in central and western Europe in the late eighteenth century provided the motivation for social elites to locate national spirit (*Volksgeist*) in the distant, timeless folk peasantry. Herder's writings in particular were instrumental to the formation of folkloristics and to the popular association of folk music with anonymous composition, rural pastoralism, oral transmission, and naturalism. Herder postulated that the presence of folk music and poetry benefited the nation as a whole; nonetheless, it was not found in equal measure everywhere. It was the task of social elites to find and nurture the production of folk music in the "common man," among whom it was thought to emerge spontaneously and instinctually.

Matthew Gelbart's research modifies this narrative insofar as it stresses the pivotal role of English and Scottish intellectuals in shaping the concept of folk music—or, as it was more commonly known in the eighteenth century, "national music" (2007). Within eighteenth- and nineteenth-century evolutionary theories, Scotland was the site of the most ancient stage of musical and social development; the combination of the physical qualities of the highland landscape, biological qualities of the Scottish race, and "primitive" musical qualities (pentatonic scales, for example) all fed into representations of Scotland as the primary folk Other within Europe (ibid.: 29–50). As we will observe below, scholars and administrators in British India drew parallels between Scotland and Uttarakhand, thus exposing their desire for "the discovery of an indigenous other—both European and foreign—[that] occasioned the birth of the folk, and of folklore studies as 'the survivals of archaic belief and customs in modern ages'" (ibid.: 64).

India also loomed large in the imagination of eighteenth- and nineteenth-century European intellectuals. Several prominent scholars speculated that the origins of European folklore could be traced to India. William Jones and other scholars of the Asiatic Society documented the relics and retentions of ancient Hindu language and culture, suggesting a "universal spiritual" link between the Orient, the great classical civilizations of the Occident, and the primitive folk societies of Europe (Bennett 1993; see also Blackburn and Ramanujan 1986: 2). According to the predominant evolutionary paradigm, each of these societies was to be understood as a stage in Europe's past and as a foil for Europe's high degree of civilization (Maskiell 1999: 363). Other scholars, such as Kirin Narayan, have identified provocative parallels between Vedic and European approaches to folk. Narayan notes that such Sanskrit story collections as the Panchatantra and the Kathdsaritasdgara resemble early European folklore collections such as Grimm's fairy tales insofar as both involved the conversion of oral knowledge into literary texts composed by social elites, and both describe the cultural practices of the "common man" (1993).

If the diverse roots of the folk concept in Europe have been well studied, its emergence in the Indian context requires more examination. Scholars have been divided about the issue of whether the contemporary uses of *lok-a* reveal pre-colonial epistemologies on the Indian subcontinent or whether they were inherited in toto from Euro-American ideas about folk and Volk.[6] Frank Korom writes that the concept of "the folk" was a "metaphorical invention" born of the colonial encounter between British and Bengali social elites and that each group subsequently channeled this concept into self-serving colonialist and nationalist ambitions, respectively (2006: 39). Beatrix Hauser notes that in pre-colonial India there were no indigenous terms that conveyed the meanings that *lok-a* came to signify under British rule: "Expressions like '*lok samskrti*' (folk culture), '*lok yand*' (folk vehicle), '*lok sruti*' (that which is heard by the folk), etc., were introduced only later as synonyms for the English term, but were never fully accepted" (2002: 111).[7]

The cultural historian Rhoderick Chalmers (2004) takes an alternative position. He notes that the term *lok-a* has carried a variety of meanings in Sanskrit, Hindustani, and a plethora of vernacular South Asian languages since the Middle Ages. The most common dictionary definitions of *lok-a* are "intermediate space," "universe/world/place," "region/district/country," "inhabitants of the world," "people" (pl.), and "ordinary life or common practice" (Monier-Williams 2006). Chalmers has outlined a discursive lineage from Vedic and Sanskrit sources in which *lok* initially signified "free or open space, room, place, scope, free motion," as well as the more specific and enduring meaning "world" (for example, the *trailokya* of atmosphere, earth, and the underworld in Hindu cosmology) (2004, 245). "By the time of the composition of the Mahabharata," he continues, "lok had acquired the key connotations which remain pertinent to its deployment today: as 'the earth or world of human beings,' 'the inhabitants of the world, mankind, folk, people (sometimes opposed to king),' and more generally as 'ordinary life, worldly affairs, common practice or usage'" (ibid.). Thus, by end of the Vedic period (c. 200 BC), there was a "reasonably clear understanding of the separate sphere of lok culture . . . [as] a direct link to the temporal rather than the spiritual: what took place in the lok was the affairs of human beings within their own communities rather than the affairs of gods; discourse that took place in lok language was divorced from that conducted in the devavan, of Sanskrit" (ibid.).

Unlike the European notion of folk, *lok* does not appear to have been applied to artistic practices in ancient India; in Matanga's *Brhaddesi* (between the eighth and ninth centuries) and other Sanskrit, Persian, and Brajbhasa texts, the terms *marga* and *desi* are more common. *Marga*, often translated as "the Universal way," signified the ancient religious and philosophical arts; *desi* signified arts with a more secular, humanist, and contemporary orientation.[8] It is tempting to fold the desi-marga binary into a Eurocentric dichotomy wherein desi arts are the natural expressions of a people, village, or community (that is, folk music) and marga arts are the cultivated products of national consciousness (that is, art music). This is a problematic equivalence, however, as desi did not necessarily mark some practices as more natural, provincial, traditional, or unwritten (oral) than others. According to Ceylonese philosopher Ananda Coomaraswamy, "the distinction of *marga* from *desi* is not a distinction of aristocratic and cultivated from folk and primitive art, but one of sacred and traditional from profane" (1937: 79).[9] Moreover, if Sanskrit theorists and eighteenth-century European scholars both demonstrated the tendency to classify cultural practices in terms of high-low binaries, their method of applying these terms was distinct: medieval Sanskrit scholars allowed for more ideological fluidity between *marga* and *desi*; European ethnologists, in contrast, tended to conceptualize folk and classical as a frozen binary (Narayan 1993: 185).

Given the very different historical and political contexts in which the terms *lok-a*, *desi*, and *folk* arose, it would be foolish to expect to find conceptual equivalence, or even a clear etymological connection, between them. Yet it would also be a mistake to discount the mutual influence and semantic overlap between these concepts. As Narayan suggests, it is "because the category deshi corresponded to European notions of folk culture that the Indian elite so readily adopted this framework in their own collection" (1993: 185). The European concept of folk would find fertile ground in nineteenth-century India.

Paharis in the Nineteenth-Century Imaginary

As the British East India Company expanded its geopolitical and economic interests across the subcontinent in the early nineteenth century, the mountainous territories of Garhwal and Kumaon became attractive for a number of reasons. East India Company officers recognized the potential for developing agriculture as well as iron, copper, and gold mines in the Garhwal and Kumaon mountains. More important, the region offered access to lucrative trade routes into Tibet. Prior to the mid-nineteenth century, the North Indian economy was heavily dependent on trade via the northeast and northwest passes. In order to control trade routes, however, the company needed unlimited access to high Himalayan passes via Garhwal and Kumaon.

The Gurkha kingdom of Nepal expanded westward via the conquest of Kumaon in 1790 and then Garhwal in 1803, bringing an end to the Chand

and Panwara dynasties, respectively, and threatening the company's economic interests in the region. Trade and boundary disputes became the pretext for the company to commence the Anglo-Gurkha wars (1814–1816). Both sides incurred devastating losses before the company's army prevailed, with considerable assistance from the local Kumaoni inhabitants. In the aftermath of the war, the British annexed Kumaon and part of Garhwal as reparations and reinstated the former Maharaja of Tehri as ruler over a much-reduced portion of his former kingdom lying west of the Alaknanda River in Garhwal.

The first decades of British rule in Kumaon brought dramatic reform to the region. Large numbers of European and American missionaries, mountaineers, Orientalist scholars, and British civil servants visited and gradually settled in the region. Surveys and censuses were conducted in order to better understand the landscape and people of Kumaon and Garhwal. The hill stations of Nainital (1841), Mussoorie (1850), Ranikhet (1869), Lansdowne (1887), and Almora (1568) were developed to offer respite and recovery from illness to European tourists, civil servants, and military personnel. The hill stations also offered surveillance of neighboring states and "launching pads for commercial probes into central Asia" (Kennedy 1996: 12). The company abolished tariffs in order to boost trans-Himalayan trade and encourage cultivation of cash crops. Increased pressure from free-trade lobbies in London restricted economic opportunity in the Himalayan colonies, but the company invested heavily in infrastructure in order to increase the production of exportable commodities from the low hills and to provide incentives for economic ventures, such as opium production, that would reduce dependency on European markets (Rangan 2000). Four major projects were launched in the Uttarakhand region during the mid-nineteenth century: tea cultivation in Kumaon, which aimed to compete with Chinese tea production in Tibet; commercial production of wheat and sugarcane, which was produced on plantations owned by former company or military officers; the construction of the Ganges river canal (1841–1861); and the felling of large tracts of Himalayan timber, which was floated down the Yamuna and Bhagirathi Rivers to be converted into railway sleepers for the burgeoning locomotive industry. Taken together, these projects considerably boosted employment in the sub-Himalayan region and demonstrated the importance of the central Himalayas to the economic development of North India.

In the context of this economic activity, English-language colonialist accounts reveal a striking difference between descriptions of the Himalayan landscape—celebrated as bountiful, limitless, and health-restoring—and descriptions of its inhabitants, who were either treated as invisible, blending into the natural and idyllic landscape, or as savages representing an earlier stage of society (Rangan 2000: 50–51). As a means of satisfying multiple agendas—missionization, accumulation of capital, colonial administration, and Orientalist fantasy—most European visitors adopted a paternalistic tone when describing residents of the Himalayas, whom they alternately reviled for their primitiveness and glorified for their simple state of existence close to nature. Writing about his expedition to Kumaon in 1824, for example, the Protestant minister Reginald Heber described the Kumaonis as "a very ugly and miserable race of human beings, with large heads and particularly prominent ears, flat noses, tumid bellies, slender limbs, and sallow complexions, and have scarcely any garments but a blanket of black wool. . . . The only satisfaction to be derived from a journey through such a country, is to look steadily at the mountains beyond it, which increase as we advance in apparent magnitude and beauty" (1829: 158–159).

European travelogues played on the imaginations of readers back in Europe, stoked by a steady stream of Orientalist literature. Fanny Parkes Parlby, the wife of a minor civil servant who lived in India for twenty-four years, recorded her impressions of "Paharis"—as those who dwelt between Nepal and Kashmir were commonly described—on her first trip to the hill station of Mussoorie in 1838 thus: "The Paharis (hill-men) who had come down to bring up our luggage, were animals to stare at: like the pictures I have seen of the Tartars—little fellows, with such flat ugly faces . . . they are very honest and very idle; moreover, most exceedingly dirty" (Parlby, Ghose, and Mills 2001: 318). Her account is typical in that it reveals the dual element of fascination and revulsion, noting the famed strength and honesty of the "Pahari race" while also drawing attention to their "animal-like" behavior and appearance.[10]

In order for the colonial elites to prove their moral superiority, they needed to demonstrate the social backwardness of the Pahari both in official and unofficial sources.[11] British administrators frequently noted the excessive harshness of the short period of Gurkha rule (1790–1815), but they nevertheless extended a number of the Gurkha regime's oppressive practices, including the forced labor system (*kuli begar*) whereby male members of the hill population were mandated to manually transport British subjects and their goods across the mountain footpaths. The begar system placed excessive demands on agricultural laborers in many areas of Kumaon, and it also exacerbated the gendered division of labor in Kumaon because the departure of males left the bulk of agricultural and domestic labor to women (Fracchia 2006; Kennedy 1996: 179–180; Pathak 1987). In passages reminiscent of early-eighteenth-century condemnations of *sati* and treatment of widows in western India, male British observers frequently wrote about the deplorable conditions of women in the hills. If this discourse validated their own moral superiority, it also fixed the position of women and the gendered division of labor as a "traditional" part of Kumaoni society (Gururani 2002).

For newcomers grasping for familiarity in a foreign and imposing landscape, the Alps, Norway, the rural English countryside, and Scotland were common points of reference. The frequent comparisons drawn between the Scottish highlands and the Himalayan landscape is in part a reflection of the large number of Scots in the British civil service in Kumaon, many of whom displayed a nostalgic yearning for home.[12] Yet the presumed similarity of highland Scots and the "poor and depraved hill races" of Kumaon reveal broader European attitudes about their equivalent evolutionary development.[13] Stereotypes about the low educational and social status of Scots had long cemented their image as a "folk society" within Europe; many writers believed that the Scots provided a conceptual bridge to European antiquity (Gelbart 2007: 8). The Paharis, in turn, offered a conceptual bridge to Indian antiquity and a shared Aryan ancestry. The parallel status of these two populations led to some bizarre proposals, such as that by Brian Hodgson, the assistant commissioner in Kumaon and later British envoy to Nepal, who advocated the importation of Scottish and Irish peasants into the Himalayas to provide agricultural products to the company and to serve as a reserve army (Kennedy 1996: 151–152). Ultimately this endeavor proved too costly and impractical to implement, but it relied on the assumption of evolutionary equivalence between the mountain-dwelling peasants of Europe and Asia.

Ideas about landscape figured heavily in theories of race from early-nineteenth-century Victorian ethnology. Landscape was believed to condition the blood of a people and generate distinct races, nations, tribes, or castes within the span of a generation or two (Bayly 1995). For this reason, company officials insisted on the fundamental difference between the Pahari and their plains-dwelling neighbors to the south. Most early administrators in Kumaon had had previous appointments in the North Indian plains, and they were sensitive to the differences in social life as they entered the hills. "All mountaineers," Commissioner George Traill wrote in 1828, "unite in an excessive distrust of the natives of the low country, whom they regard as a race of swindlers and extortioners" (1991–1992 [1828]: 38). He described how hill people refused to eat plains-reared sheep, which have longer tails and were considered "a species of dog," and how plains liquor was not consumed because its method of preparation was considered impure to hill Brahmins (ibid.: 33–34). "Throughout the hill stations," remarked the British engineer and philologist Hyde Clarke, "it will be observed that the natives consist of tribes of distinct origin, having no sympathy with the people of the plains" (1881: 531).

Plains-based and mountain-based populations were thought to differ most drastically in the practice of religion and ritual life. After reviewing early colonial documents, Dale Kennedy concluded that "the caste-bound inequalities and ritual-enmeshed superstitions generally associated with Hindu communities [in the plains] were thought not to exist among Paharis, who were seen as living close to nature in simple egalitarian communities" (1996: 65–66). Yet many colonial observers came to the opposite conclusion, finding Pahari rituals both more complex and more primitive than those in the plains. In 1874, G. R. C. Williams, the assistant superintendent of Dehradun, wrote that "the inhabitants of the Doon are exceedingly superstitious. Their belief in ghosts, demons, spirits, and witches, is implicit. This may be, because the grander phenomena of nature have overawed their mind and excited their imagination" (1992 [1874]: 40). Commissioner George Traill characterized local religious beliefs as "rude and gross, displaying neither imagination nor refinement in their texture" (1991–1992 [1828]: 40); he nonetheless described local religious practice in considerable detail, noting how "every remarkable mountain, peak, cave, forest, fountain and rock has its presiding demon or spirit, to which frequent sacrifices are offered, and religious ceremonies continually performed by the surrounding inhabitants at small temples erected on the spot" (ibid.: 26). The colonial administrator's insistence on a sociocultural boundary between subjects in the mountains and the plains confirms, on one hand, a colonial strategy of "divide and rule," and on the other, a set of assumptions about race.

Himalayan Races

From the late eighteenth century, Europeans began visiting the Himalayas to improve their health and to escape the heat of the plains, which was widely believed to stimulate disease and fever. As newcomers penetrated higher and deeper into the mountains, they frequently projected their own expectations of purification and transcendence onto the inhabitants they met. The career soldier Charles G. Bruce expressed this kind of geographical determinism in his account of mountaineering in Kumaon and Garhwal: The Kumaoni peasant, he wrote, "has none of the virtues of the hillman in general. He is of slight build and of poor physique, though active. In fact, they say that their women are often better carriers than the men. . . . Their general character is like their general appearance and physique—mean and unattractive. It is a pity a better race does not own such a charming country." Several chapters later, after crossing into Garhwal, Bruce noted that "it becomes immediately more mountainous . . . and it is inhabited by a different, and much more simple people. But though much pleasanter, they are also less industrious. The Kumaoni undoubtedly likes bettering himself, but these people are very primitive. They do not wish to become better off, but are satisfied with a sufficiency of food and clothing ... and that too in a country, where Italian or Tyrolese or Swiss peasants of the Dauphine Alps would look [at] as a land flowing with milk and honey" (1910: 43).

On his visit to the territory of Tehri Garhwal in 1815, the artist James B. Fraser noted that inhabitants of the lower hills were "contemptible in size, mean in aspect, cringing in address; their intellect appears degraded, and their ignorance almost brutal" (Fraser 1982 [1820]: 67). Proceeding further into the hills, however, he spoke admiringly of the peasants, judging them superior to his Scottish countrymen in some respects. "The farther removed from the plains, the heat, and the more accessible parts of the country," he wrote, "the higher does the highlander seem to rise in activity of mind and body" (quoted in Kennedy 1996: 65). Fraser was a popular landscape engraver, and his artistic sensibilities conformed to the dominant early-nineteenth-century "picturesque" style. The majority of the sketches he made during his trip to Garhwal foreground jagged peaks, lush forests, architectural wonders, and other sublime aspects of Himalayan landscapes. Several of his images also provide details about Garhwali people during the period of military mobilization and conflict between the company's army and the Gurkha army. *Assemblage of Hill Men* (figure 1.1) shows approximately forty soldiers (*sipahis*) in a village courtyard (*chowk*) wearing *pahari* caps, shoes, and kurta-pajamas and holding bows, arrows, and swords. To the far left, separated from and facing the men, are three bare-chested women holding two infants. In the foreground, eight darker-skinned men with cane baskets (*kandi*) relax on a rock outcropping, all but one facing the soldiers with their backs to the viewer. These men are clearly shown to be coolies from the "depressed classes": aside from their darker skin color, they are depicted without shoes or head covering and wearing just one article of clothing covering the body to the knee. Fraser's image is as striking for its representation of caste and gender segregation as it is for showing us the militarization of the Gurkha regiments of Garhwal.

Colonial attitudes about Himalayan races were obviously shaped by the political and military exigencies of sustaining the empire. During the conflicts with the Afghans in 1839 and the Sikhs in 1849, the company recognized the need to expand its recruitment strategies beyond the upper castes of the Gangetic plains. The attitude that mountainous geography bred "martial races" was already well established, but the company did not recognize all hillmen to be equally adept as soldiers, and attitudes about the virility and

Fig. 1.1. James Fraser, *Assemblage of Hill Men*, 1820 (© The British Library Board, Shelfmark X502[12])

masculinity of different races fluctuated over time in relation to political and social upheavals (Caplan 1995). Perhaps because of the grudging respect earned during the fierce Anglo-Gurkha conflict (1814–1816), the Gurkhas had acquired a reputation as the quintessential martial race. During the conflict, British East India Company officers had already begun manufacturing their own "Gurkha" battalions by recruiting Sirmauri, Garhwali, and Kumaoni peasants, many of whom had previously been forced into bonded labor or army levies under Gurkha rule (Alavi 1995: 271–279). In an attempt to stimulate the "martial" characteristics of their soldiers, company officers consciously maintained many of the practices that had been established under Gurkha rule (but were forbidden elsewhere in the company army), allowing animal sacrifices during the Dussehra festival, permitting the soldiers' wives and children to live on base, and letting the curved *khukri* knife, a distinctive weapon of the Nepali Gurkha, to be made a standard part of their uniform, for example. The maintenance of these practices, alongside a discourse of fearlessness and bravery, contributed to a distinctive "hill soldier" identity that persists in the central Himalayas today. Then as now, this identity bolstered recruitment into the ranks of the Gurkha regiments and earned a degree of loyalty from mountain residents that would come to serve the company well. In 1857, for example, Gurkha regiments resisted the attempts of several anticolonial plains-based regiments to coerce them into joining the rebellion (ibid.: 281); indeed, the majority of Kumaoni residents remained loyal to the British during this crisis, which only further solidified their reputation as an honest and reputable "hill race."

Categories of Rule in the Late Colonial Period

After 1857 the British Crown, referred to in India as the Raj, assumed direct administrative control of the Indian subcontinent, and the strategic importance of Uttarakhand shifted away from production and toward extraction. Trans-Himalayan trade suffered as borax and sea salt became available from other parts of the subcontinent, tea cultivators could no longer gain access to China, and Tibetan traders of pashmina wool brought their stock directly to the factories in the plains without going through Garhwali middlemen. With the ever-increasing need for resources in the industrial South, the central Himalayan region became valuable primarily as a supplier of raw materials for industrial production. Despite the growth of hill stations and urbanization in some parts of the lower hills, it was evident by the late nineteenth century that timber was not a sustainable resource, and cash crop cultivation in the hills could not keep pace with agricultural productivity in the plains. The rapid depletion of forest resources led to new laws restricting access for local populations and the reorganization of state-controlled land under the Forest Department and Revenue Department (see Pathak and Bhakuni 1998; Rangan 2000; Guha 2000). Himalayan families were forced to diversify their livelihoods, leading to widespread internal and external migration to supplement subsistence agriculture. By the early twentieth century, Rangan writes, the central Himalayan region and its inhabitants could more accurately be described as "backward" (2000: 126–135).

Colonial attitudes toward the local population evolved alongside the shifting economic opportunities in Kumaon. Early projections of the noble savage living in a state of balance with the mountains were gradually undone by processes of urbanization, migration, deforestation, and military recruitment—processes that British rule had precipitated since the early nineteenth century. The sentiment of lost innocence pervaded much late colonial writing, as British rule was thought to have spoiled not only the physical landscape of the Himalayas but also the moral terrain of the natives. "I am told that honesty was the distinguishing characteristic in former times of the Paharis," wrote Fanny Parkes Parlby, "but intercourse with civilized Europeans has greatly demoralized the mountaineers" (Parlby, Ghose, and Mills 2001 [1850]: 331).

If one of the major objectives of colonial travelogues from the first half of the nineteenth century was to describe the innate character of distinct mountain races, colonial writing from the second half of the century was more concerned with categorization in terms of caste and race. This was largely a shift in emphasis from looking at the Himalayan populations horizontally (distinguishing Sirmauris, Garhwalis, Kumaonis, Gurkhas, and so on) to looking at them vertically, in terms of caste stratification. It is not coincidental that the European disciplines of ethnology, folklore studies, and comparative musicology also rose to prominence during this period. Being able to document and classify the cultural practices of people over such a vast territory was central to the expansion of economic interests and political control of the Raj (Cohn 1996). British administrators had surveyed and mapped the entire central Himalayan region, but in order to maintain and validate their rule, they exploited and reified differences in status among their subjects. Writing in 1905, E. S. Oakley recorded an astute observation that would become a cornerstone of postcolonial studies in the late twentieth century: "The enduring element, is the caste system under Brahmanical influence, but its constituents have continually been changing. The caste system has tended to become more and more unalterably fixed in later times of peace, and it may even be asserted that the permanence of British rule, which everywhere accepted the exact status quo to abide by, has contributed to add fixedness of caste, which in ancient times was more or less flexible" (1990 [1905]: 44).

As is well known, the Indo-Aryan migration theory spawned a variety of interpretations of race and caste in colonial India.[14] The theory, which was controversial from the beginning, posited a series of migrations (or, according to some, one large-scale exodus) of proto-Indo-Aryans from Central Asia into northwest India and Europe. First proposed by the illustrious Sir William Jones, the theory received iterations by various eighteenth- and nineteenth-century scholars on the basis of linguistic, archaeological, and cultural observations; a key piece of evidence for the Aryan thesis was the supposedly similar form and content of folktales across Europe and India (Blackburn 2003: 180).

In Kumaon, early administrators such as George Traill had proposed that Brahmin and Rajput residents had Aryan blood because they exhibited a fairer complexion and "higher culture"; the aboriginal stratum of non-Aryan Doms, in contrast, demonstrated a "low culture," a darker appearance, and a condition of slavery (1991–1992 [1828]: 25). One E. T. Atkinson (1973 [1882]) made two further distinctions that continue to influence understandings of Uttarakhandi society. First, he distinguished the "servile races" of aboriginal Doms from the "tribes" such as the Bhotiya (or Sauka), Raji, Tharu, and

Bhuksa. Although he identified tribal groups as similarly non-Aryan, he categorized them separately because they evidenced seminomadism, hunting, and egalitarian social organization (ibid.: 367–372).[15] Second, he recognized a distinction between Thul-Jat—higher-status Rajputs and Brahmins who had migrated from the North Indian plains within the past two millennia— and Khasa (or Khasiya), lower-status Rajputs and Brahmins who arrived in Kumaon and Garhwal from Central Asia during the earliest Aryan invasion.

British administrators were not the first to deploy these social categories (with the exception of the idea of "tribe"). The Chand rulers of Kumaon, who are thought to have migrated from Rajputana to the hills about 700 CE, left copper plates delineating three distinct classes of people in the central Himalayas—Bamana (or Brahmin), Khasiya (or Khasa), and Duma (or Dom)—and indicating the existence of a different penal code for each class (M. P. Joshi 1992–1993: 303). As folklore studies developed in the late nineteenth century, however, a hierarchical classification system became more rigid, and the majority of British scholarship focused on the Dom and the Khasa. These groups were simultaneously idealized and repudiated for their "primitive" state, and their anachronistic social customs were believed to preserve the secrets of ancient Indian civilization.[16] Because of their centrality in the imagination of "the folk" in later colonial and postcolonial scholarship, some further elucidation of the categories "Dom" and "Khasa" is required.

Dom

Dom is one of the oldest designations for individuals of low social rank across northern India. The term appears in the *Tantrasastras* to indicate someone who lives by singing and music. The historian M. P. Joshi suggests that the etymology of *Duma* was onomatopoeic, connoting the sound of a drum (M. P. Joshi 1992–1993: 305). Elsewhere M. P. Joshi offers evidence from the first millennium CE for the high social and ritual status of central Himalayan Shudra—a Vedic Sanskrit term for one of the four main *varna*, or social categories of early India that theoretically encompass all hereditary laboring classes—owing to their position as the guardians of oral tradition and of knowledge about the gods (M. P. Joshi 2011). By the end of the first millennium CE, however, the influx of Brahmins and Rajputs from North Indian kingdoms likely caused a realignment of the social hierarchy in tandem with an increase in the value placed on text-based sources of knowledge. During the Chand and Gurkha dynasties (c. 700–1816 CE), the term *Dom* collectively referred to all artisans and service-providing castes, including metalworkers (Tamta), oil pressers (Bhil), tailors (Darji), tailor-drummers (alternately called Auji, Bajgi, or Dholi), and other professional entertainers (Hurkiya, Mirasi, and Baddi). Members of so-called Dom castes generally followed strict social codes whose violation was punishable by death: they were prohibited from wearing gold or silver ornaments, clothing below the knees, and shoes and from carrying an umbrella in the presence of a high-caste person; they had to carry palanquins and lead ponies during the wedding ceremonies of their high-caste patrons, but they could not use palanquins or ponies in their own weddings; they had to live on the outside and lower end of a village, with their own access path, water source, cremation sites, and defecation sites; they could only live in grass-thatch huts, not those built of stone or wood; they were sometimes sold as slave property between village proprietors; and they had to bury dead cows, the flesh of which they consumed, to the detriment of their social position (Fanger 1980: 114).

British administrators prohibited many of these oppressive and discriminatory practices and initiated a number of income-earning opportunities for members of Dom castes, such as compensation for manual labor and permission to own land under the new land tenure system (Moller 2003: 264).[17] At the same time, however, British administrators inherited many of the caste prejudices of high-status groups with whom they worked closely, and they injected their own racial theories that only further oppressed Dom communities. Oakley equated the "low culture" and "unclean and degraded" status of the Dom with their "Negrolike" appearance, noting that "the Doms have a tradition that they were the original inhabitants of the country, and that they were employed by Mahadev as drummers on the joyful occasion when he adopted the Himalaya mountains as his residence" (in G. D. Upreti 2003 [1894]: v–vi).[18] Traill wrote that "if exceptions to [the] general character for honesty exist in the hills, they are to be found only in the class of Dom, or outcastes, who are commonly of loose and dissipated habits, confirmed, if not acquired, by continued intercourse with the plains" (1991 [1828]: 39).

The eminent folklorist William Crooke proposed a theory that all Doms once belonged to an "undifferentiated tribe" that was later "broken up into occupational groups which had become castes" (quoted in Edye 1992–1993 [1921]: 117). There is little evidence to support the claim that the term *Dom* is older than many of the occupational caste (jati)-specific names used in Kumaon and Garhwal. Regardless, it is likely that low-status communities have long preferred jati designations to the "Dom" label.[19] Jati identification has allowed members of these communities to vie against each other and aspire to a higher social position; the category Dom, in contrast, lumped everyone together at the bottom of the social order (Fanger 1980: 164). In 1921 the census superintendent E. H. Edye acknowledged that people had come to resent the administrative label Dom because it was used as a derogatory phrase and because there was in fact "no true 'Dom' caste, for the Doms as a whole have no sort of caste cohesion" (1992–1993 [1921]: 119). The formal rejection of the term *Dom* may be dated to the arrival of the politician and social activist Lala Lajpat Rai in Kumaon in 1913 (Viyogi and Ansari 2010; Negi and Khatri 2005). As an Arya Samaj reformer, Rai and the Dalit leader Khushi Ram sought to reject lower-caste status markers (such as the consumption of beef) and adopt upper-caste status markers (such as wearing the sacred thread and reciting Sanskrit). These reformers introduced the term *Shilpkar* to replace the pejorative *Dom*. They conducted a series of "purification" rituals in which Shilpkars received the sacred thread (*janeo*), and they led a movement to allow Shilpkars to use palanquins (*doli-palki*) during their weddings. In 1934 *Shilpkar* replaced *Dom* on census forms, and it is now the preferred official category in much of Uttarakhand. As we will see, however, changes in categorization have done little to alleviate caste stigma in the central Himalayas.

Khasa

In his monumental six-volume *Himalayan Gazeteer*, Atkinson postulated that modern-day Khasa were the descendants of Indo-Aryan "Khasa tribes" from Central Asia who settled in Uttarakhand via Rajputana (contemporary Rajasthan and Gujarat) and subjugated the Doms. Atkinson reached this conclusion on the basis of largely speculative linguistic evidence linking the term *khas* to various place names and communities listed in Vedic and Puranic literature. "The Khasas," he wrote, "who in physiognomy and form are as purely an Aryan race as any in the plains of northern India . . . are Rajputs who have fallen from their once honorable position by the necessity of living in a country and in a climate where the strict observance of the ceremonial usages of their religion is impossible" (1973 [1882]: 379–380).[20]

Atkinson's theory inspired a great deal of research on the Khasa in the ensuing decades.[21] Some scholars opined that the Khasa skirted the Indo-Gangetic plain altogether, migrating directly from the Indus valley along the sub-Himalayan range (Oakley 1990 [1905]: 132). Yet most scholars agreed with Atkinson's assessment that the "Khasa race" had maintained ancient, pre-Brahmanical rites and a system of customary laws that preceded "Hindu law" (L. D. Joshi 1929). Many ethnologists believed that the inhabitants of Jaunsar-Bawar in western Garhwal were the living descendants of a Khasa tribe, as evidenced by their light skin and facial features and by unique elements of their culture, especially the practice of polyandry.[22]

The scholarly fixation on the Khasa during the late nineteenth and early twentieth centuries is curious because the evidence for a proto-Aryan Khasa migration across the Himalayas is speculative at best. According to M. C. Joshi (1990), the *khas* root appeared in historical documents beginning only in the first millennium CE, and the lack of consistency in documentation suggests that heterogeneous and widely dispersed social groups employing some variation on the word *khas-* probably arrived in the central Himalayas well after the Vedic period. Moreover, there is little evidence that Himalayan communities over the course of the past millennium have used *Khasa* as a term of self-identification; like "Dom," "Khasa" has long been a pejorative category used to designate lower-status indigenes, many of whom had to work the land as tenant farmers (M. P. Joshi 1990: 112). The colonial fixation on the so-called Khasa tribe might be explained in part by an Orientalist desire to find the pre-Brahmanical roots of Indian civilization and to find an explanation for a variety of social customs commonly observed in some areas of the mountains that are largely unknown in the Indian plains, such as polyandry and levirate marriage (the obligation of a woman to marry her deceased husband's brother).

Another reason for the scholarly focus on the Khasa may have been the facility of mapping this category onto an already prevalent idea of folk society in nineteenth-century western Europe. Understanding the Khasa as a middle group between the high-caste groups who were more recent arrivals in the hills and the aboriginal, lowly Doms conformed to the late-nineteenth-century evolutionary theories in which folk society was projected as a middle rung between primitive society and civilized society.[23]

The Production of Folklore in Song, Ritual, Proverb, and Ballad

A critical reading of colonial categories reveals the complex interplay of ideologies of caste, race, and tribe in nineteenth-century British India. British scholar-administrators' reconstructions of Kumaoni history and their need to explain pre-Aryan survivals such as brideprice, widow remarriage, levirate marriage, and polyandry further reified the categories of "Thul-Jat," "Khasa," "Dom," and "Adivasi" (tribal). These were not purely academic categories. The three most influential commissioners of Kumaon—George Traill (1815–1835), J. H. Batten (1836–1856), and Henry Ramsey (1856–1884)—enacted successive land reform settlements based on what they assumed to be longstanding social hierarchies and divisions of labor. These reforms significantly altered the local economy and disenfranchised artisans and laborers even as their folklore was collected and sentimentalized for revealing the secrets of bygone eras.[24] The historian M. P. Joshi has demonstrated that high-status Brahmins and Rajputs in the hills (that is, Thul-Jat) took advantage of the new colonial regime by inventing genealogies (*vamshavali*) to claim inheritance from the Chand rulers (1990). These claims were among the primary means by which they could assert their dominance over land and resources and reinforce the differences in status between themselves and the Khasa, Dom, and tribal communities.

There is some evidence that the "folk" did not accept these reforms quietly. The linguist George Grierson describes a protest song most likely composed by Krishna Parai (Patti Syunara Malla, Almora District) in the aftermath of the first land settlements to occur in Kumaon in the 1830s:

> The verses (which show a striking contrast to the contented feeling of the hill people at the present time, the result of the wise administrat[ion] of the three great makers of Kumaon [Traill, Batten, and Ramsey]) . . . represent the popular dislike to the change from the happy-go-lucky methods of a native *regime* to the settled principles of British administration. The author was a professional singer, and, on the death of his only son is said to have developed "eccentricities" (such as writing poems like the one now printed). In it he attacks the land settlements, the new system of disposing of civil and criminal cases, the law which put husband and wife on the same level, and the employment of low-caste Brahmans in ministerial offices . . . the song is still remembered by old people in Kumaon but few know it in its entirety. (1901: 475–476)

It is likely that this singer was a hereditary performer from the Hurkiya caste; Hurkiya performers were famous for spontaneously composing songs about current events such as natural disasters or political reform. Protest songs on contemporary topics rarely made it into published folklore collections, however, and one must credit Grierson for publishing such "eccentricities," even if he was compelled to insist on "the contented feeling of the hill people at the present time."

Most accounts of Garhwali and Kumaoni folklore consisted of short entries about religious rituals, cultural customs, or legends and were published in the journals *Indian Antiquary* (Bombay, from 1872), *Folk-lore* (London, founded in 1878), *Punjab Notes and Queries* (1883–1887), and *North Indian Notes and Queries* (1891–1896).[25] Descriptions of music or dance were limited to highly scripted settings in which Europeans came into contact with natives, and especially royalty. In possibly the first English reference to music in the hills, Thomas Daniell, supposedly the first European visitor to Srinagar,

Garhwal, in 1789, remarked that "the Rajah [Pradhyumna Shah] appeared to make a great parade in visiting us, came in a Palanquin, was attended by a Tamtoom [drum] and a kind of brazen trumpet like that of the Chinese" (quoted in Archer 1980: 92). Europeans encountered local musicians at the annual festivals that took place close to hill stations. Many Europeans staying in the hill station of Simla (presently Himachal Pradesh) attended the annual Sipi festival, hosted by the Rana (Rajput monarch) of Koti. "Here visitors could view Paharis bedecked in their finest costumes and engaged in folk dances, archery competitions, the sale of handicrafts, and other activities that reminded Simla's first historian, Edward Buck, of 'an old English rural gathering'" (Kennedy 1996: 82).

Descriptions of music making also appear in accounts of ritual life in the hills, a favorite subject of administrator-scholars. Traill noted that "the ceremonies peculiar to the local deities are uninteresting: on particular festivals, dancing forms a principal part, when the dances are performed by any number of men, who move round in a circle with various contortions, their motions being regulated by the slow measure of song, which is sung by the leader of the party, the rest joining in the chorus" (1991–1992 [1828]: 26). The body of the ritual performer was another site of backwardness, particularly as it transgressed the norms of Victorian moral decency. The rope-swinging (*lang*) and rope-sliding (*bedwart*) rituals of the Baddi were described by several observers with a mixture of awe and fear,[26] resembling the accounts of "hook-swinging," "Tantric rites," and "nautch dances" in other parts of India.[27]

Aside from Edwin T. Atkinson, whose *Himalayan Gazetteer* has informed nearly all the subsequent research conducted in Uttarakhand, perhaps the most significant nineteenth-century folklorist in the region was the Reverend Ebenezer Sherman Oakley (1865–1935; see figure 1.2). Born in Yorkshire to a Congregational minister, Oakley studied arts at Glasgow University and theology at Airedale College, Bradford, and eventually completed his M.A. at the University of Allahabad, India. He settled in the Kumaon hills as a missionary and became the principal of Ramsay College in Almora, where he began researching the various forms of ritual life in the central Himalayas. In *Holy Himalaya*, he encourages the study of Kumaon to uncover the "secrets of bygone races and eras yet to be wrung from the buried monuments and unpublished manuscripts" (1990 [1905]: 4).

Oakley developed a deep respect for Kumaon, calling it "a great home of spiritual forces" and noting that its people "are endowed with a remarkable genius for religion" (1990 [1905]: 301). In accordance with the evolutionary theories of the day, he deemed contemporary Himalayan religious concepts

Fig. 1.2. Reverend Ebenezer
Sherman Oakley and
family, undated (courtesy
hymntime.com)

to be equivalent to those of Europe's medieval past or to those of a European child. "All races began at the same mental level," he wrote, "and human nature from the beginning being a constant quantity, the same ideas, in almost the same forms, were evolved in various countries, representing the attempt of early man to formulate some theory of the natural appearances around him" (ibid.: 174). Oakley was an ethnologist in the Tylorian mold; he prized knowledge "derived not from books, but from the living speech of the people" (G. D. Upreti 2003 [1894]: ii). At the same time, he valued folklore studies as a means of laying bare the "character and conditions of an Asiatic people" whose survivals revealed an earlier stage of religious thought. "It is not easy to distinguish between mythology and folklore," he wrote, "for both represent an early stage of consciousness when man's fancy worked with freedom and was employed to give an explanation of all things. We are apt to think too seriously of the so-called religious ideas of non-Christian peoples. They are largely relics of man's early unrestrained fancy, consecrated, to some extent, in later times, by custom and priestly adoption; but, originally on the same level as our nursery tales. To the early intelligence of our remote ancestors everything was alive" (Oakley 1990 [1905]: 174–175). As we will explore in chapter 5, the condescension and infantilization of local rituals and beliefs was to become a persistent theme in the study of folk religion.

The production of colonial folklore—like much contemporary ethnography—necessarily involved collaborations between Western and native elites. For obvious reasons, colonial scholars required the linguistic and cultural expertise of native scholars, and the latter needed the cultural capital of colonial scholars. Oakley collaborated closely with two of the most important native folklorists of the region, Tara Dutt Gairola and Ganga Datt Upreti.

Pandit Ganga Datt Upreti (1834–1910), a native of Almora, showed prodigious linguistic abilities as a young man, teaching himself Farsi, Urdu, Hindi, Sanskrit, Nepali, English, and Latin (S. P. Saklani 2001: 268). He became deputy collector and then senior assistant commissioner in Garhwal District, and he took an interest in the study of folklore. On official expeditions throughout Garhwal and Kumaon, he recorded and collected thousands of local proverbs and stories from "old men of respectability and knowledge" (G. D. Upreti 2003 [1894]: i), later publishing them with the assistance of Oakley, who is listed as co-author, under the title *Proverbs and Folklore of Kumaon and Garhwal*. The proverbs are presented in Devanagari, with romanized transliteration and English translation and explanation, and they are grouped into two hundred categories, from "Courage under Despair" to "Peculiarities of Low Hill People." Ganga Datt Upreti believed that these proverbs offered "an insight into the character, habits, customs and traditions of the people" (ibid.: iii), and he focused on the proverbs as survivals, for "with the changes of time everything of antiquity is receding further out of sight, and is liable to disappear altogether" (ibid.: i).

Collections of proverbs were central to the colonial enterprise because they featured the speech of the colonized "isolated from the situation of its production" (Raheja 1999: 119). Proverbs could be selectively inscribed to maintain the "illusion of consent" and to affirm colonial perspectives about the unchanging traditions of Hindu society, as well as the backwardness of Himalayan subjects (ibid.: 120). Oakley begins his introduction to Upreti's volume thus: "The Oriental must have his epigram. It is one of the chief necessaries of his life, and an untold solace. . . . The wisdom of the East consists in such sentences and proverbs *rather than in any sustained effort of the reason*, and consequently they assume much greater importance than in Western lands, and furnish better materials for a thorough study of the character and conditions of an Asiatic people than any other source of information can supply" (G. D. Upreti 2003 [1894]: xxi, emphasis added).

In the last sentence of his own preface, Upreti seems aware of the contemporary political implications of his compendium: "Perhaps it is hardly necessary to caution my readers against misunderstanding some of these homely sayings, *and regarding as indications of the 'depravity' of the people, maxims which are obviously framed in an ironical sense and not seriously meant*" (G. D. Upreti 2003 [1894]: iii, emphasis added). Here Upreti betrays a hint of caution about the supposedly scientific enterprise of folklore studies. Many of his collected proverbs reinforce the low status and condition of poverty of the Dom and Khasa, for instance, "*Duma dagarhi gugeli.* A quarrel with a low-caste man is like playing with human excreta (i.e., degrading to oneself)" (ibid.: 288; see also 232, 234, 247, 248, 270, 302, and 377). One senses his discomfort with the knowledge that European readers might selectively draw from this collection of random, decontextualized proverbs to form a negative impression of *all* Kumaonis.

Another critical folklorist of this period, Tara Dutt Gairola (1875–1940), was born in the princely state of Tehri Garhwal. Gairola had a long and productive law career in Dehradun and Srinagar, and as the editor of *Garhwali* magazine he wrote in support of the uplifting of Shilpkars (Negi and Khatri 2005). In his spare time, he collected heroic ballads and devotional songs performed by local bards from the Hurkiya caste, eventually publishing them, with Oakley as co-author, under the title *Himalayan Folklore: Kumaon and West Nepal* (1977 [1935]). The text offers English translations of thirty-two stories from his own collection and sixty-five tales from Oakley's and Upreti's collections arranged into five categories: "Legends of Heroes," "Wit and Wisdom," "Animal Lore," "Bird Folklore," and "Ghost and Demon Lore." A large number of ballads detail the romantic trysts and battlefield exploits of warriors and kings who lived between the fourteenth and sixteenth centuries. References to music and musicians appear often in the stories, but rarely in a positive light. Music is frequently used to deceive or entrance someone, and musicians either lead warriors into battle with their drumming or they are maligned figures, impersonated by thieves, beggars, or heroes in order to avoid detection (ibid.: 21, 140, 222–226).

Like early Orientalists, Gairola valued contemporary folklore primarily as a means of interpreting regional history; the royal genealogies orally maintained by the bards formed the basis for reconstructing the lineage of Chand and Panwara dynasties. Yet his approach to folklore had an anticolonial slant: "The Europeans consider Indians as an inferior race," he wrote, and "the intelligentsia, the townsmen of India, look down upon the masses [of] the rural population, as ignorant and superstitious rustics. In the same way, the high castes of Hindus look down upon the depressed classes as untouchables, whose very shadow would pollute them. . . . It is also my belief that by a sympathetic study and understanding of the folklore of the various peoples of the world, the great truth will be discovered that all are closely related, in spite of their accidental differences, and that, in the great purpose of God, all nations of mankind are made of one blood, of one heart and mind, to dwell together on this earth and fulfill one united destiny" (1926: 29, 32).

Couched in the Enlightenment-tinged rhetoric of universal sameness is a subtle critique of the divisive discourses of caste and race promulgated by the colonial administration. By the presentation of regional stories and ballads, he sought to demonstrate that the medieval kingdoms of Garhwal and Kumaon were as noble and civilized as any in the world. He was also outspoken about the shortcomings of British folklorists like Edwin T. Atkinson: "With due deference to that great scholar I am constrained to say that his descriptions are very meagre, and even the pedigrees of the various kings given by him are not authentic. He does not describe the political and social conditions of that period correctly and leaves an unpleasant impression on the mind of the reader that the society was barbarous and uncivilized and devoid of all the noble qualities of head and heart" (Gairola and Oakley 1977 [1935]: 8). After confronting the demeaning characterizations of Himalayan peoples that accompanied earlier folklore studies, Gairola offered a more uplifting message: "It will be evident to any [unbiased] reader of the ancient folklore of the Himalayas that the people of those days, under the inspiration of their religion, compare favourably with any other nation of that age in heroism and other moral qualities" (ibid.: 21).

The production of folklore in late colonial India required the close collaboration of British and Indian scholars. The former obviously benefited from the linguistic skills and cultural familiarity of the latter; the latter gained personal prestige and, at times, a feeling that they were contributing to the documentation of their regional history. Although I have been unable to locate any personal correspondence between Oakley, Gairola, and Upreti, it is clear from their published statements that they shared great mutual respect and that Oakley treated Gairola and Upreti as associates rather than assistants.[28] As was common throughout India in the late nineteenth century, all three men treated the collection of folklore as an amateur endeavor—if still a scientific one—while engaged in educational and legal careers. And all three clearly believed that the collection and publication of Kumaoni folklore would advance the study of universal principles of thought and human history. Nevertheless, the differences in status and orientation between a British missionary and an Indian civil servant should not be minimized, and there are subtle signs that folklore fulfilled a different purpose for each of them. According to Oakley, it showed that Kumaonis, for all their "remarkable genius for religion" (1990 [1905]: 301), must ultimately accept Christianity and discard Hinduism because it promotes caste and division and leads people to blind faith. Upreti's and Gairola's motivations for participating in colonial folkloristics are less transparent and were likely ambivalent. Yet folklore offered a means of confronting colonial ideologies about the central Himalayas and of India more generally. "The colonizing world formed images, and the colonized became aware of those images of themselves and often used the same images to create anti-colonial and postcolonial identities" (Briggs and Naithani 2012: 247). Folklore offered a space in which colonized elites could shape the discourses of caste and race and portray a level of societal development and historical grandeur in Uttarakhand that was equal to any other "nation of that age."

Conclusion

Although the term *folk* does not appear in North Indian texts until the end of the nineteenth century, the origins of a folk concept may be traced to a number of ideological precursors. The Sanskrit concepts of lok-a and desi, while not equivalent to the folk concept taking root in western Europe in the late eighteenth and nineteenth centuries, were ideological antecedents that marked lower-status, mundane creations as different from higher-status, divine creations. The expansion of the British colonial empire generated a desire for a specific kind of folk subject, one that would validate the racial and cultural superiority of the colonizers. The European encounter with Himalayan landscapes had a direct bearing on the characterization of those who dwelt there. The Himalayan landscape was initially considered forbidding and dangerous, but it also yielded economic development and recovery from disease. In the same way, Paharis were a manifestation of the classic paradigm of the "noble savage": on one hand, they were fearful primitives only slightly more developed than animals, and on the other, they were people living in an Edenic paradise in perfect equilibrium with nature (Kennedy 1996).

In the late nineteenth century, the political and economic pressures of direct rule led to the reimagining of the central Himalayas as an area of military expansion and resource extraction. The idea of an undifferentiated Pahari folk subject was no longer tenable; rather, Himalayan races were distinguished on the basis of their innate character and ability to serve the British army with loyalty and courage. The Indo-Aryan migration theory provided the purportedly scientific rationale for scholar-administrators to reify the already extant divisions within Kumaoni society between "Aryan" Thul-Jat and Khasa, and between "non-Aryan" Dom and tribal groups.

Folklore was a powerful vehicle for maintaining the social hierarchy. As a method of inscription, folklore was produced by and for British and Indian elites, and it necessarily reflected and replicated their innermost values and goals. "The colonized was asked for 'folklore,' asked to record it, and asked to translate it—and could therefore not remain unaware of the concept and object of 'folklore'" (Briggs and Naithani 2012: 247). High-status Rajputs and Brahmins (Thul-Jat) such as Gairola and Upreti acquired positions of power and prestige within the colonial administration, and producing folklore was one of the ways they could shape European impressions of Himalayan society, even if they were obliged to use the methods and language of the colonizers. The Khasa were the favored subjects of folklore because of their presumed indigeneity, their lower social positions as agricultural laborers and artisans, and their maintenance of primitive social practices that were seen as survivals from an earlier age. The Dom, consisting of low-status singers, drummers, and other artisans, were the anonymous transmitters of oral folklore that Thul-Jat converted into written knowledge. The mediation of writing ensured that the authentic experience of folk remained within the circles of literate urban elites and that the compiler and arranger was able to demonstrate his own cultivation by selecting the "most polished, attractive, significant . . . and most typical representative of various types" (Lampert 1982: 11).

For colonial ethnologists, the value of collecting Himalayan folklore lay in reconstructing an ancient Aryan society rooted in a medieval past predating the arrival of Gurkha and British rule. Contemporary proverbs, ballads, and rituals were vestiges of the glorious classical past of Kumaon. Oakley and other British folklorists sought and found parallels with the tales of medieval Europe, which provided evidence for the theory that "all races began at the same mental level" (Gairola and Oakley 1977 [1935]: 174). Native scholars such as Upreti and Gairola valued folk idioms because they revealed a royal Kumaoni history that could "compare favourably with any other nation of that age." Keenly aware of European depictions of degradation and backwardness in the Himalayas, these scholars sought to elevate the position of Kumaoni society, upgrading it to a classical status. Upreti and Gairola treated Himalayan folklore as their personal inheritance, but they did not appear to count themselves as part of the folk; there was a need to locate the latter elsewhere and in another age. Within the emerging discipline of folkloristics, the folk concept was part of a "scientific" discourse that sought to identify the collective, timeless, rural Other and to position the scholar or observer at a distance from it (Blackburn and Ramanujan 1986). The repositories of folk culture were not individuals but collective bodies connected through heritage, a mythic past, and a set of marked traits. As Kirin Narayan explains, "There was clearly a preexisting notion brought over from Europe of who the folk were: they were not Brahman pandits of the sort that Orientalists were consulting about Sanskrit texts, nor were they British-educated Indians. Rather, they were the 'lower classes' steeped in tradition" (1993: 182).

It is noteworthy that the ballads, religious texts, stories, and proverbs collected by these folklorists usually came to them in the form of songs or pitched recitations accompanied by one of several percussion instruments. In the absence of written documentation, Gairola, Oakley and Upreti relied on hereditary musicians and balladeers (Shilpkars) as their primary informants. Yet we know next to nothing about these performers from their texts. Gairola wrote that the ballads, "preserved in the memories of the local bards, who are the descendants of the *Hurkias*, the family bards of the Kings and chieftains, whose heroic deeds they sang, are more likely to be accurate than the pedigrees in the Gazetteer" (Gairola and Oakley 1977 [1935]: 15). This sentence is all we learn about Gairola's primary informants, who remain nameless in the text. Even the anthropologist Marc Gaborieau, who wrote the introduction to the 1977 reprint of Gairola's *Himalayan Folklore*, tells us that the Hurkiya are "begging musicians . . . who do not have a wide repertory: they usually sing fashionable songs and make their women sing and dance (i.e., prostitute them)" (ibid.: xvii). Such characterizations of hereditary performers are part of a long history of Shilpkar anonymity and misrepresentation extending from the late nineteenth century to the present.

2 Mohan Upreti and the Assimilation of Folk Music in Nehruvian India

This chapter examines the crystallization of the folk concept in the policies of the Nehruvian state and the writings and cultural performances of urban intellectuals in mid-twentieth-century India. In particular, I focus on the contributions of Mohan Upreti (1925–1997), a Kumaoni composer, author, director, performer, political activist, and folklorist who was perhaps most responsible for the dissemination and codification of folk music at mid-century. Supported by a mixture of private and state patronage, Mohan Upreti brought attention to indigenous performance idioms in the Uttarakhand Himalayas at a time when most Kumaoni elites were interested in moving to the urban plains and distancing themselves from local performance idioms. I examine four influences—North Indian classical (Hindustani) music, the populist productions of the Indian People's Theatre Association, the music of Hurkiya balladeers in Kumaon, and the cultural institutions of the central Indian government—that cumulatively shaped Upreti's approach to Kumaoni folk ballads, the artistic form for which he is best known as a theater composer and performer.

Inheriting the Dualism of Folk and Classical

Born in Almora, Mohan Upreti was the eldest son of Heera Upreti and Kishori Chandra Upreti, a forest office superintendent and avid patron of music and theatrical performance. During Mohan Upreti's childhood in the late 1920s and 1930s, Almora was a hub of cultural and political activity. Mohandas K. Gandhi, Rabindranath Tagore, Swami Vivekananda, and Sister Nivedita were among the prominent national figures to visit or live in

Almora in the first decades of the twentieth century. As a member of one of
Almora's more prominent Brahman families, Upreti was immersed in theater
and North Indian (Hindustani) classical music throughout his childhood.
In annual performances of the Ramlila, a theatrical enactment of scenes
from the Ramayana epic, Upreti enacted the roles of Ram, Lakshman, and
Ravana. Although the Ramlila is performed across Uttarakhand and much
of Uttar Pradesh, Bihar, and Madhya Pradesh, a distinctive operatic tradition
has been performed annually in Almora for the past century and a half. The
Almora Ramlila is sung through and draws extensively from Hindustani
raga and *tala*, as well as the music of Rajasthan and the music of minstrel
performers.[1] In addition to the extensive training that Upreti received as part
of these annual performances, he received training from his grandfather
Revadhar Upreti and his uncle Chandra Shekhar Pant, both of whom were
well-known Hindustani vocalists.

Upreti was also influenced by the eclectic artistic productions of the India
Cultural Centre in Almora, founded by Uday Shankar in 1937.[2] The center
was the culmination of Shankar's effort to develop an artistic pedagogy that
blended folk arts and Indian classical music and dance with international
styles. Shankar leveraged his international stardom to assemble a talented
faculty that included the multi-instrumentalist Baba Allaudin Khan, the
Bharatanaytam dance instructor (*nattuvanar*) Kandappa Pillai, Ambi Singh,
and the Kathakali dancer Sankaran Namboodri. Soon he was able to attract
a range of talented students including Lakshmi Sastri (later to marry Uday's
brother Rajendra and become the well-known Hindustani vocalist Lakshmi
Shankar), Zohra Sehgal, Guru Dutt, and Uday's own younger brother Ravi
Shankar. Uday's staging of the Ramlila is an example of how he fused so-
called classical dance styles with local folk elements: the performers moved
along a road lined with oil lamps between two hills representing Ayodhya
and Lanka, while the spectators lined the roads, becoming ritual participants in a kind of open-air theater. Among the many folkloric dances that
Uday Shankar choreographed was *Ghasyari Geet*, which he modeled on the
graceful movements of the female grass cutters in the hillsides surrounding
Kumaon. Shankar went on to present this item in dance recitals in China
and Mongolia in the 1940s, a fact that undoubtedly left an impression on
the young Mohan Upreti, as did Shankar's efforts to fuse folk and classical
elements. Upreti's composed "folk ballads," particularly those from later in
his career such as "Ramleela," "Lal Gulab," "Inder Sabha," "Sanjhi Virasat,"
"Meghdoot," and "Amir Khusrau," reveal influences from village-based Kumaoni song, dance, and poetic forms, as well as melodic frameworks (raga)
and rhythmic frameworks (tala) from Hindustani music. Before exploring

Upreti's life and artistic approach in more depth, it is worth considering the genealogical relationships between folk music and classical music in northern India at mid-century. A large body of literature in ethnomusicology and related disciplines has been dedicated to understanding the emergence of the concept of classical music in South Asia, as well as the motivations behind classicization within the performing arts. Many scholars have been quick to acknowledge that folk music is an equally fluid and contested discursive domain, but the ways in which this concept emerged, and the ways in which folk and classical (and the processes of classicization and folklorization) have been ideologically intertwined, have been interrogated only recently.[3]

Indian society underwent monumental changes in the decades leading to independence, with urban migration, industrialization, and the decline of the landholding aristocrats (*zamindars*) and royal courts all contributing to the growing economic clout of the middle classes. A newly urban elite sought to "classicize" the performing arts as a way of legitimating their activities by drawing from older sources of social and spiritual authority. The influential pedagogues S. M. Tagore (1840–1914), V. N. Bhatkhande (1860–1936), and V. D. Paluskar (1872–1931) were among those invested in reforming modern music to fit their conception of the ancient heritage of pre-colonial ("Hindu") India. As has been well documented,[4] these reformers shared many of the modernist, cosmopolitan values of the European colonial elite, and they sought to codify and reform Indian classical arts (*shastriya sangeet*) by emphasizing early treatises as sources of authority and by creating systems of notation, institutions, classification schemes, and orchestras using Indian instruments. While conforming to a broader set of ideas about "classical" music, these reformers also celebrated the uniquely Indian essence of largely oral, improvised music based on raga and tala, with little direct musical influence from the West (Weidman 2006). For these reasons, modernist reformers identified Indian classical music as a potent vehicle for nationalist sentiment.

As described in chapter 1, the concept of folk began to appear in Orientalist scholarship concerning India in the late nineteenth century. European and Indian scholars inscribed their knowledge of rural communities in collections of ballads, songs, stories, and proverbs. The term *folk music* served as a catch-all designation for a loosely defined repertory that frequently was characterized by what it was not—classical music. Folk music came to be identified by many intellectuals by its *lack* of refinement, status, and abstract theoretical knowledge. The English scholar Arthur H. Fox-Strangways, one of the pioneers of contemporary ethnomusicological fieldwork and ethnography, offered a glimpse into his own understanding of these labels when he transcribed and recorded several songs performed by a group of "cheerful and honest" Garhwali migrants from Mussoorie who had arrived in Allahabad for training as rickshaw pullers (1914: 51–72). When a man from the First Gurkha Regiment revealed that one of the items he had performed was in *Raga Behag*, Fox-Strangways remarked, "That its singer knew so much about it as that, not to mention its carefully balanced sections (the same as in our National Anthem), removes it from the category of folk-song proper" (ibid.: 56). To Fox-Strangways, the song did not meet the criteria for a folk song because of its symmetrical form and refined quality, and because the singer was able to verbalize theoretical knowledge about the music.

Indian government officials also perpetuated the idea of folk music as cruder and simpler than classical music. The Minister for Broadcasting and Information for almost a decade beginning in 1952, B. V. Keskar, understood folk music to be at a lower level of musical evolution:

> Just as in language side by side with Kalidasa there might be a cheap novel, so in music there might be cheaper forms. There are the simple forms of music [that] can be understood by everybody. Even the fisherman will understand it. That is why we call it folk music. It is meant to please and charm the mass of people. We produce a book for a little child or we produce books [that] the ordinary man in the street can read; we produce the highest books on science or the finest piece of literature by Shakespeare or Kalidasa. In music also there are the simplest forms to the very highest and most abstract. (1967: 48–49)

Such attitudes were commonplace among mid-twentieth-century European and Indian intellectuals, and to some extent they persist today.[5] It remains common to find descriptions of the relation between classical music and folk music as an evolutionary progression, such that folk music is conceived as a spontaneous and infantile reaction of the masses to their environment that could only evolve into classical music after careful cultivation, elite patronage, and abstraction through the development of notation and theory. For some, folk music is principally valued as one important *source* of classical music but remains rooted in a primitive stratum of Indian society and is inextricably tied to social function (e.g., Ghosh 2004: 20; see also Manuel 2015: 86).

A reverse assumption—that classical arts devolved into folk arts—also finds endorsement in some scholarship. This assumption may be found, for example, in studies that seek to position the central Himalayan region as the birthplace of orthodox and textual expressions of Brahmanism that gradually degenerate into the "jungly" Hinduism of the common people (Sarkar 1917). Research concerning the relation between oral and written traditions of the Mahabharata is another area in which folk and classical have frequently been cast in evolutionary terms. John Leavitt has described the ways the "relatively fixed Sanskrit text has served as a main source for some oral tellings" of the Kumaoni Mahabharata (2000: 72). Although he is careful not to suggest that *all* oral tellings derive from a Sanskrit urtext, Claus Zoller (2001) nonetheless faults him for assuming primacy and holism within the Sanskritic tradition and for adopting Ramanujan's "classicist" bias in explaining the transformation within folk epics according to four "derivative" processes: fragmentation, domestication, localization, and contemporization (Ramanujan 1993). Both Leavitt and Zoller make reference to Chandola's (1977: 18) tripartite Folk-Classical-Folk model of the Mahabharata tradition, in which the first "folk" connotes something like "original," and the second "folk" means something like the localized adaptation that has been filtered through the "classical" tradition. Given the historical depth of many regional epic traditions, however, Zoller argues that it is impossible to establish definitive origins or direct lines of influence between folk and classical versions; instead he posits the existence of a "proto-Mahabharata" from which both of these traditions emerged. Such debates demonstrate the degree to which cultural expressions in the central Himalayas continue to be interpreted in terms of an interactive relationship between two distinct streams, with *classical* signifying text-based traditions and *folk* signifying oral traditions.

High-status Indians educated in English-language schools in semi-urban settings have tended to grow up removed from village-based cultural practices, and this distance has exacerbated prejudices when confronted with so-called folk music and dance. Nonetheless, negative portrayals of folk culture have been as much the products of the contradictions inherent in classicization as they have been direct responses to so-called folk performance. Attempts to elevate the status of Indian classical arts were hindered by the need to accommodate the presence of the large numbers of professional female, lower-caste, and Muslim hereditary musicians. In order for classical music and dance to become emblems of Indian modernity, these stigmatized performers and elements needed to be reformed or purged. Indian dance forms including Bharatanatyam (Allen 1998; Soneji 2012), Kathak (Walker 2014), and Kathakali are examples of classical forms that have been reformed. Following the ideological pattern of modernist reform elsewhere, these forms are frequently described as having been "revived" when they are in fact newly constituted in accordance with cosmopolitan values and presentational norms (Turino 2003; see also Livingston 1999).

The persistent characterizations of folk traditions as provincial, timeless, and infantile have led some contemporary scholars to conclude that the folk concept was ill equipped to serve the needs of cultural nationalism. In his

assessment of print media in late-nineteenth-century Tamil Nadu, Stuart
Blackburn concluded that printed folklore "was found to be too native, too
redolent of backward traditions, to be capable of assuming the public mantle
of a political nationalism" (2003: 16). In contrast to classical literature such as
the Tamil Sangams, folk literature was deemed to have questionable morals
and imprecise antiquity.

By the 1940s, however, nationalist reformers were rethinking the political and social repercussions of rebuking folk culture and folk performance.
One of the benefits of the folk category was that it gave cultural reformers
a discursive space in which to position many low-status performers from
subordinated or "backward" musical traditions. Folk music began to be rei-
magined as a resource that could benefit the new nation. Some intellectuals
made a conscious effort to reclaim folk music and folk musicians from the
margins of society and to use them in the creation of the national patrimony.
One of the leading Indian anthropologists of the 1940s and 1950s, D. N. Majumdar, established the Ethnographic and Folk Culture Society of Northern
India in 1945 with the aim of studying the country's "thirty million tribals . . .
and many [Scheduled Tribe] groups that derive from the tribes." He railed
against the destructive influences of missionization and colonization on the
tribal populations and advocated "rais[ing] the criminal tribes from their
stagnation and squalor" so that all of India might become civilized (1946:
xii).

In his study of the Sauka, a community of trans-Himalayan traders living
on the border of Uttarakhand and Tibet, the Kumaoni anthropologist Naresh
Chandra wrote:

> There is now hardly any possibility of a diversity of opinions on the importance
> of *the preservation of folk-songs of our people, who have escaped the influences of
> the new hybrid culture* and have thus been able to preserve from its ravages the
> native beauty of their social customs and simple pastimes. . . . As these tribal
> people become aware of the more "advanced" cultures around them, they begin
> to be *obsessed by a consciousness of [their] backwardness and awkwardness.* They
> are desirous to bring their native culture more in line with that of the outside
> world, and thus folk cultures and folk songs are pitched in a struggle for exis-
> tence. (quoted in Pangtey 2006 [1949]: 106, emphasis added)

This passage marks the temporal and spatial boundaries of folk culture
in opposition to the "advanced cultures around them." Urban ethnologists
sought out folk culture in an essentialized space (the village) and time (pre-
British or pre-Mughal history, or an "unchanging present"), and among a reified people (tribals, scheduled castes, remote hill populations).[6] They viewed
folk culture as being in a perpetual state of decline and needing protection;

tribal people could not accomplish this task by themselves because they were "obsessed by a consciousness of backwardness." Majumdar's and Chandra's research agendas were rooted in a discourse of preservation and protectionism, but they also believed that folk communities formed a valuable part of the national patrimony. It is especially noteworthy that Chandra incorporates the music of the Sauka—one of the more marginalized communities of Uttarakhand—into the repertoire of (presumably Indian or Kumaoni) folk music, signaling a shift to nationalist or regionalist discourse. If folk music continued to mark a position of alterity and marginality within the nation, it also marked the possibility of sameness, of a collective heritage that could be claimed by each and every citizen. The goal of folklore studies at mid-century was thus to reclaim "the folk" from the margins and convert their cultural practices into a collective resource for the nation.[7]

Many urban intellectuals turned to folk music and dance for raw materials that could be used to create populist art that would articulate the goals of the leftist movement in India. The role of the Indian People's Theatre Association (IPTA) in the 1940s and 1950s, discussed in more detail below, was particularly important in this regard. Yet the political legacy of this organization may be less important than its creation of a sense of value among urban Indian audiences for indigenous folk forms. In contrast to classical music, which struggled to find a mass following among diverse social classes (despite the efforts of All India Radio in the 1950s), folk music became valuable precisely because of its ability to "please and charm the mass of people." It was assumed that all regions within India had a corresponding folk music, making it a natural vehicle for the expression of cultural regionalism and cultural nationalism.

The study of folklore became a way for nationalist cosmopolitans, in the words of German folklorist Konrad Kostlin, to demonstrate "their own contribution, and this often in reaction to feelings of inferiority in regions which were, in more than one sense, colonized" (quoted in Bendix 1997: 184). Indian scholars may have inherited theoretical and methodological approaches from European folkloristics, but they also *responded* to colonization by identifying with and asserting ownership over regional folklore as part of the national patrimony (Narayan 1993: 187).[8]

IPTA and the Search for Authentic Folk

In the early 1940s, Upreti and his four siblings became heavily influenced by the leftist political and artistic movements sweeping across much of North India. Upreti followed in the footsteps of many of his male relatives and peers and moved to the urban plains for higher education, graduating in 1949 with a dual degree in diplomacy and international relations and vocal music from Allahabad University. In the same year, Upreti joined the Communist Party of India (CPI). Under the mentorship of fellow Almora native Puran Chand Joshi, who served as the first general secretary of the CPI, Upreti also became heavily involved in the Indian People's Theatre Association as a performer and composer. After the India Cultural Centre in Almora closed in 1943, many of its faculty members, including Uday Shankar and his family, applied their artistic vision to supporting the IPTA from its inception in July 1944. The IPTA was the first national-level artistic organization to utilize village-based regional forms; it incorporated aspects of performance traditions from diverse regions in India—notably urban theatrical forms such as *jatra* in Bengal and *tamasha* and *powada* in Maharashtra—to create new works with the goal of unifying the working classes against fascism and imperialism (Bharucha 1998: 32–45). According to Aparna Dharwadker, "the IPTA's traditionalism was the first major modern reaction against two deeply entrenched colonial practices: a century-long denigration of 'corrupt' indigenous forms by the colonial and Indian urban elite and the thorough commercialization of urban proscenium theatre by bourgeois Parsi entrepreneurs. Folk theater thus answered the need for *noncommercial* forms that were already familiar and appealing to 'the people'" (2005: 312). By reaching back to so-called premodern forms of cultural expression, the urban functionaries of the IPTA were attempting to make the "political message of opposition to fascism, imperialism, and capitalism accessible to mass audiences in both cities and villages" (ibid.). That these political developments occurred in the realm of theater is significant; it must be seen as a response to the growing popularity of Parsi theatre and Hindi cinema, both of which were widely denigrated as overly "Western" (Anand 1950).

By the time Upreti became involved in the IPTA in 1949, the organization's influence was already waning because of its submission to the political agenda of the Communist Party of India. Yet Upreti was deeply influenced by the method of fusing diverse artistic genres to create a political message that could be understood by urban and rural audiences alike. Directors, playwrights, and performers in the IPTA worked together to rewrite and restage the same plays in multiple languages, incorporating either urban or rural idioms depending on the performance setting (Bhatia 1997: 433). "Though still patronizing of folk forms," Dalmia writes, "the IPTA's intentions were beyond revivalist or conservationist: there was an agenda of communicating with rural audiences . . . and an unsentimental awareness that folk forms needed to change with the times" (2006: 164). Upreti had studied musical forms from many parts of India, but he was, by his own admission, reluctant to embrace the village-based artistic forms of Kumaon because of a deep-seated prejudice against activities associated with lower-caste performers in the hills. He later attributed his feelings of shame concerning village-based music to a colonial inheritance from his forefathers in British India, some of whom had campaigned against the performance of folk song and dance because of long-held discriminatory attitudes (Bajeli 2006: 132).

All of this changed for Upreti in 1955, when he and several colleagues trekked to the home of Congress leader Pratap Singh Bisht in Naugaon, a village near Almora, and encountered Mohan Singh "Reethagadi" Bora (figure 2.1). In the Reethagad *patti* of the Almora District, Bora had become a renowned Hurkiya, or bard, who accompanied himself on the hurka. He was an extremely charismatic performer who had been steeped in ballads and village performances since his youth; somewhat unusually, however, he was a Rajput rather than a Shilpkar. His upper-caste background would have made it easier for him to mix with Upreti and other high-status intellectuals and politicians. Puran Chand Joshi, who was also present on this occasion, described Bora as a "non-commercial musician . . . beyond the buying and selling powers of the marketplace" who performed melodies and texts that were not his own but had "originated and reverberated in the Himalayas for ages" (quoted in Bajeli 2006: 163). For Upreti, the experience of hearing Bora perform was nothing less than a conversion experience. He wrote that he "felt for the first time that [this music] was such a precious cultural treasure of which not only Kumaon *but the whole of Indian music could be legitimately proud.* . . . His musical vibrations and compositions gave a glimpse of the infinitely changing landscape of the mountain ranges—all this and much more I witnessed, felt and experienced, internalized and acquired during that night which changed the entire course of my life" (ibid.: 22, emphasis added). Upreti began learning many styles of song from Bora, and he frequently referred to him as a guru. There is no formal tradition of *guru-shishya* discipleship in the traditional musical systems of the central Himalayas, but it is noteworthy that Upreti—who had extensive training in Hindustani music—framed his relationships with Bora in these terms. According to P. C. Joshi, "opting for a life-long dedication to folk music [signaled] a fundamental break from his Brahmanical upper-caste conditioning which did not allow for such 'descent into lower depths,' for adopting the hurka, the musical instrument played by low-caste folk singers, and for 'degrading' [himself] by putting [onto a] high pedestal a musician from a caste lower than his own as his *guru* for [his] whole life!" (ibid.: 151).

For Upreti and his peers, Bora was a paradoxical figure: idealized, heroic, proud, connected to the rural landscape, a "voice of the masses," but also

Fig. 2.1. Mohan Singh Bora
("Reethagadi") performing with
the hurka, undated (courtesy
Himanshu Joshi)

irrevocably backward, noncommercial, and unable to adapt to the exigencies of modern life. Bajeli noted, "[Upreti] was of the opinion that it was very difficult for the traditional artist, who performed in the open air without any theatrical props, to act on the modern stage. They tended to be like a fish out of water. But [Upreti] had always expressed his gratitude to traditional artists who are the true creators of folk wealth. He organized special evenings to give a rousing welcome to folk artists, especially to his Guru Mohan Singh Bora. Folk artists were frequently invited from the hills. They were also given exposure [in] the electronic and print media" (2006: 43). According to P. C. Joshi, "the same Mohan Singh who had performed for us in his natural setting, the lap of his Mother Himalaya, [performed] again in the drawing room of Miss Nirmala Joshi, the First Secretary of the Sangeet Natak Akademi. . . . The same poet-musician torn out of his own milieu, his native and natural environment appeared almost to be a shadow of his former self" (2000: 20).

The promotion of this "natural" folk artist of the Himalayas exposes a discourse of authenticity that is reminiscent of the attitudes of John and Alan Lomax, Cecil Sharp, and other participants in the English and American folk revivals. Yet while Upreti was susceptible to a certain romanticization of village folk artists, his goal was not cultural preservation per se; in fact, he was concerned that collection and collation of folk culture oriented toward mere preservation had done little to revive the cultural life of ordinary people "We have treated our folk heritage in an elitist manner," he wrote, "without caring to see beyond its formalistic aspects. Its content has rarely been touched for other than academic purposes" (Bajeli 2006: 128). Upreti's solution was to treat folk art as a malleable tool of expression that could be adapted to reflect a modern sensibility. "We cannot," he warned, "project rare folk forms created by the collective genius of the masses hundreds of years ago in a different socio-economic position, [as] a museum piece. Folk art can never be extinguished, just modified to fit modern consciousness. . . . As folk art assimilated primitive art, so the modern consciousness can assimilate folk art" (ibid.: 134).

As recounted by Joshi, Bajeli, and Upreti himself, this chance meeting with Bora was the spark that motivated Upreti to reinvent himself as a champion of Uttarakhandi folk arts. Instead of using folk arts to serve political interests, which, he believed, had been the downfall of the IPTA, Upreti, drawing on the writings of the Russian novelist Maxim Gorky, would use folk arts for the aesthetic needs of all. What distinguished folk communities from non-folk ones, he wrote, "was the absorption of the individual within the whole" (Bhattacharya, Upreti, and Parmar 1967: 96).

Institutionalizing Folk Music within the Nehruvian State

In 1955, shortly after adopting Bora as his guru, Upreti started a theater group in Almora called Lok Kalakar Sangh (Folk Artist Collective). Upreti's productions started to garner attention within Uttarakhand after he received a UNESCO grant that enabled him to research and compose new works based on local folkloric elements. He used this group to stage many of the songs, dances, and ballad forms that he had learned from Bora, and he began to sing compositions on stage while accompanying himself on the hurka, an indigenous pressure drum. The hurka carried associations with Shilpkar bards, and Upreti's public adoption of the instrument caused an outcry from within his family, which was among the highest-ranking Brahman families in Almora (figure 2.2).[9]

The success of Lok Kalakar Sangh was short-lived. In 1962 longstanding border disputes between India and China ignited in a brief but costly war waged at various points along Uttarakhand's border with Tibet. Indian patriotism swelled during and after this conflict, and members of the Communist Party of India were jailed in large numbers. Upreti was arrested on suspicion

Fig. 2.2. Mohan Upreti performing
with the hurka, undated (courtesy
Himanshu Joshi)

of being a Chinese sympathizer, and he spent ten months in prison. After the
war he was released on the condition that he live outside Uttarakhand. Cut
off from his artistic community, Upreti went through a protracted period of
depression until he was able to settle with friends and relatives in Delhi.

In 1968 Upreti started a Delhi-based theater company called Parvatiya
Kala Kendra (Center for Hill Arts) along with his friend Brijendra Lal Shah.
Upreti's approach to music direction was daring and progressive, and the
company brought together performers from diverse backgrounds, including several high-caste women and at least one Shilpkar drummer, Kali Ram.
Naima Khan was a Muslim performer who worked alongside Upreti for
decades; while most members of the company knew that they had been ro-
mantically involved for years, their eventual marriage in 1975, when Upreti
was fifty years of age, caused yet another minor scandal in the orthodox
Brahman community of Almora.

Upreti was eager to confront such taboos, and he began to resent the conservative elements within Almora society. According to his younger brother,
Bhagwat Upreti, who also performed in this group, there had been growing
sentiments of jealousy and backbiting directed toward Mohan Upreti on the
part of conservative elites in Almora.[10] Few individuals within the Brahman
community were ready to support Upreti's progressive stance toward using
women and lower-caste artisans in his performances, and some resented his

Communist politics. On the few occasions when the company performed in Almora, the response was muted and indifferent.

After 1968, Mohan Upreti no longer needed support within Almora. He was well positioned to take advantage of the cultural policies of the Nehruvian state and of the large and influential Kumaoni migrant class in Delhi. Early in his first term as prime minister, Nehru recognized the threat posed to the new nation by secessionist movements and by calls for regional statehood across the subcontinent. As a way of accommodating many of these demands, the States Reorganization Commission's 1954 recommendation led to the creation of fourteen new regional states and six centrally administered territories within India. The commission elected not to carve a separate hill state out the mountainous districts of Uttar Pradesh, despite the longstanding call for such a state by a small but powerful faction of social elites in Kumaon (Husain 1995). Nehru was keenly aware of the risk of backlash by activists in Uttarakhand and other parts of India whose regionalist demands went unheeded. For this reason, perhaps, he felt that "special attention [should be directed] to folk performers from the nation's peripheries along with tribal artistes" (Roy 2007: 76). Even if all ethnolinguistic groups in the nation could not be represented by their own regional state, he recognized the importance of artistic expression as a form of political representation. Nehru conceived of folk culture, as Srirupa Roy notes, "as a national and natural resource—available in abundance but requiring careful monitoring, management, and harvesting by the state" (ibid.). By encouraging folk performances among marginalized communities from around the subcontinent, the state could claim to offer a platform for regional diversity while restricting antinationalist sentiment.

Upreti's role as an ambassador of Uttarakhandi folk music was only possible with the growing migration to the cities during the late 1940s and 1950s. Encouraged by industrial growth and educational opportunities in the cities, large numbers of migrants entered India's four largest urban areas from Uttarakhand and other economically depressed rural areas. Most urban migrants were men who were unable to return to their villages for long periods of time. New arrivals sought out individuals from their extended family or their mountainous district, thereby forming mutual support networks. Some of these networks grew to become regional migrant associations, drawing individuals from all corners of Garhwal and Kumaon. In Delhi, Uttarakhandi migrants established cultural institutions like Akhil Garhwal Sabha, Kumaon Sabha, and Uttarakhand Yuva Manch, all of which were vital to forming artistic alliances and collecting financial support for cultural performances.[11] Colonial administrators had used the term *Pahari* for all residents of the central and western Himalayas, but the term never had much relevance for local communities in the mountains or the urban plains. The vast majority of migrant organizations in Delhi, Chandigarh, and Mumbai stressed distinctive Garhwali and Kumaoni identities.

As the primary beneficiaries of state-funded cultural performances and recordings, Upreti and his contemporaries directly shaped the stylistic development and canon formation of folk music and dance. Parmar notes that "rural musicians who came and settled in towns for livelihood also contributed to the emergence of [new genres;] . . . without abandoning the basic characteristics of their original styles, they were required to evolve a new type of musical discipline especially when they came into contact with radio, television and film" (1977: 61). Adapting village musical forms to urban presentational contexts and recorded media was not always a simple process. The temporal limitation of recording was one significant challenge. Local heroic ballad forms (*panwara*, *vir gathae*, and *barh geet*), for example, typically required hours or days to perform. The performance of rural styles was also not desirable for some urban migrants whose sentiments of nostalgia, hope, and loss required new cultural forms that communicated a cosmopolitan sensibility.

Mohan Upreti, along with Jeet Singh Negi, Mohini Sharma, and Keshav Anuragi, was among the first Uttarakhandi artists to leverage the influence of gramophone recordings through the state-owned Gramophone Company of India, Ltd. (also known as His Master's Voice, or HMV). Upreti made several recordings for HMV in the early 1950s, including the infamous "Bedu Pako" (see below).[12] Upreti also broadcast regularly on All India Radio, an ideal platform from which to popularize his renditions of anonymous village-based folk songs as well as his own folk-inspired compositions. Upreti, along with such contemporaries as Jeet Singh Negi, Govind Chatak, Uma "Satish" Shankar, and Chander Singh Rahi, developed thirty- to sixty-minute programs that often focused on the music of a particular subregion within Uttarakhand (for example, Jaunsar, Rawain, or Tehri) or an indigenous song type (for example, *bajuband*, *mangal geet*, or *thadya-chaunfla*). All India Radio stations in Lucknow and Delhi were the first to broadcast Garhwali and Kumaoni music on "regional folk" programs in the 1950s. The extremely popular "Uttaraini" request program on AIR Lucknow helped establish the reputations of Upreti and others as legitimate folk artists. Taken together, these programs popularized genre categories and markers of stylistic authenticity that would be used to identify and evaluate the folk music of the region.[13]

A number of Garhwali and Kumaoni migrants, including Mohan Upreti, Mohan Lal Babulkar, Govind Chatak, and Chander Singh Rahi, supplemented radio broadcasts and gramophone recordings with academic publications.[14] Across India urban intellectuals returned to their native regions to document the folk arts. Their research was supported by a dramatic increase in the number of private and state-funded publishers, archives, museums, and academic departments specializing in regional folk studies. The Ethnographic and Folk Culture Society of Northern India (1945), the Folk Music and Folklore Research Institute at Calcutta (1965), the Folklore Institute at the University of Mysore (1967), and the Folk Institute of Meerut (c. 1975) were among the earliest folklore programs in the country. The Sangeet Natak Akademi and the Indian Council for Cultural Relations, both initiated in the early 1950s, patronized Upreti's productions and supported scholarly efforts to collect and classify various types of folk songs, dances, proverbs, and ballads via performances and publications.

Upreti's compositions for the stage drew from Kumaoni songs and dances, especially the long ballad forms (panwara and vir gathae) that he learned and transcribed from Mohan Singh Bora. Upreti composed the music for more than a dozen "folk ballads" premiered by Parvatiya Kala Kendra, including *Rajula-Malushahi, Ajuwa Bafaul, Mahabharata, Rasik Ramola, Jeetu Bagdwal, Hill Jatra, Bhana-Gangnath, Haru Heet, Rami Baurana,* and *Gori Dhana.* Upreti is often credited with introducing an operatic through-composed style of theater to cosmopolitan audiences in Delhi, and he most likely drew on his early exposure to the Almora Ramlila, as well as his study with Bora. Probably his most famous production was a 1981 adaptation of *Rajula-Malushahi,* a romantic ballad that is known throughout Kumaon. This ballad tells of the forbidden love between the son of a king from the medieval Katyuri dynasty and the daughter of a Bhotiya trader. Upreti recorded and transcribed three versions of this ballad performed by Bora from Almora and two Shilpkar balladeers—Joga Ram from Bageshwar and Gopi Das from Kausani—and he later published a comparative analysis of all three versions (H. C. Upreti 1981; see also Meissner 1985). His stage adaptation of *Rajula-Malushahi,* directed by Brij Mohan Shah, incorporated aspects of the singing styles and narrative devices used by all three ballad singers. "Rajula-Malushahi ballad seems to be breathing its last," Upreti later wrote. "The old generation of singers [and] audiences is vanishing fast. One should not wait for a new ballad singer to be born to pick up the broken thread. That thread is broken forever. The ballad is no longer going to be re-created and re-fashioned by the community in its old style. If it has to survive, it must find a place in the contemporary medium of artistic communication" (M. Upreti 2001: 203).

Upreti's adaptations of folk ballads for contemporary audiences shows clear influences from his early years with the IPTA, but productions he led

after the late 1960s also reveal a new nationalist imperative as the steward-
ship of Indian folk art moved to state-funded institutions such as the Sangeet
Natak Akademi. Within the IPTA, folk was understood as "the vital resource
that classical traditions drew upon for their inspiration and sustenance"; in
contrast, scholars of the Sangeet Natak Akademi "saw the many folk forms
as the many offshoots as the one, the classical Sanskrit theatre" (Dalmia
2006: 172). In his writings, Upreti does not clearly line up on one end of
this ideological spectrum or the other, but the compositions from later in
his career—for example, *Ramleela*, *Lal Gulab*, *Inder Sabha*, *Sanjhi Virasat*,
Meghdoot, and *Amir Khusrau*—reveal strong nationalist influences and the
more direct application of Hindustani raga and tala. Kumaoni inflections are
still present in these works, but they are ensconced within the stylistic idiom
of Hindustani music.

It is not surprising that the cultural boundaries of Upreti's academic studies
and creative endeavors, like those of other state-funded folklorists, replicated
the political boundaries of regional states or divisions (Narayan 1993: 189;
Bharucha 1990: 198); Garhwali scholars tended to write only about Garhwali
folklore, Kumaoni scholars about Kumaoni folklore, Bengali scholars about
Bengali folklore, and so on. The Sangeet Natak Akademi and regional min-
istries of culture also introduced a tiered competition format for festivals
whereby performance groups that won competitions at the local block level
would move on to the district level, the division level (Garhwal or Kumaon),
the state level, and finally the national level. Such folkloric competitions are
important modernist devices through which the state builds a distinct repertory of regional folk songs and folk dances.

The Song and Drama Division, originally established in the 1954 as a branch
of All India Radio, was another institution that was critical to the codification of folk music in Uttarakhand. Mohan Upreti's longtime collaborator,
Brijendra Lal Shah, was deputy director of the Song and Drama Division in
Nainital, one of the first national branches. The goal of this organization was
to adapt indigenous dance and singing styles into variety shows that could
entertain rural audiences and in some cases could be used to communicate
government policies. All artists were required to learn and perform codified
folk performance genres from multiple regions of India. Artists from the
Nainital (Kumaon) and Dehradun (Garhwal) branches, for example, learned
and performed folk dances from Chattisgarh, Bengal, Rajasthan, and other
parts of North India. Following a common strategy used by professional
folkloric ensembles in other national contexts,[15] this initiative ensured that
one or two musical and choreographic styles from each subnational region
would become codified and disseminated to nonspecialists across the country.

Finally, Upreti was also involved in staging the tableaux representing Uttar Pradesh during the January 26 Republic Day Parade, which was and continues to be one of the principal ways the state showcases the diversity of regional folk cultures as a means of generating nationalist sentiment. As Srirupa Roy describes it, "the [Republic Day] displays presented culture as a territorially discrete, politically eviscerated, and temporally static 'resource' that can be mined by citizens, communities, and the state. In the tableaux of the Republic Day parades, moreover, culture was always a variable endowment: it belonged to the 'folk' rather than the city-dweller, the artisan rather than the factory worker, the dancer rather than the militant" (2007: 10; see also de Maaker 2013).

Each of the state-funded institutions discussed above—HMV, All India Radio, the Sangeet Natak Akademi, the Indian Council for Cultural Relations, the Song and Drama Division—has shaped the work of Upreti and other cultural entrepreneurs in codifying regional folk arts throughout the country. If Mohan Upreti's stint with the IPTA implanted a belief that folk was to be found among the rural peasants, and if his encounter with Mohan Singh Bora marked a turning point in his identification with his own (village-based) folk arts, the institutionalization of folklore by the Indian state made a different kind of impact. Upreti's reliance on patronage from state institutions and wealthy individuals nurtured his performances of folk music in urban spaces to the exclusion of rural spaces. Upreti continued to celebrate Kumaoni villages as the source of folk authenticity in his writings, but he

Fig. 2.3. Mohan Upreti, c. 1980
(courtesy Himanshu Joshi)

refined and performed his folkloric productions almost exclusively in urban spaces. He was able to leave his mark on the national theater scene in Delhi and to perform in at least eight countries on government-sponsored tours, but after the 1950s he was almost completely divorced from village-based folk performance. Upreti was part of a growing number of cosmopolitan performers who conceived of folklore "as a source of vitality for the urban stage" while ultimately "divorcing folk forms from their context of meaning" in rural areas (Dalmia 2006: 200).

"Bedu Pako": An Enduring Legacy

Upreti's legacy continues to be felt mostly outside of Uttarakhand. Under his leadership, Parvatiya Kala Kendra became one of the most prominent theater companies in Delhi, and since his death in 1997, the company has continued to perform old and new works under the direction of his wife, Naima Khan Upreti, and later his brother, Bhagawat Upreti. Mohan Upreti also emerged as a prominent advocate of the public patronage of folklore during the 1970s and 1980s. Indeed, it is remarkable that despite being jailed as a potential traitor by the Indian state, he ended up working so closely with state institutions, directly shaping policies concerning folklore. In one publication he offered a three-point plan as a roadmap for the state to develop folk arts: "i) a national grassroots organization, primarily of folk artists, should be formed on IPTA lines, wedded to long-term social objectives but free from political exigencies, ii) a Central Institute of Folklore should be established for research in the scientific documentation of folk art, iii) a folk dance and song ensemble should be formed to serve as a national performing troupe of art" (Upreti, quoted in Bajeli 2006: 134–135).

Upreti's most enduring legacy *within* Uttarakhand is the song "Bedu Pako Baramasa," which he is credited with composing in 1952 along with the lyricist Brijendra Lal Shah. Upreti recorded this song on gramophone for HMV, but he made it famous through theatrical performances in which he would sing and dance while accompanying himself on the hurka. According to an anecdote that has become legendary in Kumaon, when Upreti performed "Bedu Pako" with characteristic flair at a national folk festival in Delhi, Prime Minister Nehru selected it as his favorite and dubbed Upreti the "Bedu Pako Boy" (see figure 2.4).

"Bedu Pako" is a strophic song consisting of couplets, each of which touches on a unique spiritual, geographical, or culinary aspect of Kumaoni life. The meaning of the first couplet, which many performers use as a refrain, is that the *bedu* passion fruit ripens throughout the year, while the

Fig. 2.4. Mohan Upreti with P. C. Joshi, his wife, Rubi, and Mohan's brother, Bhagwat Upreti, singing "Bedu Pako," undated (courtesy Naima Khan Upreti PAHAR Collection)

kafal berry ripens in April. The song uses a gapped five-note scale common to much village music from Uttarakhand and corresponding to Raga Bhupali in Hindustani music. Its catchy melody has a narrow range and two short phrases; it is set to a six-beat rhythmic meter called *khemta* that is frequently performed using an alternation of two-against-three beat patterns.

This song has only become more popular since Upreti's death; it is the unofficial folk anthem of Uttarakhand, a kind of sonic index of the region used in films, cassette and VCD remixes, mobile phone ringtones, and a national Coca-Cola campaign featuring Aamir Khan as a farcical mountain guide who hums the tune. As more than one bagpiper has told me, "Bedu Pako" is obligatory during mountain weddings, processions, festivals, and regimental marches. Uttarakhandi geet is currently disseminated on a popular website called bedupako.com.

The popularity of this song has engendered a number of different reactions that speak to multiple and conflicting conceptions of a folk song and the folk artist. I spoke with one Kumaoni music producer who was uncomfortable with labeling "Bedu Pako" a folk song. In his opinion, a song composed as recently as 1952 and popularized through stage, gramophone, and radio performances should not be called a folk song any more than Upreti should be labeled a folk artist. "A whole generation of people is looking to capitalize on the name of folk," he opined, "when they are, in fact, burying it."

Others expressed ambivalence not about the folk designation as such but, rather, about the credit given to Upreti and Shah as composers. I spoke with many Shilpkar musicians who perform this song on almost a daily basis but did not know how old it was nor who had originally composed it; most were unaware that Upreti was the official composer. Several interviewees, including some of Upreti's own relatives, believe that multiple variants of the tune used in "Bedu Pako" have been in circulation since at least the late nineteenth century. According to them, Upreti and Shah can be credited only with codifying one particular version of an older folk song.

Does a folk song need to originate in a village setting? If it is altered, does it remain a folk song? Which is an authentic folk artist: Mohan Singh Bora or Mohan Upreti? Both? Neither? Such questions are disputed in contemporary Uttarakhand, underlining the politicized and contested meanings of the folk concept and complicating the legacy of Mohan Upreti.

Conclusion

Using Mohan Upreti as a case study, this chapter has traced the emergence of a new folk paradigm under the cultural nationalist priorities of the Nehruvian state. In the late nineteenth and early twentieth centuries, native and colonial scholars collected proverbs, songs, ballads, and so on as a means of better understanding and ruling those at the cultural and economic margins of the colony, namely women, tribals, and lower castes. Given the populist priorities of the Nehruvian government, however, the discourse of folk was instrumentalized to articulate the national and regional identities of, presumably, all Indian citizens. Urban intellectuals sought to justify the creation of new regional states on the grounds that linguistic and cultural homogeneity cut across diverse class and caste strata within a particular region. Patronizing folk arts, moreover, became a way for the state to accommodate and celebrate cultural heterogeneity within the nation while defusing antinationalist sentiment.

Alongside this shift in ideology came a shift in methodology. It was no longer enough for urban intellectuals to go into rural areas and collect and preserve folklore. These collections needed to be assimilated and reworked to become products of "modern consciousness," to use Upreti's phrase. The locus of folk art had shifted from the mountainous village to the plains city, from the open air to the stage, and from the spontaneous creations of rural singers to the meticulously composed productions of high-status artists like Upreti. As Rustom Bharucha wrote, "quite literally, [folk] has become a nomenclature for a wide range of supposedly non-urban performance traditions, that are primarily enjoyed by urban audiences" (1990: 199). Although Upreti and his colleagues regularly honored Bora as their guru and as the "true creator of folk wealth" (Bajeli 2006: 43), it was ultimately they who presented Himalayan folklore to the modern nation, and it was they who ultimately assumed the title of folk artists.

In many ways, Upreti was a radical and a trailblazer: a Communist activist jailed during the Sino-Indian war of 1962, an anti-caste agitator who publicly performed on the hurka, and an atheist who married a forty-year old Muslim woman against the wishes of his family. Although he was not in favor of using his music to serve the goals of a political party, his choice of performers and musical materials demonstrated an alignment with subaltern populations and a blatant disregard for caste and class structures. "With a view to identify himself with the masses," Bajeli wrote, "[Upreti] started to de-class and de-caste himself" (2006: 23). By his own admission, this was not an easy process. Like most individuals who hail from orthodox, upper-caste families in Uttarakhand, Upreti selectively valued certain aspects of his cultural environment (Ramlila performances and Hindustani music) while inheriting the caste stigma associated with local instruments and hereditary performers. Only after his involvement with the Indian People's Theatre Association and his exposure to a variety of rural musical forms from around India did he come to identify the music of Kumaoni Hurkiyas as part of his cultural heritage.

Mohan Upreti followed a well-trodden path for music and theater personalities of the post-independence period, including Habib Tanvir of Chattisgarh, Bupen Hazarika of Assam, Chandrashekhar Kambar of Karnataka, K. N. Panikkar of Kerala, Ratan Thiyam of Manipur, Jhaverchand Mehgani of Gujarat, and Khaled Choudhury of Bengal. All of these figures embraced folk arts as the cornerstone of political activism and as a legitimizing source of regional distinction within the nation. All were inspired by early involvement in the IPTA, and all became involved in regionalist politics and state-funded folklore projects. These artists' promotion of regional folklore at mid-century resembles the early-twentieth-century *indigenismo* movement in the Andean region of South America. In that context, educated mestizo or *creolo* (non-indigenous) populations sponsored and presented folkloric performances in celebration of the indigenous population. As Tucker notes, "by allowing interpreters to inhabit a fictive indigeneity for the duration of performance, they became a means to enact appreciation for indigenous heritage" (2013: 40).

How do the activities and ideals of these individuals compare to those of the reformers of Indian classical music? Classicization has usually been discussed separately from folklorization, but it is fruitful to see them as intertwined processes. I have already discussed the ways in which the concepts of folk and classical are frequently framed within an evolutionary paradigm: the elevation of classical music in India required that folk music be positioned as both the source of and repository for "impure" elements. Beginning in the 1940s, however, many nationalist artists and activists recognized the value of reforming folk music in order to serve the needs of a new nation. Like Bhatkhande and Paluskar, Mohan Upreti had a desire to valorize this music as emerging from a golden past, and he was concerned with the decay and loss of musical traditions in contemporary hereditary communities. Like the classical reformers, Upreti first sought to orally assimilate music from a guru and then to inscribe and codify this knowledge in the form of publications, recordings, and the creation of new artistic forms. Finally, reformers in both camps depended on state-funded institutions to disseminate their pedagogical methods and to create value for this music within the middle classes of urban India. Folklorization and classicization have been the twin processes of modernist reform in modern India.

3   Turning Dying Folk into Living Folk

The Musical Activism of Narendra Singh Negi

On my first visit to the town of Pauri, Garhwal, in July 2005, I walked from the bus stand through small, crowded lanes in the bazaar, stopping periodically to ask people the location of Narendra Singh Negi's house. The shopkeepers all pointed vaguely in the same general direction. As I walked through the bustling bazaar, I became aware of Negi's voice emanating from cassette and VCD players in several of the shops. This was a mutual love affair: Negi had always claimed Pauri as his home, and, just as evidently, Pauri was eager to claim him as its most famous son. After a few wrong turns through ever-narrowing alleys, he warmly received me in his home (see figure 3.1).

Narendra Singh Negi is Uttarakhand's best-known artist, and there is no close second. Although there were many pioneers in the music industry before him, Negi's success as a songwriter and recording artist has been unprecedented and has opened pathways for every subsequent artist from the region. His songs are adored by Uttarakhandis of every age, residence, class, caste, and gender demographic. To hear his fans speak of him is to hear them describe a living legend, someone who represents the pinnacle of artistic achievement. Perhaps more significant, in a region that has suffered the symptoms of cultural and economic poverty for centuries, Negi's songs have made many people feel proud of being Uttarakhandi even as they have articulated the emotional and physical challenges of everyday life.

This chapter examines Narendra Singh Negi's career as a songwriter and performer as it coincided with the rise of the Garhwali music industry from the early 1980s until about 2010. During this period, Negi's music was disseminated via radio, film, cassette, VCD, and mp3 formats, and in a sense his

Fig. 3.1. Narendra Singh Negi (center) and Pritam Bhartwan with the author, 2013 (courtesy S. Fiol)

narrative can be read as one of technological progression, as newer media have built on and modified older ones, reaching ever-larger numbers of listeners. Indeed, Negi's success can be attributed to the simultaneous dissemination of his music in all of these formats. From the perspective of local consumers, it is possible to read the progression of sound technologies over the course of the past half-century as having led to greater access and more diverse content, mirroring some of the discussion of democratization in Peter Manuel's work on cassette and VCD cultures (1993, 2014). Yet from his own perspective as a working musician, Negi offers a narrative of progressive degradation, as the socioeconomic and political contexts surrounding each new medium's emergence resulted in greater exploitation and loss of control for the musician, ultimately leading to the decreasing production and inferior quality of commercial vernacular music. As I trace Negi's career path through this chapter, then, I seek to illuminate the particular configurations of social, political, capital, and legal relations that have cohered around each new technological medium, thereby creating a rupture in the experience of past forms and practices.

The narrative of Negi's career that I present raises a number of issues that are relevant to the study of small-scale vernacular recording industries more generally. They include the structural inequalities between regional and national music companies, the ideological differences between state-owned and privatized media, and the aesthetic balance between cosmopolitan and vernacular elements. Uttarakhandi geet as a commercial genre is identified first and foremost by the use of the Garhwali, Kumaoni, or Jaunsari language, but it has other distinguishing stylistic features as well. Songwriters such as Negi use a plethora of melodic, rhythmic, and verbal codes and emotional registers that collectively index village life in Uttarakhand. Negi refers to these as "folk elements" (*lok pada*). In his words, "You have to see whether there's a folk element in the [music] or not! If not, then reject it. If there is, then record it. Because [through these] songs—Garhwali geet, Kumaoni geet—folk will be made after fifty, sixty, one hundred years. But it will only happen if [people] record and play it."[1] From Negi's perspective, vernacular recordings that incorporate authentic folk elements are most likely to become tomorrow's folk songs.

The key question is, what constitutes a folk element? Although Negi presents the matter in a rather straightforward fashion—folk elements simply exist and must be carried forward through recordings—the idea of the folk element is inherently slippery and multivalent. Some so-called folk elements are clearly rooted in village-based expressive practices, but many are not or are only very tenuously so. The long history of vernacular music recording has generated its own musical and social discourse of folk, one that not only interacts with but also deviates significantly from village-based praxis. Ultimately the origin of a specific folk element matters less than its semiotic effect: it should signify a connection to rural Uttarakhand in the mind of the listener. Elsewhere I have outlined the specific processes by which producers construct Uttarakhandi geet in the recording studio, drawing from a well-known stock of folk elements (Fiol 2013a). Here I am primarily concerned with the broad arc of Negi's career and the ways in which the selection and presentation of folk elements in his music have been mediated by his approach to social activism and by the broader political, economic, and technological conditions of commercial music production. The evolution of technological forms and processes within the vernacular recording industry is particularly relevant, because the possibilities and constraints of each new technological medium have directly informed the way folk is understood and deployed.

This chapter contributes to the main goal of this book—denaturalizing the folk concept in India—while also demonstrating how the political intent and aesthetic range of the folk concept shifted significantly beginning in the early 1980s. As discussed in chapter 1, the concept of folk arts (lok sangeet) in the Indian Himalayas was first formulated through late-nineteenth-century Orientalist scholarship and colonial administrative policies rooted in essentialisms of geography, race, and caste. In the decades following independence, explored in chapter 2, the upwardly mobile elite sustained the idea that folk music was subservient to classical arts (*shastriya sangeet*), but folk music also came to be positively valued as a token of plebeian identification, anti-colonial nationalism, and cultural regionalism. These earlier valences of folk music continued into the 1980s and 1990s (and persist today), but the semiotics of the folk concept also expanded significantly during this latter period. Spurred by the growth of political regionalism and the economic liberalization that opened up new regional markets across South Asia, folk music became a potent concept invoked by regional politicians, recording artists, and diasporic audiences. Following Negi's lead, hundreds of semiprofessional singers from Garhwal and Kumaon have recorded songs in urban studios far from villages, some of which are subsequently labeled *lok geet* (folk song) or *paramparik geet* (traditional song) on album covers. While retaining earlier layers of meaning, folk has become an essential ingredient in creating a successful brand in Uttarakhand, reflecting the tightly intertwined relation between identity politics and capitalist accumulation worldwide. In the words of the Comaroffs, folk music has become one of the "universally recognizable terms in which difference is represented" (2009: 24).

The first section of the chapter examines the political, cultural, and economic developments that led to the growth of the Uttarakhandi music industry in the 1980s and 1990s. The second presents a narrative of Negi's musical career, focusing in particular on the articulation of folk elements within the contexts of recording for radio, cassette, and video compact disc. The final section considers Negi's position as a musical reformer and social activist. Negi's engagement with folk music in commercial recording is contextualized as part of a broader effort to professionalize hereditary musicians and to reform and raise the status of folk music in Uttarakhand.

The Emergence of a Vernacular Music Industry

The first vernacular recordings made in India date from the beginning the twentieth century, when European talent scouts began looking for popular music and musicians to record on gramophones. Hughes (2002), Farrell (1993), and Kinnear (1994) have documented the strategies used by British, German, and Indian gramophone companies to enlist local performers to record for "vernacular catalogues" and to establish lasting regional markets across South Asia. Producers and talent scouts sought ways to distinguish their products from those of their competitors by adopting regional, ethnic, and religious labels for their products and creating distribution channels that reached remote corners of the empire. The vernacular catalogues in Tamil Nadu, for example, featured a number of "folk genres" (*paramap padalkal* in Tamil) that satirized the "rural bumpkin" (dhobis, milkmaids, "gypsies," and so on) as a commercial strategy to appeal to the colonial elite (Hughes 2002: 466).[2]

Commercial recordings of Himalayan musicians were not made until many decades later. Himalayan territories were difficult to access, and the low population density offered a relatively small market for gramophone and film productions. The mountainous terrain also dissuaded companies from investing in cinema halls, thereby limiting the reach of film to Uttarakhandi populations in the lower foothills and in the urban plains. By the late 1970s, however, conditions were ripe for the emergence of a vernacular recording industry in Uttarakhand. Peter Manuel dedicated a chapter of his path-breaking monograph *Cassette Culture* (1993) to regional music production across the subcontinent. He emphasized in particular the influence of inexpensive cassette technology, which democratized musical production and propelled the formation of new consumer markets in all corners of India. Since the late 1980s it has been possible to make the claim that in most areas of South Asia, vernacular recorded music has been consumed as much as or more than has Hindi-language film music (ibid.: 156). Manuel did not treat all vernacular music industries as equal, however; he explained that some industries were more financially successful than were others, and that some better reflected the cultural diversity of their respective regions than did others. One of the reasons why the Garhwali music industry was disproportionately large relative to its population of approximately five million Garhwali speakers, Manuel opined, was that most people in the region share a lingua franca; in regions that are linguistically more diverse, such as Himachal Pradesh, music markets are smaller but more varied stylistically (ibid.: 162).

Several other factors also contributed to the rapid growth of the Uttara-khandi music industry. In 1962, spurred by the brief Sino-Indian war, the Indian government funded the construction of several roads cutting across Uttarakhand to facilitate the transportation of military provisions to the front lines. It is difficult to overestimate the effect that road construction had on cultural life in the mountains. Once the roads were converted into national highways, they became the major arteries of the regional economy, expand-ing opportunities for tourism, trade, and road travel at the same time they diverted resources away from the footpaths and pilgrim trails that had long sustained the local economy.[3]

The development of the news industry also benefited the incipient music industry in Uttarakhand. Anup Kumar (2011) describes the "hyperlocalization" of Hindi news media from the 1980s, as news organizations sought to attract readers beyond urban centers. Two of the most prominent and long-standing Hindi-language newspapers, *Dainik Jagran* and *Amar Ujala,* utilized the national highways to distribute their dailies to Uttarakhand beginning in the late 1980s. These newspapers became important means of advertising vernacular films and recordings. Moreover, the distribution network established by the print media directly benefited the young music industry, as print and music products were frequently distributed together via the same networks of wholesalers, drivers, and independent retailers.

The expansion of state-run media, particularly All India Radio, also contributed to the growth of the vernacular recording industry. Beginning in the 1950s, AIR stations in Lucknow and Delhi regularly broadcast programs of Uttarakhandi music, but these broadcasts only reached the lower foothills of the Himalayas. In January 1978, as part of the state's effort to expand the medium of radio throughout the country, the Information and Broadcasting Ministry of the central government opened a 100-megawatt AIR station in the plains city of Najibabad in northern Uttar Pradesh. At forty kilometers from the southern border of Uttarakhand, AIR Najibabad's programs reached the inhabitants of northern Uttar Pradesh, western Bihar, and most of the Garhwal and Kumaon hills. Much of the news, topical programming, and music broadcast on AIR Najibabad, such as the Vividh Bharati program, was relayed from the Mumbai and Delhi AIR stations. Yet for six hours each week, programs featuring Uttarakhandi vernacular music were broadcast in thirty- and forty-five minute-segments. In order to represent the aesthetic preferences of its diverse listeners, the programming schedule was structured by subregions within Uttarakhand: Jaunsari folk on Sunday and Friday mornings, Garhwali folk on Monday, Wednesday, and Saturday mornings, and Kumaoni folk on Tuesday and Thursday mornings. This broadcasting policy was a continuation of the Nehruvian state's desire to promote subregional artistic expression as a way to incorporate cultural differences at the margins of the nation (see chapter 2).

The proximity of AIR Najibabad to the Garhwal and Kumaon hills enabled large numbers of hereditary musicians to travel to the station to broadcast their music. Station staff members also went on field expeditions to remote mountain valleys in order to locate and record village artists. Radio staff artists sought out musical specialists from Baddi, Bajgi, and Hurkiya hereditary communities because the musical traditions that they represented were deemed at risk of disappearing. I interviewed several current and former AIR employees who regarded these field excursions as difficult but gratifying experiences in which they discovered "untouched" Uttarakhandi folk songs. One former employee valued the experience of making such discoveries in remote villages and of locating the "original" sources of folklore. The recordings from these excursions were taken back to the studio to be edited and reassembled into programs that would fit into the categories of folklore that were in the process of being codified.[4] The approach to Himalayan folk music propagated by AIR Najibabad was in many ways consistent with aforementioned approaches from the late colonial and post-independence periods; underlying these perspectives was an essentialist ideology of folk music as a timeless and original expression of the village-based, low-caste hereditary artisan. As I examine below, this conceptualization of folk music conflicted with Narendra Singh Negi's more organic and fluid understanding of the concept.

Each of the factors mentioned above—the existence of a lingua franca, the accessibility of inexpensive sound reproduction technology, the construction of roads, the expansion of print media, and the extension of state radio broadcasting—played a role in encouraging the growth of the vernacular music industry throughout the late 1970s and 1980s. Yet an equally important reason for the tremendous growth of the industry was the trailblazing path of Pauri's native son, Narendra Singh Negi.

The Voice of Uttarakhand

Narendra Singh Negi was born on August 12, 1949, in the picturesque town of Pauri. Perched on a steep mountainside and surrounded by rich agricultural land and renowned temples, the town of Pauri has long nurtured a disproportionate number of artists relative to other areas of Garhwal. This can be attributed to the town's historical access to the urban plains through trading routes along the Ganges River valley and to its proximity to Srinagar, the erstwhile capital of the Garhwal kingdom until 1804 and the educational center of Garhwal since the 1970s.

Negi showed artistic promise at a young age while performing in school festivals and local Ramlilas. As a young man he took an interest in Hindustani music and began performing tabla with his cousin, the blind *khyal* singer Ajit Singh Negi. He earned a degree in tabla performance from Prayag Sangeet Samiti in Dehradun, and later he received his BA in music from Garhwal University in Srinagar. After returning to Pauri, he began working for the

Suchni Vibhag (Information and Public Relations Department) of the state
government, a post that he would occupy until 2005. As a hobby, Negi began composing songs modeled on the slower, sentimental genres of village
songs (*khuder, bajuband,* and *ritu geet*). His first break came in 1977, when
he was asked to audition for AIR by Keshab Anuragi, a Garhwali who was
the executive program director of the station in Lucknow. I spoke with Negi
about this period.

> SF: It was fortunate that there was a program director [at AIR] who was from
> the hills [*pahari*]. Was that an advantage for you?
>
> NN: Yes, yes. The advantage was like this. At that time, I played tabla. They had
> taken me for some program in Lucknow, to play tabla. But I also sang a song,
> and when he saw me on stage and heard me singing, [he was surprised]. Then
> he gave me a form and asked me to sing for the audition. I went to [AIR]
> for the audition with the filled form, and gave it to Anuragi-ji. The day of
> my audition, my throat was closed [*awaz baith gai*], and I told Anuragi-ji
> that it would be difficult for me to sing. He said, "Don't worry, just sing the
> lower part of the composition [*asthai*]." As happens in lok geet the first part
> is lower [in pitch]. So I sang, and the other judges in attendance said they
> couldn't hear my voice. But he said, "His voice today is a little off, but I have
> heard him before," and passed me.
>
> SF: There was a big committee there? But Anuragi-ji was the top?
>
> NN: In folk there was no one else, right? In Garhwali folk his decision alone
> was respected. The others were [specialists in] Hindi music: one for ghazals,
> for this, for that.[5]

It is significant that Negi's first break came from Keshab Anuragi, one of the
seminal figures in the early years of the Garhwali music industry. Raised in a
family of hereditary dhol drummers (Bajgi) in Pauri Garhwal, Anuragi was
widely respected for his deep knowledge of indigenous vocal and percussion
music.[6] Despite having opportunities as a professional folk artist, Anuragi aspired to become a Hindustani vocalist. His qualifications and his being from a
Scheduled Caste community eventually secured for him a series of influential
positions at AIR, but according to his contemporaries, his lack of accomplishment as a classical vocalist was a source of constant frustration.[7] It is ironic that
Negi, a non-hereditary, high-caste musician who turned from classical to folk,
was given his first break by Anuragi, a hereditary, low-caste musician who was
unable to make the transition from folk to classical. The diverging trajectories
of these two men's careers speaks volumes about the links between caste and
musical identity with respect to professional aspirations.

Negi and a handful of other Garhwali artists, including Chander Singh
Rahi, Jeet Singh Negi, and Uma Shankar ("Satish"), became regular per-

formers on AIR Lucknow, performing both traditional and newly composed material. Their recordings were featured on the weekly *Uttaraini* program, on which disc jockeys read letters and took song requests (*farmaishi geet*) from Uttarakhandi soldiers training far from home and from families in Himalayan villages sending greetings to their kin in the plains. Although the range of the broadcasts did not extend much beyond the foothills, Negi was nonetheless able to cultivate a devoted following. I met elders in several villages who recalled how they used to assemble with heightened anticipation around a single radio receiver in their village square once a week between 5:45 and 6:45 p.m. to enjoy these songs and hope for a message from a relative who had migrated to the plains or had enlisted in the army. As discussed in chapter 2, All India Radio was one of the main instruments through which the government disseminated a canon of folk musical styles rooted in regional states throughout the country. At first, AIR programs dedicated to regional folk music offered staff artists the flexibility to broadcast idiosyncratic interpretations of traditional genres or original compositions modeled on such genres. Yet as state ideologies about folk music, popular music, and classical music evolved, the conventions of radio programming became much more circumscribed.

In 1978, soon after joining AIR in Lucknow, Negi was reassigned to AIR Najibabad. Madhuri Barthwal, the director in charge of regional folk at AIR Najibabad from 1978 to 2012, recorded dozens of musicians from Uttarakhand on twelve-inch reel-to-reel tapes in the studio and in the field. She edited these recordings and added her own narration to create sound documentaries that were broadcast on bi-weekly thirty-minute programs. In my conversations with Barthwal, she insisted that young artists who come to AIR should develop their own musical style by singing "anonymously composed, locally rooted, and ancient folk songs" rather than their own compositions.[8] She had absolute confidence in her ability to identify an authentic folk song from any subregion of Uttarakhand because she recently had compiled and analyzed approximately four hundred songs from the region for her doctoral dissertation and had received her PhD in music from H. N. B. Garhwal University. If a singer passed the AIR audition but did not know any folk songs from his or her particular area, Barthwal taught the singer several songs from her extensive folk song collection. Only after a singer had attained the rank of B+ and had recorded for a minimum of five years did she permit him or her to supplement folk material with more recent compositions.

Barthwal's approach echoes the official government position concerning the role of regional All India Radio stations, which is, in her words, "to protect the 'dying' traditions of folk song from the *kichri* [a dish of mixed rice and pulses] of modern songs." She had particular disdain for contemporary vernacular music produced in Delhi, which she felt was promulgating inauthentic versions of folk music. It is significant that, aside from programs featuring indigenous music from Garhwal and Kumaon (which make up about 15 percent of AIR Najibabad's total musical programming), the station broadcasts Hindi film music, contemporary Maithili and Bhojpuri recordings, and commercial Uttarakhandi recordings from the 1970s and 1980s but excludes contemporary Uttarakhandi geet. The network has a long history of regulating programming content on the basis of purist ideologies; the bans on harmonium and film music during parts of the mid-twentieth century are among the best-known examples (Rahaim 2011).

This policy of regulating folk music, and Barthwal's role as the gatekeeper of this process, have generated criticism from several artists, none more prominent than Narendra Singh Negi. Part of Negi's critique is admittedly personal, because many of his more recent compositions have effectively been excluded from the category of "folk music" and from vernacular radio programming. Yet he also bristles at Barthwal's policy of requiring singers to record only folk songs from their particular subregion because it limits the organic movement of musical styles and motifs from singer to singer and from place to place. Negi believes that such a restrictive policy negates one of the core functions of a folk song, which is to disseminate historical knowledge and provide commentary on recent events. He shared with me a story about a local singer who was not allowed to record a song on AIR about the disastrous 1952 flood that occurred in Satpuli, near the hill station of Mussoorie:

> Have you seen this river? Before there was no bridge above it. The vehicles were [parked] below, alongside the river. It was a skinny river, and during the rainy season, there was some block of the water source higher up. Some rock was lodged. And when the rock was released, all the water in the river came rushing and swept away the vehicles. A lot of people died in that flood. And soon, folk songs were made about it. . . . But if you say, "Sir, that song from '48 or '49 cannot be recorded," then how in the next fifty years will anyone come to know about the flood in Satpuli? Now if earthquakes come, if there is a tragedy, and if the new songs about this will not be played on Akashvani [AIR], then the next generation will never know that there was an earthquake! One should think from [listening to] these songs that such things have happened in the past. It is history. So if today we decide not to record these songs, then after fifty years we will realize that no one knows what happened fifty years back.
>
> Which time do we save? [The songs from] seven hundred years ago? What happened to the creations from four hundred years ago? In the fifty years to

come, what will be the folk songs? You can call it anything you like: traditional song, new song, modern song. Maybe it is fifty or forty years old, [but after] one hundred years it will become a folk song. It is a circle out of which some songs will fall and become extinct and some others will prevail.... Folk [should not] become fixed. If we have 100 songs, and all of our lives we only have that [many], it won't become 101. We have to move it forward. We [may] lose some things as well. If we have one hundred songs today, then one hundred years later we may only have fifty or forty, or perhaps even more will become extinct, leaving three or four. It's like when you have animals you need to do breeding. If you have fifty elephants, then to save those fifty you need to breed them. It's the same with songs. You need to breed new ones. Nowadays requests for some songs are made, and you hear [them] for two to four days and they disappear. So you need to record new songs, otherwise whatever songs you have will be forgotten in forty to fifty years, surpassed by even newer ones.[9]

Negi's approach is similar to Barthwal's insofar as he is concerned with a body of songs that may be identified as folk after passing from being individual creations into part of a communal repertoire. Yet his approach differs in that he understands folk music as a body of continuously evolving resources that contemporary artists need to carry forward and make meaningful in the present. Folk music represents not a body of old texts and tunes confined to a premodern, communitarian mode of existence but a living form of historical knowledge that must be nurtured and regenerated song after song, generation after generation. Not surprisingly, commercial recording is an important part of Negi's vision for regenerating folk music. With the decay of indigenous systems of patronage and hereditary knowledge, the recording industry has an increasingly critical role to play in sustaining the folk song repertoire. Negi continued:

Before, what we called folk was the Beda [or Baddi] people, who would sing going house to house, village to village. [Their music] didn't become popular in one listen. You had to listen several times. And when they came through again, you would listen again. After hearing a Beda once, you might only be able to hear him again after three or four months. This is why it took years for a song to enter the people's repertoire [*juwan*]. And in a year, maybe once, at the time of Baisakh festival, we call it Bikhod, we [would] dance and sing [these songs] in the village: *thadya geet, chaunfla geet, jhumeilo*. These songs became popular slowly, over time. There are certain songs that people were singing two hundred or three hundred years ago as they traveled, and people continue to remember these.

Now the situation has changed. Today the song first is played through Akashwani [radio] or Doordarsan [television] or cassette. Now the days of popularizing through visiting home after home are over. Now you won't find Beda. Now that change has happened. Through the medium of cassette, people listen when they want. And through radio and TV, you'll find new songs to listen to. Before, it took one hundred years for any song to become popular; today if the song is good, it becomes popular in a single night by way of TV, cassette . . . so the definition of folk also changes.[10]

In recent decades, commercial media have replaced itinerant performers as the suppliers of new material, and songs are being learned and transmitted much more quickly than in the past. But Negi maintains that a folk song is very different from a popular hit, though the same musical content can appear. The difference between a folk song and a popular hit does not lie in formal aesthetic criteria but, rather, in its relation to time: a folk song needs to withstand the test of time and go through a "filtering process" requiring generations of adaptation and sedimentation within a community. As he relates:

> NN: I once saw villagers in Jaunpur [western Garhwal] . . . singing a song [while dancing]. But I couldn't recognize the song, and I couldn't even understand the words. Afterwards they told me, "Negi-ji, this is your song."
> SF: So in their own way they changed your song?
> NN: Exactly. This is what's so special. There is a "filter" at work, and for this reason songs last for one hundred, two hundred, three hundred years. Today the songs that we call *chancheri*, you cannot know how these were written two hundred years back. The original song was something else. But over time the filter was working, and changes in the melody were introduced so that people would enjoy it more, and certain words would be linked to other words so that it would reflect their life. So this filtering over time is what has allowed the songs to come in the form that we have them, and they may be two hundred or three hundred years old. Today these [songs] are perfect; there is no need to change them. People cut them and reformed them so much, and have revealed these forms to us today. This is how much filtering has happened.[11]

Negi's objective as a performer and songwriter is not simply that his songs become popular, but that they become lok geet, outlasting his own life and fame. In the autobiographical song "Bol Jab . . ." Negi explains: "Tomorrow when night turns to day, new shrubs will spring up, and dead branches will become posts used to support new creepers. I'll be gone tomorrow, my brothers, but my songs will remain with you."[12]

> After 100 or 200 years, only the songs will remain. And for several even my name will not remain. Like in the old bhajans, Meera inserted her own name,

Kabir inserted his own name . . . they maintained their contribution [*dan*]. When my name is not in the songs, my name will gradually be detached from these songs, and then only the songs will remain. If they have the strength to remain, then they will remain. In this way lok sangeet will be made.[13]

The Shift to Cassette Production

If radio provided exposure to village-based styles of music and dance and allowed Negi to build a public following for his own compositions, it was the cassette revolution that catapulted him to regional celebrity. In 1982 Negi decided to record a cassette after witnessing the unfortunate experience of three of his colleagues. As he related it:

NN: In the eighties, Gopal Babu Goswami and . . . Diundi, Bakashpati Diundi, and Raj Kishore Mishra. They were from the Song and Drama Division in Nainital. So what did they do, they made an EP [with a] company, a small one. This EP is small—four songs come, two on one side, two on another. So that EP was made by Polydor, no? So they contacted them and said that for every EP sold, we'll give ten rupees.

SF: So there was a royalty system?

NN: Royalty. HMV was the only one to follow royalties. And this other, Polydor, also did royalties. In this day and age, they don't give royalties—if they did, then I'd be living well! [laughs] So, they made EPs. Now EPs were rising, but the EP player was owned only by very "big people." In Pauri maybe there was no one with a player. In this there was the need for a needle, and the needle was not readily available.

SF: Have you ever seen one here in the hills?

NN: Yes, I have. [But] here in Pauri I've never seen one. So just as [this EP] came out, T-Series came with the cassette system. And what did they do? The songs of the three of them were put on one cassette. [T-series] pirated the EP and put it on a cassette. The cassette was very popular.

SF: They came at the same time?

NN: [nodding] The EP was expensive; the cassette was cheap. And the cassette player was very cheap as well. And the record player was very expensive, not every man could buy that. So after that, those artists didn't receive even one rupee in royalties. Polydor closed down.[14]

Negi took this as an omen, and a few months later he arrived on the steps of Saraswati Studio in Daryaganj, Delhi, with the goal of making his first cassette. Negi cobbled together twelve thousand rupees (approximately US$300 at that time) for the recording, much of which was borrowed. After three days of paying session artists, the money was used up and Negi was still unhappy with several of the tracks, so he visited a Garhwali industrialist in Delhi who agreed to lend him more money. Negi drew the cover art for the album to save on costs, and he went from alley to alley assembling the casing, ribbon, and spools. He told me about the process:

> NN: It took a whole month [to make the cassette] and I had to borrow [money] from many people. I made a promise: I won't come to Delhi again. It was very hot, and I cannot bear the heat.
>
> SF: So in the studio did you have any help? From the director?
>
> NN: No, no one. They are "commercial" people. They play music and then leave. They take your money and leave.
>
> SF: Did you use a studio tabla player, or your own?
>
> NN: No, none of them were mine, they were the studio tabla players.
>
> SF: And the director?
>
> NN: No, no one, I was the only one. I made five hundred cassettes, and promised that I will not go there again. Then I said for all the money I put in, to cover my expenses, one cassette will be sold at twenty-eight rupees. . . . So one man's hotel was here [in Pauri]. He had bought a tape recorder. He came to my home and ate and said he heard that I brought a cassette. I said yes, but I won't sell them one at a time, I will give it to the person who takes all of them. How long can I sell one at a time? So he forcibly came inside and threw down a fifty-rupee note and took one cassette and ran away. . . . Then he played it in his shop. And people started asking, "Where did you get this from?"
>
> SF: Had you first recorded these songs on the radio?
>
> NN: Yes, I had been singing them from 1977, and the radio made them popular. Those compositions were very close to folk, and the people really appreciated it a lot. Then there was a boy here who has a tailoring shop. He came to me and said, "I need two hundred cassettes." I said take two hundred, and later he came to me and said, "Uncle-ji, chachaji, I will make your next cassette." Then he took another one hundred cassettes. And in three days they were sold out.
>
> SF: In the third day?
>
> NN: Yes, the third day. Two hundred were sold the same day. There was so much *craze* for these songs in those days. That is why these days, I tell these kids to make a song popular through the medium of radio, and then use the cassette medium. But nobody wants to use that long route.[15]

The rural musician struggling in the industrial city is a trope in popular music narratives in many places, and Negi's emphasis on the difficulties of traveling to the urban plains and the perils of working with commercially motivated people is a familiar theme for many artists from rural parts of India. Despite these early struggles, Negi soon became adept at negotiating with multiple music companies. Saraswati Studio bought the rights to the first two albums and contracted with Negi to record several more albums (*Garhwali Geetmala* vols. 1–4). Negi then chose to record his next ten albums with Rama Cassettes, started in the early 1980s by the Punjabi entrepreneur Ram Ajmani, who had established a successful wool company. The commercial success of Negi's recordings helped established Rama Cassettes as one of the leading music companies specializing in North Indian vernacular music (Garhwali, Kumaoni, Nepali, Punjabi, Haryanvi, Jaunsari, Himachali, Bhojpuri, and Ladhaki). Between cassette releases, Negi traveled to Mumbai to compose and record music for seven Garhwali feature films.[16] The cassettes featuring Negi's film songs were extremely popular, but the films themselves never garnered much attention because of the uneven distribution of electricity and cinema halls in the central Himalayas.

Negotiating with multiple music companies and using radio to establish his reputation became essential to his early popularity and his ability to court patrons for more lucrative stage performances. The low production costs and the plethora of music companies and recording studios in the 1980s and 1990s ensured that Negi and a growing number of other musicians were able to compete for a piece of the vernacular market, but rampant piracy and the lack of a royalty system meant that even the most acclaimed musicians were not able to earn a sustainable income from recording.

In Search of the Folk Element

For most of Negi's fans, his early analog studio recordings represent his best work, if they did not achieve the level of commercial success of his later productions. Negi's supple voice and formidable songwriting skills are combined with sensitive flute, harmonium, mandolin, sitar, dholak, and tabla accompaniment. On the early albums Negi's interest in foregrounding various "folk elements" is already apparent. On each of his albums, he modeled at least one or two tracks on village-based styles of singing and dancing; in many cases these songs are labeled lok geet (folk song) or paramparik geet (traditional song) on the album cover. For instance, the song "Ghughuti Ghuraun Lagi" (1983) weaves a tapestry of sights and sounds encountered in the month of Chait—such as the *ghuraun* call of the *ghughuti* bird—when women who have left to marry return (or long to return) to their natal villages. The lyrics and melody of this song are adapted from a large stock of "songs of longing" referred to as *khuder geet* in Garhwal (see chapter 5).

Even when his texts and tunes do not show the direct influence of a particular genre of vernacular song, Negi's early compositions focus on themes concerning out-married women, soldiers, and migrants. The regional anthem "Bavan Garhu ku Desh" (1983) condenses the history of each of fifty-two forts (*bavan garh*) in Garhwal that later became unified in the fifteenth-century Panwar kingdom. The hit song "Chali Bhai Motor Chali" ("Drive On, Brother," 1983) offers a humorous parody of bus travel on mountain roads.[17] The popularity of this song prompted bus drivers to install cassette players on their buses to attract passengers; this is an interesting example of a song directly engendering technological change, rather than simply being a product of such change.

Negi's fans and critics are particularly appreciative of the way he incorporated typical Garhwali phrases in the lyrics of his early compositions. Many listeners have praised the pure (*shuddh*) form of the Garhwali language that Negi utilizes in his songs and his avoidance of Hindi words to a greater extent than most of his contemporaries. His lyrics generally conform to the Srinagari dialect of Garhwali spoken in the districts of Pauri, Tehri, and Chamoli, but he also employs phrases from other subregions (for example, "Rashmi Rumel," which is rendered in Rawaini). When Negi comes across unfamiliar Garhwali phrases in published sources or in conversations with elders, he notes them and often incorporates them into later works. The resuscitation of older phrases contributes to what many people identify as the sentimental quality of his music. Some of Negi's songs also employ *tukbandi*, end-rhyming couplets in which the first line's meaning is irrelevant but matches the prosodic rhythm and rhyme of the second line; this is a common feature of many village genres, including the free-rhythm improvised song known as *bajuband* in Garhwal and *nyoli* in Kumaon.[18] Because of the influence his songwriting has had on a younger generation of artists, Negi receives credit for spearheading a revival of Garhwali literature.[19]

If most people agree on the textual folk elements in Negi's songs, there is less agreement about musical folk elements. A number of sonic features used in Negi's songs and in the majority of Uttarakhandi geet are not necessarily specific to the region but correspond to a more generic "folk style" used across North India and especially the Himalayan region (Dinnerstein 2012: 80–82). For example, binary melodic form (*asthai-antara*) separated by instrumental breaks and bounded by an introduction and a coda, antiphonal sections using a male chorus and a female chorus, and free-rhythm improvisatory passages on the bamboo flute (bansuri) at the beginnings and ends of the track are characteristics of commercial vernacular songs produced in Nepal, Himachal Pradesh, and Ladak. The bansuri is regarded by many in the music industry as the quintessential Himalayan folk instrument, and a free-rhythm cadenza on the bansuri is considered an essential sonic element in Uttarakhandi geet. As Andrew Alter notes (2014: 65–79), the folk status of the bansuri is ironic given that this instrument (and its cousins the *muruli* and the *algoja*) are almost never encountered in noncommercial musical settings in Uttarakhand, though once they may have been more prevalent.[20]

The instrumentation used on Negi's albums is not vastly different from that used in other vernacular commercial genres such as Bhojpuri geet or Nepali geet: dholak, tabla, guitar, mandolin, octopad, flute, and electronic samples form the core. Nonetheless, Negi has been innovative in using indigenous instruments such as the hurka (a type of pressure drum), the dhol-damaun, and the binai (mouth harp) on several recordings, and he has helped design a dhol that can be tuned precisely and used for studio recordings. The electronic samples he chooses—musette, oboe, bagpipes, or accordion—are indicative of the preference for reedy timbres found in much Uttarakhandi music. In melodic terms, Negi's compositions draw from a wide range of modes, but most conform to one of several gapped five-note scales that predominate in the village music of the central Himalayas (roughly corresponding to the Hindustani ragas Durga, Bhupali, Dhani, and Brindabani Sarang). Negi's singing voice has a somewhat constricted, nasal timbre that one can identify as a general trait of singers from Uttarakhand. He also uses a variety of vocal ornaments such as quick runs, mordents, and glottal stops that characterize many styles of village singing.

Negi has made an attempt to preserve village-based rhythmic patterns in his recordings. For example, "Cho Chamale" is based on a field record-ing of a five-beat chancheri dance-song performed at a festival in Chamoli District. Negi explained that studio accompanists recommended altering the rhythm to conform to a four-beat pattern, but he wanted to maintain the original rhythm because it is linked to a specific dance pattern of four steps forward, one step back. Retaining this rhythm was linked in his mind to preserving this style of dance in Chamoli. Drawing on his background in tabla performance, Negi has also written songs corresponding to cycles of seven, ten, and twelve beats, none of which are particularly common in the village music of Uttarakhand. The majority of Negi's songs utilize kaherva (eight-beat), khemta (six-beat), and *chanchar* or *deepchandni* (fourteen-beat) rhythmic cycles found in a plethora of regional and light-classical styles across North India. Even if the overall cycles are consistent with other repertories, however, the internal arrangement of accents and drum strokes—most of which are derived from the dhol-damaun or hurka-thali repertories—is what gives Uttarakhandi geet its unique character. When discussing his early ana-log recordings with me, Negi expressed dissatisfaction with the rhythmic articulation of the tabla and the dholak. He felt that the "folk feeling" of the rhythm was being sacrificed because there were no Garhwali accompanists working in Delhi and Mumbai at the time who would be able to correctly render such rhythms. This situation would begin to change in the mid-1990s as Garhwali percussionists began working in the industry as session musicians, explicitly modeling their drumming patterns on the dhol-damaun and hurka-thali repertoires.

In this brief discussion of textual and musical elements in Negi's music, I have sought to highlight the multivalent nature of the folk concept. In some cases, Negi has made a point of directly connecting his songs to music and dance styles found in rural Uttarakhand. In other cases, sonic elements (such as the free-rhythm introduction on the bansuri) have little connection to contemporary musical practice in Uttarakhand but have become indexical of Himalayan folk music, presumably because this is how studio musicians residing in Delhi, Dehradun, or Mumbai imagine Himalayan folk music sounds or should sound. Such imaginings may be at least in part rooted in the long history of sonic representations of the Himalayas in Hindi films (Fiol 2016). Finally, the discourse of folk also crosses over any specific local reference and encompasses a more general set of aesthetic choices used in many North Indian musical genres (for example, the use of dholak accompaniment and asthai-antara form). Negi uses the metaphor of a filter to refer to the gradual process of transforming commercial recordings into folk songs, but this metaphor seems equally apt for describing the process of sifting through the various discourses of folk music to construct vernacular recordings.

Political Engagements

Negi's employment in the Uttar Pradesh government's Information and Public Relations Department from 1972 to 2005 was critical to his success as a songwriter, offering him valuable opportunities to travel the length and breadth of Uttarakhand and study the musical and linguistic diversity of the region. Yet Negi's position as a state employee sometimes conflicted with the political expression in his songs. For example, "Dam ka Kathir" ("Because of the Dam," 1989) foreshadowed the sorrow that many residents of Garhwal would feel following the lengthy construction of a controversial dam over the Bhagirathi (Ganges) River (completed in 2006) and the subsequent flooding of the historic town of Tehri. Although the song did not explicitly endorse a political position, it was widely interpreted as supportive of the growing anti-dam movement in the 1990s, and the song was banned from All India Radio.

Negi was also a vocal supporter of the Uttarakhand movement. At various times in the twentieth century, beginning with the failed effort of a group of

Kumaoni Brahmins in 1917, regional elites attempted to establish a separate mountain state.[21] The formation of states in other parts of India following independence was based on calls for linguistic or ethnic homogeneity; in contrast, the Uttarakhand movement, as well as the regional statehood movements in Jharkhand and Chattisgarh, gained traction because of the idea that governance from afar denied people opportunities for economic development (Mawdsley 2002). According to Chakraborty, "Uttarakhand can be marked as the first people's movement in independent India in which ethnic, linguistic, and religious considerations either have not existed or remained in low key. The main issue for debate [was] the problem of distribution of resources" (1999: 67).

Regional leaders in Garhwal and Kumaon often agreed on the economic and social problems facing the hill people, but they disagreed about whether to agitate for a separate state or an autonomous region within an existing state. Factionalism between political groups in Garhwal and Kumaon and between centrist and leftist parties flared up frequently, complicating the matter of political unity. The calls for separatism became more acute, however, when incorporated into longstanding social movements organized to protect the forest rights of villagers (the most well-known of which was Chipko, or, as it became known in the West, the "tree-hugging" movement), to establish universities in the hills, to prevent the damming of rivers, to plant trees, to prohibit the sale of alcohol, or to wipe out untouchability.

In the early 1990s several developments coalesced into widespread demand for a separate regional state. The initial spark was the Uttar Pradesh government's implementation of the recommendations of the Mandal Commission, which required that 27 percent of government and civil service jobs be reserved for members of Other Backward Castes (OBCs), on top of a preexisting 23 percent quota for members of Scheduled Castes (SCs) and Scheduled Tribes (STs). Most Garhwalis and Kumaonis resented this high percentage of enforced reservations, because OBCs in their region made up only 2 percent to 5 percent of the population, unlike Uttar Pradesh, with its large population of OBCs. The state government's refusal to retract this law led to massive strikes and protests and provided the impetus for various groups to demand a separate state outright.

The movement for statehood entered a more violent phase in October 1994, when several buses full of Uttarakhandi protesters on their way to attend a rally in Delhi were detained by police in central Uttar Pradesh. When the protesters tried to continue their journey, the police restrained them with force, raping and beating some of the protesters. As news of these events reached the mountains in the following days, many responded with violence, leading to a twenty-four-hour curfew in many parts of Kumaon and Garhwal. The dishonoring of Uttarakhandi women became a rallying cry for regional statehood. It was thus the feeling of "cultural and social discrimination/ humiliation" (P. Kumar 2000: 93) directed at the plains-based government that finally generated a collective movement (andolan).

In the absence of unified regional political leadership, writers, musicians, and grassroots activists living in the mountains were instrumental in articulating the needs and desires of the movement. The Hindi-language print media and regional-language newsletters and pamphlets carried a number of the slogans and songs used in the movement, voicing the grievances of the public (A. Kumar 2011). The compositions of activists and singers such as Girish Tiwari ("Girda") and Narendra Singh Negi helped establish awareness of the problems facing the region. As a government employee, Negi could not directly criticize the state in his works; nonetheless, in songs such as "Khoja Ve Sani" ("Find Him Out"), composed in 1989, Negi gave voice to the frustrations of poverty, environmental degradation, urban migration, and corruption that boiled over during the Uttarakhand movement:[22]

Nau farein vikas ka binash	Who has destroyed our mountains in the
Kain kari yu pahaduku	name of development?
Lheki nau sudharkubBigad	Who has caused further degeneration in this hill
Kain kari yu pahaduku	region after swearing to regenerate it?
Khoja ve sani, pachana ve sani	Find him out, identify him.

Despite Negi's ability to express deeply held and widely shared sentiments in such songs, his commercial recordings had a limited effect on the Uttarakhand movement. Commercial music production, largely confined to Delhi, was removed from the source of political strife in the hills. Even people within the music industry who were sympathetic to the cause feared government censorship. In late 1994 Negi recorded the album Utha Jaga Uttarakhandyu ("Rise up, Uttarakhandis!"),[23] which documented the political demands and the violence of the Uttarakhand movement, which had reached its climax in that year. The producers at Rama Cassettes in Delhi initially refused to make this album because of the political risks and because they were not convinced of its commercial potential. There was little precedent for protest albums in the region, but Rama producers ultimately were persuaded when Negi offered to record his next album at a reduced rate if there was a negative financial return on this album.[24] The album sold well, but Negi received a warning from the district magistrate to abstain from any further involvement in the movement.

Negi's role in the political landscape of Uttarakhand has always been one of a removed and critical observer. Although he has at times been a vocal supporter of Uttarakhand Kranti Dal, a regional political party that has struggled to win seats against the nationalist parties, he has consistently refused offers to stand for election or to formally endorse any party platform. In this respect he departs from a well-established pattern of Indian musicians' and film actors' entering state-level politics.[25] Yet Negi's role as a removed critic of the state who gives voice to the sentiments of common people has arguably been much more powerful than any influence he could hold in political office.

Politicization and Digitalization

By the mid-1990s Negi had become the most influential and successful vernacular recording artist in Uttarakhand. The inability of distributors to keep up with local demand for his cassettes contributed to the creation of illegal dubbing stations in the more remote parts of the region. Vendors would keep one original copy of each album at their kiosk, and listeners would come and request songs to be added to a personalized "made-to-order" cassette or CD. For the extra labor of dubbing, the retailer made considerably more profit than he or she would make by selling the original album and avoided the fee normally paid to the distributor as well as the fee normally paid for an entertainment license. Following Negi's example, large numbers of novice singers began pooling their money and traveling to Dehradun or Delhi to hire studios and accompanists in the hope that they, too, could become famous. This large supply of commercial singers from nearly every village in Uttarakhand gave rise to a musical cottage industry in which many albums were produced by regional companies (or self-produced by local singers) and distributed only within a limited geographic area.

In 1994 India's largest music company, T-Series, owned by Gulshan Kumar, bought the rights to Negi's next album for twenty-five thousand rupees (US$600). At the time it was common practice among all music companies to pay artists less than half of the contracted amount by check; the remainder was paid in cash in order to avoid taxes. As with "majors" and independent music companies elsewhere, T-Series recruited vernacular artists only after they had established one or more hits on regional labels (in Negi's case, with Saraswati and Rama). Negi's success with T-Series led to increasing numbers of invitations to perform at festivals, political rallies, private parties; many of these invitations came from Uttarakhandi communities in Dubai, Oman, Australia, New Zealand, and the United States.

At about the same time Negi joined T-Series, commercial studios were switching from dual-track analog to multi-track digital recording. This technological transformation led to a radical change in the musical process and product. Musicians began to be recorded in temporal and spatial isolation, thereby fragmenting the social experience of music making. At the same time, multi-tracking technology led to the possibility of recording and mixing a seemingly infinite number of tracks per song. While most commercial Garhwali songs from the mid-1990s required no more than thirteen tracks, by 2005 most songs contained more than fifty tracks, many of which were cloned to produce a fuller sound in particular sections.

The shift to digital multi-tracking allowed for the contemplation of each line of the sonic texture in isolation from others, potentially expanding the ways Negi and other producers thought about and sonically engineered the folk element. Studio staff became increasingly concerned with the concept of the folk element as a quality of performance that inheres in specific stylistic gestures and nuances. In the production of one of Negi's albums, for instance, I witnessed the sound engineer and bansuri session musician recording a free-rhythm improvisatory cadenza. The producer described the playing as "mountain style" (*pahari shaili*) because of the pentatonic modality and the distinctive ornamentation and heavy reverb added to the melodic line. Digital multi-tracking may be responsible at least in part for new conceptualizations of the folk element because producers are, in effect, isolating and then editing detachable musical moments, bringing attention not only to overt choices of tune, text, or instrumental timbres but also to embodied and fleeting qualities of style.

In 1999, the first video compact disc album was launched in Uttarakhand. This digital medium soon supplanted the cassette as the dominant production format even as it extended the life of cassette recordings when artists' back catalogues were re-released with new videos. Negi initially resisted working in this visual medium for two reasons: first, he feared the loss of revenue that might result from the ease of pirating VCDs, and second, he did not believe he had the visual appeal to appear onscreen. Yet several VCDs of dubious quality appeared on the market, and people began thinking that Negi had produced these albums because the songs were his and his name was on the cover along with his photo. Legally he could do nothing to prevent the production of these knock-offs, so he decided to begin producing official VCD albums of his own back catalogue with T-Series.

The dominance of the VCD format throughout the early part of the twenty-first century created an emphasis on visual reproduction throughout the industry, and this in turn created a new urgency to visually capture the folk culture of Uttarakhand, which had been granted regional statehood in 2000. Most such VCD albums feature scenes of costumed, lip-synching youth danc-

Fig. 3.2. Cover of Narendra Singh Negi's album *Jai Maa Nandadevi* [Victory to Mother Goddess Nanda] (T-Series VCD, 2000)

ing in remote settings in the hills, interspersed with stock images of flowers, waterfalls, mountain vistas, and famous pilgrimage sites.

Negi has also created a number of VCD "folk albums" intended to revive a particular village-based musical style within a particular context (such as weddings, rituals, or festivals). These albums usually include verbal commentary describing the tradition being presented and the need to revive it as a valued part of the region's cultural heritage. In each case, Negi has undertaken significant research, often in collaboration with local folklorists and academics.

For instance, the VCD album *Jai Maa Nandadevi* ("Victory to Mother Goddess Nanda"), recorded in 2000, was based entirely on field recordings of dance-songs that were once performed in the villages of Chamoli District in honor of Nandadevi, one of the most popular forms of the goddess in Uttarakhand (see figure 3.2). A number of industry insiders have credited the commercial success of this album with generating an explosion in VCD production in the first decade of the twenty-first century.[26] Negi's VCD album *Chancheri Jhamako* (2007) consists of eight varieties of chancheri, a circular dance-song genre performed by men and women during festivals in central and eastern Garhwal. The videos show male and female dancers singing tunes and texts that similarly have been adapted from field recordings made by the folklorist Nand Kishore Hatwal in the Chamoli district. *Haldi Hath* (2003) consists of musical items that were once performed during Garhwali wedding ceremonies by semi-professional female singers (*mangaliya*). Observing the decline of this practice, Negi planned this album as a series of tracks that could be successively played during marriage ceremonies as a substitute for live performance.

Negi's most popular VCD was also his most politically confrontational (see figure 3.3). Written shortly after his retirement from government service, "Nauchami Narayana" (2006) utilized folk elements to parody the Congress-led state government. At the time he was serving as an unofficial advisor on the state government's Culture Committee, which was headed by Narayan Datt Tiwari, the chief minister of Uttarakhand. Negi's frustration with Tiwari's inaction regarding proposed recommendations in the areas of cultural policy was part of his motivation to write "Nauchami Narayana." Appropriating stylistic elements from local possession rituals, or jagar (see chapter 6), he sharply satirized the two national political parties in India, the Congress and the Bharatiya Janata Party (BJP), for their mismanagement of Uttarakhand since 2000. The song title is intended as double entendre; Narayana is a local name for the Hindu god Krishna dancing to nine rhythms (*nau chami*), but it also references the name of Narayan Datt Tiwari. While the text mockingly praises the god-man Nauchami Narayana, images on the VCD of the amorous, blue-skinned Krishna cross-fade against clips of an actor impersonating the chief minister while playing the flute and dancing with women in the garden of his Dehradun residence.[27] One of the most comical passages of the song describes Tiwari indiscriminately handing out *lal bati*, the red flashing lights mounted on cars that signify officialdom. Negi is exposing the Congress government's notorious practice of conferring VIP status on low-level officials through government handouts.

Negi's reputation in the music industry as a dependable hit-maker was well established, and he had little trouble convincing Rama Cassettes to produce a politically charged album this time around. The timing of the album's release, just months before the state assembly elections of 2007, reassured the producers at Rama that there would be a return on their investment. Indeed, "Nauchami Narayana" became the best-selling song in the history

Fig. 3.3. Cover of Narendra Singh Negi's album *Nauchami Narayana* (Rama Cassettes VCD, 2007)

of Garhwali-language popular music, selling fifty thousand copies in its first week and more than one million copies in all (Kazmi 2006; Gusain 2010). From my home in Srinagar I heard the song broadcast from the party headquarters of both the BJP and the regional Uttarakhand Kranti Dal on nearly a twenty-four-hour rotation. Tiwari's Congress-led government responded aggressively to the album's release, censoring the video album, restricting Negi's opportunities to perform the song publicly, and later releasing its own

VCD parodies of Negi's song.[28] Yet the political damage had already been done, and the crackdown only enhanced his image as a voice of the oppressed, leading one national newspaper to proclaim Negi the "Dylan of the hills" (*Telegraph*, Calcutta). It is difficult to measure the effects of a single song on a complex political environment, but most analysts agreed that "Nauchami Narayana" was a major factor contributing to the defeat of the Congress party in the Lok Sabha elections (Juyal 2006).

Following this episode, each newly elected state government has feared being on the wrong end of Negi's pen. In 2011 Negi critiqued the BJP-led government of Chief Minister Nishank Pokhriyal in the song "Ab Kathga Khailo." State officials purportedly offered Negi a large bribe not to release the album; he politely declined. Negi's position as a poet of the people likely is linked to his command of local folk elements and the subversive power of his music, which acts as a counterweight to politics as usual.

In 2008 Negi partnered with the Garhwali businessman Ravindra Lakhera, a hotel magnate in New Zealand, to form Himalayan Films, the first music production company owned and operated by Uttarakhandis. This entrepreneurial effort was motivated by Negi's longstanding concern that the commercial development of the region's music was primarily benefiting non-Uttarakhandis. The statement published at www.himalayanfilms.com underlines the centrality of the folk concept to the company's mission. It reads: "[Himalayan Films] has been set up to promote local folk and it aims at working for the preservation and conservation of the hill folk music. The Himalayan Films is planning to release one number per month. The Company has signed many young artists and is looking for new talent. [The] Company's move to promote local folk is considered a good sign for Uttarakhandi folk as the company has an experienced artist like Narendra Negi in its board."

At about the same time this company was launched, however, vernacular music production across Uttarakhand took a nosedive with the transition to mp3 and mp4 downloads, online streaming videos, and satellite television channels dedicated to round-the-clock music videos (Nowak 2014). In 2015, Himalayan Films had a total of twenty-three albums in its catalogue, many of which appeared in multiple formats; this is far from the projected production rate of one album per month. As a performer and producer, Negi is despondent about the effects of the new media; he believes that hit songs are becoming redundant only days after they are released because of overexposure. Consumers have free access to vernacular music through so many channels that they no longer expect to pay for it. As a result, regional companies are no longer willing to invest in new productions, and most of them have closed (see Manuel 2014). Large companies like T-Series continue to buy up albums by the most popular Garhwali singers, and these are now distributed for free via their T-Series regional music Youtube channel, largely as a way to advertise other products. All this has led to a reduction in the quality and overall number of Garhwali recordings. Since retiring from government service in 2005, Negi has relied on live shows in India and the diaspora for his income; for the first time since 1982, he has gone more than three years without releasing an album. There is no economic incentive for him to do so, and because he already has the reputation of Uttarakhand's best-known artist, there is no promotional reason to do so, either.

Negi as Social Activist

Many listeners enjoy Negi's lyrics precisely because of the references to village life, but some have been critical of Negi for singing about what they see as an outdated and essentialist role of the hereditary musician. Negi once received a letter from a Dalit student organization at Garhwal University that included the following passage: "All of your cassettes have become very famous, [but] when you use [words like] wooden mallet (*lakud*), 'dhol,' and 'Auji,' this increases casteism. One point is that India is ready to move beyond the 20th century. . . . You can understand our meaning. We just don't like the use of these words. Our 'mood' is disturbed when we hear them. When we write our [caste-given] names, we do not believe ourselves to be at all inferior" (N. S. Negi 2002: 5–6).

Negi seemed perplexed as he told me about several incidents in which individuals from Shilpkar backgrounds took offense to his use of song lyrics that carried caste-specific and, in their view, pejorative associations.

> NN: So the SC [Scheduled Caste] people said, "Why are you bringing us in[to] the music every time?" They have a *complex*. They say, "Don't mention Das and Aujis and dhol playing, people don't refer to them."
> SF: You used the word *Das* and they opposed that?
> NN: Yes, I used it and they opposed it. In Rudraprayag, there is an association of SC teachers, and we got a letter from a teacher [saying,] "Negi-ji, we really like your songs, but in this song 'Tilu Bakhri' you have tried to increase casteism and so many people from the village are upset." So I wrote him a letter and said if you want to play politics then do it somewhere else, not with culture. I said that you should understand the sense of the song. In our society, we have [been] given the job of playing dhol to a group of people. Is it my fault? This is a tradition that has been going on [and as long as] I am seeing it with my own eyes, I will write about it. And see, I didn't even say anything bad about these people. But you can't say that these castes are not

there in Garhwal at all, or that they are over. You can't say that, you can't stop anyone from writing history. I have written it before and I will keep writing it in the future. There have been two or three incidents such as this. . . . They have an inferiority complex. It is not the fault of the Das. They also have a right to pursue their own work. Every Brahmin is not doing puja, and every Thakur [Rajput] is not in the army. So even they have the right to choose and leave and get a new job. But it is a question of the art, which is only with them and no one else. And we want to preserve that art. We are not saying that only you should play. We are saying, "How can we preserve the art that you have and send it out to people?" Because I can sing lok sangeet, but I can't sing jagar in the style of jagar.[29]

Up to a point, Negi's response to this letter demonstrates a perspective similar to that of Madhuri Barthwal and many other Garhwali folklorists. Folk music has traditionally been the sole responsibility of hereditary musicians. He admits that individuals should have the freedom to choose any profession and that caste specializations are not binding, but he also understands dhol playing as the socially designated job of a certain group of people. Something essential to the region's cultural heritage would be lost if Shilpkar musicians were no longer able or willing to perform their hereditary functions.

Where Negi differs from Barthwal and other traditionalists is in the approach he advocates for preserving the hereditary practices of Shilpkar communities. In public lectures and in print, he has criticized the hypocritical stance of folklorists who favor keeping instruments such as the dhol-damaun free from commercial influence while calling for Bajgi musicians to maintain their dying traditions. Consistent with his views of folk music in general, Negi feels that commercial recording, stage programs, and competitions are avenues towards revitalizing Shilpkars' performance traditions and improving their economic and social status. To this end, he has created opportunities for a number of Shilpkar musicians to record albums in Delhi and to become part of the folk orchestra Himalaya Nad (discussed in chapter 4). He has also made plans to introduce a dhol competition in which performers from each subregion would compete, with the first- and second-place finishers moving to the district level and finally to the state level. I raised the question of how he would adjudicate such a competition, and he responded that performances would be judged on the basis of presentational criteria, such as how the musicians present themselves and maintained their instruments and how clearly and accurately they played each item. We discussed the problem of judging accuracy in the context of complex and non-standardized dhol-damaun repertory, but Negi insisted that certain items could be evaluated on formal criteria; for instance, any performance of *naubat* (a set of rhythms played near a temple or fort that traditionally marked the time of day) should exhibit nine distinct rhythmic cycles, even if the articulation of each individual cycle might vary between subregions. He also advocated scheduling the competitions in the morning to prevent excessive drunkenness among the participants.

Negi has been outspoken in his view that AIR Najibabad should hire a permanent Shilpkar drummer to properly represent Uttarakhandi music; he has criticized the fact that traditional forms such as jagar are presented on the radio with tabla accompaniment because there is no staff artist who knows how to properly play hurka or *daunr*.[30] This outspokenness led the AIR station manager to ban Negi from performing on the radio or from receiving any state awards. As a means of fostering employment for Bajgi drum makers and raising the status of the dhol-damaun, Negi also has proposed to the Uttarakhand Ministry of Culture that the Western drums used in school assemblies in each of the more than five thousand schools in Uttarakhand be replaced with a dhol-damaun. According to Negi, the minister of culture dismissed this proposal on the grounds that the people would not be able to change their perception of the lowly dhol. For Negi, this reaction was further evidence of the state's lack of support for local folk music and musicians. "Instead of saving the dhol, it is imperative that we save the dhol player," Negi says, continuing,

> They should be given the benefit of the electronic media and [be allowed to] make cassettes that will get them money. [Then] they can keep two or three dhols in their home and improve the standard for their children. I am trying to improve the status of [the dhol] so that one day they will jump [up] and say, "This is our instrument, where are you taking it?" And so we keep the dhol in our program and give it respect and also respond to people who say, "Don't keep the dhol in the concert." [My response is] that dhol is not exclusively yours. It belongs to your grandfather and father, and it is ours—it is for anyone who respects it.[31]

Note that, in contrast to the previous passage, he identifies the dhol as the property of the collective rather than the property of a particular caste community. He is personally invested in sustaining this tradition because it is part of a regional cultural heritage with which he strongly identifies. Yet by his own admission, the strategy of promoting Shilpkar musicians in the vernacular music industry has not been successful. As chapter 4 shows, few Shilpkar musicians have succeeded in maintaining a foothold in the industry, and those who have succeeded face significant challenges such as a lack of social and financial support, caste prejudice, and different cultural expectations of musicality and musical training. Faced with the declining position of the Shilpkar performer in both commercial and traditional settings, Negi posits an alternative approach:

> In the Bhuvaneswari seminar, I said we should take the dhol from their weak shoulders and take it on our own. Their shoulders are weak because they don't have the advantage financially and socially. The weight of such a huge tradition like dhol cannot be borne by them and their children. . . . I asked if they will put the dhol around their children's neck, so that the tradition lasts. It's not that we want to forcibly take the dhol off their shoulders, [but] if they don't want to play and don't want their children to play, then we have to put it around our necks if we want to preserve the tradition in the hills.[32]

That Negi means this quite literally is evident on his VCD recording of "Nau Durga Naraini,"[33] in which he simulates playing a dhol throughout the video; although Negi has never learned to play the dhol, he recognizes that for a Rajput man of status even to *simulate* playing the dhol is an important political act. Much like Mohan Upreti's controversial adoption of the hurka, Negi's embracing of the dhol is a sign of regional cultural heritage and of his own form of cultural activism.

Yet Negi's cultural advocacy is undeniably rooted in caste privilege. As an upper-caste man, he has the *choice* of when and how to align with subaltern drummers and their music. In some cases, he promotes dhol performance as a Shilpkar art form; elsewhere, noting the weakness of Shilpkar communities, he states that a new generation of upper-caste composers, performers, and scholars (the "we" to whom he refers) now have the responsibility to gain and maintain this knowledge. Since about 2005, increasing numbers of high-caste, non-hereditary musicians have followed Negi's lead, creating mass-mediated albums that include dhol-damaun, hurka-thali, and a variety of textual and musical folk elements.[34] As the vernacular industry has become ever more closely wedded to the folk brand, Negi and other high-status recording artists have to a large extent supplanted Shilpkar performers and have transformed themselves into the new folk artists. Their compositions and adaptations of village-based genres have gradually filtered into festival dance-song repertories, political rallies, and wedding celebrations.

Conclusion

The career of Narendra Singh Negi has followed a trajectory similar to that of Mohan Upreti. Both men came from high-status families in the hills, and both received an education in classical music in the plains. Both men began artistic careers with the support of family and patrons in Delhi, and both developed their artistic sensibilities in a time of political volatility. Finally, both men advanced their careers through folklorization, which involved the selective adoption of elements from narrative and musical performance rooted in village practice and the adaptation of these elements to cosmopolitan performance media through modernist reform.

Yet the political and economic context of Negi's career (1980–2010) has been strikingly different from that of Upreti's (1950–1980). Economic liberalization has created a flood of commodities and job growth in urban sectors and a boom in vernacular entertainment industries (Beaster-Jones 2016). State-operated media failed to keep up with the shifts in consumer taste, and artists increasingly turned to private music companies, which offered greater artistic freedom and greater compensation. Whereas the sphere of influence for Upreti's staged folk ballads was limited to Delhi-based intellectuals, Negi's commercial recordings reach millions of people. Whereas Upreti changed from Communist activist to patriotic nationalist during his career, Negi has moved from longstanding state employee to outspoken critic of the regional government. The slow simmer of desire for a separate state of Uttarakhand boiled over into a mass movement in the early 1990s, with Negi and other artists and intellectuals leading the charge.

Under these different political and economic conditions, the presentation and meaning of folk music has also changed. Although still informed by nationalist cultural processes and notions of tradition and heritage, folk music has increasingly been marketed as a commercial brand that represents the new regional state and can appeal to diverse audiences at home and abroad. Within the vernacular music industry, folk music does not only present a canvas of rural forms and practices upon which cosmopolitan creations are modeled; it has also become an essentialized quality of place indexed through discrete sonic emblems and that are packaged into sound commodities. Within the music industry and the regional political environment, "folk" is the label for a particular kind of sensibility and a distinctive brand that marks Uttarakhandis from the inhabitants of other regions of India.

I have offered one version of a history of music and technology in the Garhwali recording industry. Using the reminiscences and experiences of a single musician—albeit the best-known musician in the region—is one way of acknowledging the partiality and idiosyncrasies of any attempt to account for such a history, while also offering a sense of continuity that is grounded in embodied and lived experience. Through Negi's story, we can appreciate how each new medium of production and dissemination has piggybacked on the social and technological relations of earlier media; at the same time, however, this narrative illuminates the experience of rupture and insecurity that accompanied each new technological innovation.

Negi has consistently articulated a value for the "folk element in his vernacular recordings, but I have attempted to show how the possibilities and constraints of each medium have engendered new ways of conceiving and instrumentalizing the folk element. On state-controlled AIR, the idea of folk music was highly circumscribed by professional musician-caste identities, village provenance, and the discourse of cultural loss. Negi has advocated a more elastic notion of folk music that includes many varieties of song that filter into the communal repertoire from various sources. In the context of the Delhi-based vernacular music industry, however, Negi initially faced the challenge of constructing folk in an environment that was culturally and geographically removed from Uttarakhandi performers. By the beginning of the twenty-first century, however, the presence of more Garhwali instrumentalists in Delhi and the technological developments in digital multi-track recording and video production allowed Negi to accentuate folk elements on both the micro level, as an element of style in each layer of the recording, and the macro level, in the large-scale production of folk albums. In chapter 4 I consider the effects that the commercial craze for folk music has had on the lives and careers of Shilpkar performers. As Negi's and Upreti's careers make clear, the process of turning dying folk into living folk is enmeshed in a parallel process of separating the folk sound from the folk body.

4 The Folk Sound without the Folk Body

Sohan Lal and the Rhizophonics of Dhol-Damaun

Since the 1980s, the growth of political regionalism and of the privatized music industry in India has created opportunities for cultural entrepreneurs to codify national and regional heritage and to forge new income-earning opportunities. In Uttarakhand and a variety of other regions, lok sanskriti (folk culture) has been celebrated in the official state discourse and has become a major brand in vernacular culture industries. Shilpkar musicians in Uttarakhand would seem well positioned to take advantage of this trend. Indeed, a few, including Chander Singh Rahi and Pritam Bhartwan (see chapter 6), have capitalized on recording opportunities and have become well-established public performers. A number of other artists from Shilpkar backgrounds have found work in the vernacular music industry but have concealed their caste background by changing their surname or marrying out of caste. The vast majority of hereditary musicians in Uttarakhand, however, have neither the opportunity nor the desire to become involved in the commercial music industry. The reasons for this include the shift in patronage networks from rural landowners to urban, plains-based institutions; the emphasis on shared, nonspecialist styles of music and dance on commercial albums; the prevalence of caste-based prejudice among industry insiders; the impoverishment of most Shilpkar families, linked to the rampant abuse of alcohol and challenges to mental and physical health; and the lack of familiarity with cosmopolitan values and the process of studio production.

The confluence of these factors has led to a paradox within the industry whereby vernacular recordings celebrate and raise the profile of folk music while communicating an ambiguous or disdainful attitude toward the

hereditary folk artist. Conforming to the hallmarks of modernist reformism, cosmopolitan producers selectively include certain folk elements that
are believed to signify the rural heritage of Uttarakhand and subsequently
highlight, extend, blend, and embellish these elements for urban stage
programs and studio recordings (Turino 2000: 15–17). Because Shilpkars'
bodies—regarded as polluting and primitive—cannot be reformed as easily
as their music can, we are left with a situation in which studio producers
separate folk sounds from folk bodies and emphasize sonic elements that
can be easily detached from the body.

A useful concept in this context is rhizophonia, described by Jason Stanyek
as the "fundamentally fragmented yet proliferative condition of sound reproduction and recording, where sounds and bodies are constantly dislocated,
relocated, and co-located in temporary aural configurations" (2014: 119).
Stanyek advances rhizophonia in place of the popular concept of schizopho-
nia first theorized by Murray Schafer (1977) and later by Steven Feld (1996),
critiquing the latter as "a problematic, tautological term that seems to describe
an exception (sound severed from source) to some impossible, full presence
(sound as identical with its source)" (Stanyek 2014: 119). Stanyek's articulation of the unceasing processes of dislocation, relocation, and co-location in
contemporary sound reproduction is persuasive, as is his claim that "personhood is distributed" through the chain of recorded sound production—"but
not all the elements involved in its distribution have the same ethical claim"
(ibid.). I am particularly interested in fleshing out this last observation by
focusing on rhizophonic processes across social networks in which power is
unequally distributed. What are the ramifications of cosmopolitan producers'
and music directors' electronically producing melodic or rhythmic motives
that evoke (absent) Shilpkar musicians in the minds of Uttarakhandi listeners? Unlike Stanyek and Feld, I am not interested in exploring rhizophonic
or schizophonic-mimetic processes within the "global space of circulating
commodities" (Feld 1996: 9). My scale is more circumscribed and ethno-
graphically grounded. I explore a context in which Shilpkar musicians know
and collaborate with higher-caste producers and music directors even as they
are often marginalized by the latters' decisions, and one in which listeners
are connected to producers through distribution networks and community
alliances. In this intimate setting, the ramifications of rhizophonia are all the
more interesting because all participants are aware of them.

This chapter draws primarily on the work of Sohan Lal, my dhol teacher
and close collaborator since 2007. I focus on his experiences as a hereditary
drummer because they are typical of those of many other Shilpkar musicians
in Uttarakhand. At the same time, Sohan's story is exceptional in that he is

one of the few individuals from his community of hereditary drummers to have established a professional career in both rural and urban contexts, for lower- and upper-caste patrons. He is also exceptional for his musicianship, his knowledge of drum making, and his outspokenness about the injustices of the conventional caste hierarchy.

Sohan Lal

I first met Sohan Lal and his older brother, Sukaru Das, in March 2007 in Srinagar (Garhwal), where my wife and I were renting part of a house.[1] I had long wanted to own a set of dhol-damaun drums and to begin learning the repertoire, and I had heard about Sohan's abilities from a number of artists and scholars in Garhwal.[2] I had also heard that he was an unusually outspoken advocate for Shilpkar musicians in Uttarakhand and that he recently had been elected headman (*pradhan*) of his village in Tehri Garhwal. After I spoke to Sohan several times by phone, he overcame his initial skepticism and agreed to come to Srinagar with his brother to spend a week making drums and teaching me. My landlords, who lived in the other half of the house, were an upwardly mobile Rajput family who had migrated from a nearby village a couple of years earlier. I anticipated that they might be sensitive to notions like caste pollution, and so I booked a hotel room for Sohan and Sukaru to sleep in after we had finished our daily lessons.

Sohan, a slight, energetic man in his late forties with bright eyes and a quick smile, arrived a little more than a week later. I received him and Sukaru at the bus stop, and as we approached my home, I heard a neighbor calling out sarcastically, "We see you have *special* guests!" Soon thereafter, my landlords bolted shut the door to the common area of the house where the washbasin was located, presumably to prevent my guests from accessing the water source. If Sohan was uncomfortable he did not show it, and we continued with our music lesson. But later that evening, after my guests had retired to their hotel room, the landlady visited and made clear her opinion that inviting a Das into an upper-caste home (even my half of the home) was *not* acceptable. My attempts to appeal to her sense of social justice did not succeed, and as her tenant I ultimately had to abide by her wishes.

The following day we resumed lessons at the hotel. While I was documenting the process of drum construction and simultaneously learning to perform various patterns on the dhol-damaun, several of my higher-caste friends dropped by, watched our lessons for some time, and eventually left. Over the course of the next several days, one friend called and approached me repeatedly, asking if I could share recordings of our lessons with him because he was interested in learning but did not think it appropriate to learn from a Shilpkar. I brought the matter up with Sohan. What follows is part of our conversation.

> SF: I think when they saw me learning, they thought, "We also want to learn this." And I was thinking, here is your [fellow villager], but still you don't want to learn this from him.
>
> SL: [laughing] Of course!
>
> SF: Then they asked, "Can we get this recording from you?"
>
> SD: Don't give them that!
>
> SF: No, of course not; this is for my own research.
>
> SL: Listen, I'll tell you. Our traditional teachers, they didn't used to teach this to [high-caste people]. There's a reason for this, a very big reason. Maybe a skin was brought and what will they say? This is something that should have been discussed yesterday. You must know why our people haven't taught this. There was injustice [*anyay*]. So now, now they may think these people [Das] are next to us and we should learn, [because] someone from America is learning.[3]

Sohan described many instances of such injustice to me. During a large-scale festival in Dehradun, he was asked to direct and coordinate a performance involving dozens of dhol players, but after the performance he noted that the cultural entrepreneur who had organized the event had stolen the limelight. "I put in so many days of hard work," he related, "only to pick up the newspaper and find that [this person] had taken all the credit, when he doesn't know the first thing about the dhol."

He also gave many examples of social discrimination in villages throughout Uttarakhand. Sohan's father, like his grandfather before him, used to have to play naubat everyday at sunrise and sunset at the Chandrabadni temple located ten kilometers from their village. Twice a year the family would receive payment in kind for this service, but his father received no food or accommodation at the temple, and he was forced to sleep in the open under a tree. When Lal became village headman in 2003, he lodged a case against the Chandrabadni temple committee and passed a new rule that any future drummer performing this service should receive food, money, and a room in the temple complex.

As the leader of a large group of hereditary performers, Lal is responsible for negotiating all compensation, travel, and accommodation arrangements with his patrons. After many difficult experiences, he has learned to be very explicit about the kinds of lodging, meals, and payment his group requires. "Many times we have left the village [performances] and have come home without taking money," he told me. "We have played all night and avoided drinking. These rascals would give us liquor like milk and [our] people would play out of fear. Sure, lots of people drink when there is a wedding, but [our people] used to drink out of tension." During a wedding gig I attended with them in 2007, Lal and his band were told by the hosts to remain at the edge of the ceremonial space in direct sunlight for hours while wedding guests sat in chairs under the tarp, they were given chai without milk when all others were drinking chai with milk, and they were invited to eat only after every guest had finished eating. These experiences of discrimination in rural areas are so prevalent that Lal pre-screens his patrons, agreeing to perform in a village function only if he is promised clean accommodation and his own means of transportation. In general he avoids eating or drinking whenever possible because of the potential conflict with conservative, higher-caste people.

Lal's ability to decide where and when he performs is an indication of his entrepreneurial abilities and his recent rise in status. In general, this degree of choice is rarely evidenced by individuals belonging to the Bajgi drumming community. *Bajgi* (lit. "one who plays or sounds"), also called Auji in some regions, is the caste designation for the largest group of professional musicians in Uttarakhand. As with the Damai of Nepal, the traditional occupations for Bajgi males were drumming and tailoring, but in recent decades many have migrated to urban areas and learned other skills. The relative rank of the Bajgi community varies by subregion, but typically it lies along the lower to lower-middle end of local caste and class hierarchies. For those who remain in the village, drumming is a hereditary duty; there is little choice about whether to play, nor is there much opportunity to negotiate the remuneration or conditions for playing. In every village in Uttarakhand, drummers are required to play the dhol and the damaun (figure 4.1) for their higher-caste patrons for calendar-based rituals (ancestral rites, festivals) and life-cycle rituals (births, naming ceremonies, *disabhent*,[4] weddings, funerals). One consequence of these hereditary duties is that Bajgi families are geographically dispersed across villages throughout Uttarakhand. At certain times of the year, however, drummers travel long distances to lead processions of local deities or lead wedding parties to and from the bride's residence (*barat*).

In exchange for performing these duties, drummers were once remunerated by the village in kind (*kar* or *dadwar* in Garhwal, and *khaukiya-gusai* in Kumaon) in the form of measured amounts of food, clothing, and jewelry and a token monetary offering. This system has been abandoned in all but a few interior regions of Uttarakhand, and most Bajgi families survive on

Fig. 4.1. Sukaru Das (left, with the damaun) and Sohan Lal teaching the author (with the dhol), 2005 (courtesy S. Fiol)

remittances sent by family members employed in urban areas, supplemented by meager resources accrued from drumming, tailoring, and subsistence farming. Extreme poverty and alcoholism plague this community. Packets of village-brewed alcohol (which, ironically, are distilled by Shilpkar families themselves in many villages) are regularly given to drummers as a substitute for cash payments.

High-caste patrons continue to enforce a code of conduct for subservient members of artisan communities. The latter have been discouraged by regular acts of caste-based discrimination and have had little opportunity to develop the kind of caste consciousness evident in other parts of India, most visibly in the Dalit movements (Fanger 1980: 160–164; Rathore 2016). The population of service-providing castes has always been relatively small in Uttarakhand, making up less than ten percent of the total population. Shilpkar settlements continue to be evenly and widely dispersed.

Drumming across Caste and Class Boundaries

Sohan Lal was one of three children born to Granti Das and Longhi Devi, both of whom transmitted their extensive knowledge of local songs, ballads, and drumming patterns to their children. In addition to drumming, Lal and his older brother, Sukaru Das, learned how to sew and mend from their relatives.

Shortly after passing the eighth grade, Sohan Lal quit school and joined the staff of a local NGO, Sri Bhuvaneshwari Mahila Ashram (SBMA). The organization was founded in Anjanisain, Tehri Garhwal, by the late Swami Manmathan, a social crusader from Kerala who worked for decades to improve the condition of women, children, and Shilpkar communities in Garhwal. Lal worked for SBMA as a drummer for approximately ten years; he joined a team of activist-artists who traveled across Uttarakhand and performed skits addressing the ills of alcoholism and the need to visit health clinics. This work exposed him to the issues of discrimination and poverty that Shilpkar musicians faced in all parts of Uttarakhand. The work also allowed him to develop his abilities as a drummer. Throughout his travels, Lal regularly recorded and interviewed elderly Bajgis, learning new compositions and improving his knowledge of building instruments. During this time, he was also developing another hereditary occupation. He set up a small tailoring business on the road above his village where he sold cloth and rented equipment for weddings.

In 1999 Lal was invited to participate in a forty-day workshop called Dholi Bacao, Dhol Bajao (Save the Dhol Player, Play the Dhol). This workshop was part of a larger project, funded by the Ford Foundation and organized by the NGO Rural Entrepreneurship for Art and Cultural Heritage (REACH), to document the dhol-playing tradition of Garhwal and to foster entrepreneurship and economic sustainability among Shilpkar musicians. Local folklorists, foreign scholars, and several instructors of North India tabla invited and interviewed hereditary drummers from different parts of Garhwal with the aim of recording and transcribing the existing drumming repertoire and isolating the subregional differences in drumming style. The organizers believed that a written theory needed to be created in order to transcribe and preserve an art form that is quickly disappearing. The interviewers guided the repertoire choices and asked the drummers to recite *bols* (beat patterns) for each item before playing.

I spoke with one interviewer with a background in tabla performance who expressed disappointment in the lack of a systematic theory of bols in the dhol-damaun repertory. He explained to me that centuries ago, the standardization of the dhol repertoire was possible because of the cultural authority of the *Dhol Sagar* (Ocean of Drumming), an enigmatic treatise that now survives only in fragments within oral tradition. The disappearance of this document has resulted in the splintering and dilution of knowledge across Uttarakhand. His perspective corresponds to that of many regional scholars who rue the disappearance of the *Dhol Sagar* as a unified authoritative text rooted in Sanskrit theory and Hindu cosmology.[5] In these accounts the *treatise* becomes a sign of lost tradition and prestige, and the contemporary Bajgi performer becomes a relic of past greatness. Many Bajgi performers can recite long passages from the *Dhol Sagar* from memory, and many of these passages have been copied out and handed down from generation to generation. A systematic study of the content and of the relation between the oral and written materials is lacking, but if done it would likely reveal a fragmented and adaptive historical relation between inherited practices and innovations, rather than demonstrating the gradual corruption of a single authoritative text.

The ethnomusicologist Andrew Alter, who attended the REACH workshop, has described several of its methodological dilemmas (2014: 87–94). The interviewers focused on the role of the dhol in their transcriptions but largely excluded the damaun. In some ways this omission was natural since the dhol is the lead instrument and theoretically can be played apart from the damaun (though in common practice, this only occurs in the northwest portion of Garhwal); the strokes of the dhol are also louder, more variable, and more important in marking large-scale shifts in the rhythm. Yet as Alter notes, the omission of the damaun in transcriptions was an unfortunate oversight. The damaun does not simply fill in between the strokes of the dhol but also "serves to emphasize the metric character of the dhol's pattern when/if a metric cycle is present" (ibid.: 90). The damaun provides crucial micro-rhythmic information that contributes to the way the overall pattern is heard and experienced. The ways in which the damaun subdivides the stronger beats of the dhol can be highly variable; Keil's notion of "participatory discrepancies" (Keil 1987) might be invoked to describe how the damaun adds groove to the overall rhythm.

The interviewers carried over certain assumptions from their knowledge of tabla playing. Rhythmic patterns on the tabla are also produced by the interaction of two drums; unlike the dhol-damaun pair, however, they are played by a single individual and are conceived of as a single rhythmic expression. This has facilitated the development of a systematized vocabulary of bols that tabla players use as a mnemonic and didactic device. Many Shilpkar drummers also use bols to transmit and remember rhythms on the dhol-damaun, but they do so in a much more flexible and idiosyncratic way that reflects the variability within this oral performance tradition, as well as the nuances of local speech dialects. Whereas recited bol syllables and drum strokes tend to have a one-to-one relation in tabla discourse, village drummers in Garhwal primarily use bol patterns as imitations of groups of sounds (rather than individual strokes) produced by two distinct but interlocking instrumental parts. Alter convincingly demonstrates this point by showing how bol recitations may alternately emphasize only the dhol pattern, only the damaun pattern, a composite of the two, or neither (2014: 87–94).

In addition to the goals of documentation and analysis, the REACH workshop also sought to improve the economic position of Shilpkar musicians by expanding their patronage opportunities to include wealthier, middle-class people living in urban areas. The workshop attempted to accomplish this goal in several ways. First, musicians were encouraged to expand their ensembles from two or three instruments (dhol, damaun, and sometimes mashakbaja) to between eight and ten instruments (dhol, damaun, daunr, naggara, mashakbaja, ransingha, bhankora, *shehnai*, binai, and muruli). All of these instruments are indigenous to Uttarakhand (with the exception of the mashakbaja, or bagpipe, which has gone through a process of indigenization over the past two hundred years after being introduced by the British Army), but they are not typically used in large-ensemble formats.[6] Second, performers were encouraged to present themselves in a more uniform and attractive way; workshop participants pointed out which instruments were in need of polishing, repair, or replacement, and musicians were offered financial assistance to purchase matching kurta-and-pajama sets for all of the performers in their ensemble. Third, performers were encouraged to adapt their traditional repertoire to meet the demands of the contemporary patron. The workshop organizers stressed that many traditional items such as panwara and jagar needed to be truncated and modified to fit the needs of the setting. Musicians were also advised about how to sing in front of a microphone and how to arrange their songs to accommodate a more expanded instrumentation.

As a means of actualizing these goals, organizers put together a folk orchestra consisting entirely of Shilpkar performers that was given the name Himalaya Nad (Eternal Sound of the Himalayas). The expectation was that members of this ensemble would later return to their respective villages and form their own folk orchestras based on the model of Himalaya Nad. The organizers were hopeful that these ensembles could spark a revival in indigenous music among middle-class patrons who had long preferred to hire plains-based brass bands for weddings and private performances rather than local hill bands. Narendra Singh Negi (see chapter 3), a workshop participant, was invited to be the arranger and director of Himalaya Nad, in large part because he was one of the most respected musicians in the region and one of the few individuals who had extensive experience performing and composing in styles from various parts of Garhwal. Sohan Lal and about a dozen other Shilpkar musicians were invited to perform in the ensemble.

Over the course of a few days, Negi worked with the musicians to try to create a program that would be presented at the Virasat Festival in Dehradun in 2001. He soon became overwhelmed by the challenges. The use of instruments with variable dynamic range (used for either indoor or outdoor contexts) required selective miking techniques. Balancing the sounds of various percussion instruments proved especially complicated because rhythmic patterns are hierarchically organized in dyads, with "lead" instruments (dhol, daunr, and hurka) accompanied by "follow" instruments (damaun and thali). Another problem was that the performers came from different regions with highly variable drumming repertoires. While many of the names of drumming items are shared across the region (for example, *barhai, dhunyal, shabd,* and *naubat*), the manner in which these are performed varies from one family of drummers to another, the result of both subregional stylistic differences and personal idiosyncrasies. To make matters worse, the performers of the hurka and dhol were unaccustomed to being asked to learn and *follow* a rhythmic pattern played by someone else; the idea of melding their individual part into a large ensemble was a new one.

Negi decided that the ensemble would perform a very short prelude together and then switch to a medley format, featuring small groups of instruments in turn: daunr-thali, binai-hurka-thali, dhol-damaun-*mashakbin*, and so on. The biggest obstacle of the entire project, according to Negi, was that the performers were not willing to learn; they came with a fixed repertoire and were not willing or able to develop beyond it. "I was not able to achieve what I wanted to achieve, mainly because these people are not *musicians*," he claimed. "They don't have technical knowledge of what they are playing, and cannot learn what I am trying to teach them." [7] Negi cited the lack of group cohesiveness, organizational skills, self-confidence, professional decorum, and pride in the art form as the main obstacles facing the professionalization of Shilpkar performers. Several days before the performance, Negi grew frustrated with the project and quit his position as director. His collaborator Ram Charan Juyal stepped in and hastily completed the preparations. The performance at the Virasat Festival was warmly received by the audience, but according to several participants, the performers were less than satisfied by the experience.

Fig. 4.2. Sohan Lal's ensemble Himalaya Nad, undated (courtesy S. Fiol)

After the Virasat performance, members of the group had been instructed to return to their villages to start their own folk ensembles. Several groups were successfully launched through this initiative, and some received financial support to purchase costumes. At present, however, Sohan Lal's group is the only one spawned by the REACH workshop that continues to perform. It is clear that he absorbed much from his participation in Himalaya Nad. In fact, Lal adopted the same name for his own group, which performs extensively throughout Uttarakhand and in migrant communities in other parts of India for diverse occasions including weddings, birthday celebrations, regional and national festivals, healing rituals (jagar), and receptions at the airport for arriving political figures. His group currently consists of about thirty-five members of his extended family; during the wedding season Lal divides the troupe into three or four smaller groups in order to maximize income-earning opportunities. Depending on the budget of the client and the requirements of the occasion, Lal gathers a team of four to twelve performers, all attired in blue kurtas with white pajamas and Pahari caps (figure 4.2). In addition to the standard instrumentation of the Pahari hill band (dhol, damaun, and mashakbin), Sohan Lal uses the double-reed shehnai (played by the bagpiper, who attaches a reed to the chanter), a set of natural horns (the ransingha and the bhankora, also called the turi), and a Casio keyboard with a portable amplifier. His groups are invited to perform for urban and rural audiences from diverse backgrounds; consequently, they have prepared a range of commercial Garhwali, Jaunsari, Kumaoni, and Hindi film songs, as well as local items that traditionally would be performed by the Bajgi community. During weddings, for instance, Lal's group performs processional rhythms during the barat, and it performs rhythms of invocation (*barhai*) and auspicious songs (*mangal geet*) during important moments of the ritual; at other times, however, the group accepts requests for commercial songs or plays a range of local hits to encourage people to dance.

Studio Recording

Sohan Lal's involvement with local NGOs and government-funded initiatives has given him exposure to a range of music industry insiders who have been interested in reforming and preserving the dhol-damaun repertory. One of these individuals is Negi, who in the early 1990s convinced Lal and a number of other hereditary performers to make recordings of divine and heroic ballads (jagar and panwara). Negi believed that making commercial recordings was an important way for artists to promote themselves and create opportunities for live performances. Negi's own career amply demonstrates this fact. Yet when he offered Bajgi musicians the chance to make studio albums, he was often met with reluctance, refusal, or outlandish demands for compensation. Negi could not understand these musicians' inability to recognize what were to him the obvious benefits of studio recording. If one examines the studio experiences of Sohan Lal and others, however, these reactions become more understandable.

Most studio recording takes place in East Delhi, across the Yamuna River between Noida and Ghaziabad, more than a day's travel for most village musicians in Uttarakhand. East Delhi became a hub of regional recording beginning in the 1970s because of inexpensive real estate, the large concentration of migrants settled in the region, and the presence of large music companies such as T-Series. It is central for Uttarakhandis arriving in one of two northern bus terminals, ISBT (from locations in Garhwal) or Anand Vihar (from locations in Kumaon). Shilpkar musicians are less likely than are higher-caste individuals to have friends and family members living in Delhi. They also tend to be less familiar with the urban market economy, leaving many susceptible to the corruption for which Delhi is notorious. For his part, Mayur Nichani, a producer and studio owner in the regional capital of Dehradun, hopes that the drawbacks of Delhi will encourage more musicians from the hills to utilize his studio. He stated,

> See, [the reason] my studio does good is, I'm near to the hills. So most of the
> musicians . . . are living up in the hills. So it's actually very difficult for them to

go and live in Delhi. And in Delhi there are many cheats, you know? They'll have to first spend on transportation, then they'll have to spend on what they're eating, their food and everything, plus they'll be staying over there. Three things: accommodation, eating, and to and fro. And the real musicians are from the hills. . . . But people have this psyche that we've got this work from Delhi [so it's better, even though] they might go and spend more [there]. They might get inferior quality, you know? But still they'll want to go there. Though in Delhi there are some people who are using, you know, curtains for sound proofing . . . and you can hear the horn of a truck [in the recording] also. But still they'll go to Delhi, they'll get cheated over there, and they'll come back. Until now, say 70 percent of the audio work is being done in Delhi. Only 30 percent is being done in Uttarakhand.[8]

Nichani was speaking of the general risk of financial exploitation in Delhi for all performers arriving from the hills; yet in my experience Shilpkar performers were particularly vulnerable. For example, in the past several decades, a number of Bajgi drummers have traveled to Delhi studios to make commercial recordings. In all cases that I have heard about, they were either invited by upper-caste singers from the village (in which case they performed as rhythmic accompanists, and their names rarely appear on the album jacket) or they were invited by music companies to record solo albums. One such album, titled *Uttarakhanda Gaja Baja* (T-Series), features Devendra Kumar, Suresh Lal, and Moti Lal performing on dhol, damaun, and mashakbin (figure 4.3). Images of the instruments appear on the album cover but not the performers themselves; this is symptomatic of the aforementioned tension between idealizing folk music and negating the folk artisan. Such tension became evident during recording sessions I attended in which music directors and sound engineers focused on capturing the sound of indigenous instruments but neglected the desires of the Shilpkar performers, many of whom were expected to record material for anywhere between two and five albums in a single day.

Vikram Rawat was the producer of a number of folk projects for the Rama and T-Series labels during the late 1980s and early 1990s, including several involving Sohan Lal.[9] These recordings have been quite profitable for regional music companies because they have a longer shelf life than do albums of newly composed Uttarakhandi geet, despite selling in smaller numbers initially. Recalling the studio project involving Lal, Rawat said, "We called in 'typical' players and singers. They played and sang in the same way [as they would in the village]. We had them play dhol, [and they performed] a *mandan* and *Devi jagar*. On a recording [with Sohan Lal] we spent only five thousand rupees [approximately $115]. Only five thousand we threw at [the

Fig. 4.3. Cover of *Uttarakhandi Gaja Baja: Garhwali Paramparik Dhune* (T-Series cassette, 1988)

performers] (*un par phainka*). And that was so successful—at the time of the Navratri festival 60,000 cassettes were sold."[10] All performers involved in a studio project are remunerated through a lump sum payment arrangement, which is calculated to reduce risk and bring maximum profit to the music company. Nonetheless, the payment of $115 to Lal and his partner on damaun was unusually low given that the album was recorded, mixed, and mastered in a single day, incurring minimal studio expenses, and that the album grossed $30,000 (at 50 cents per album) during a single season, according to this producer.

On several occasions I observed studio professionals using offensive language with Shilpkar performers, ordering them out of the studio immediately after recording or demanding that they perform repeated takes without rest. Although most studio professionals were uncomfortable discussing openly with me the issue of caste prejudice when working with Shilpkar musicians, one engineer, who wished to remain anonymous, was explicit:

> They don't take a bath and the moment they come over here, it's difficult for me to sit down. . . . In Delhi, everyone is in the habit of using *ji* to call anyone respectfully. But here I thought, well, how can I call them *ji* [when] they are from the remote village? Ultimately now what happens is, I'm sorry to say, "Get up" [*uttaro*], "Get out!" [*bahar jao*]. And [ordering] has become a habit. I joke

around with them also; I scold them also. Sometimes if they're not singing properly I scold them. Like maybe they haven't been to the studios before, they come and fool with the mic . . . because these things cost money . . . and naturally when we have musicians from Delhi, I have to talk to them respectfully.[11]

Such stigma and caste or class prejudice unquestionably have contributed to the reluctance of many Shilpkar musicians to participate in studio recordings. At first glance, these experiences appear to resemble the forms of verbal and physical discrimination that these musicians regularly face in rural settings. Yet I believe the studio experiences are qualitatively different because of the unfamiliarity of the setting and the different system of values in the studio. As a number of ethnographies have documented in other settings (Porcello 1996; Meintjes 2003; Scales 2004), notions of musical training in the studio environment have to do with command over a particular kind of discourse; in North India, this discourse draws on knowledge of technology, classical, folk, and film music conventions, and Western functional harmony. Anyone new to the studio environment can feel alienated by this discourse, but the Shilpkar musician is explicitly marked as ignorant of technology and studio practice. For instance, one studio percussionist commented, "Dhol players get scared. Like they are playing before the microphone, right? Psychologically they get a little scared. It's a little tough: This is a technical line, and they don't have the technical aspect. They play according to their own style."[12]

Narendra Singh Negi explained that the studio environment required an attention to detail and precision that listeners had grown accustomed to but that most village musicians were unable to provide:

These days folk has changed—it is played less in villages and more in studios, through those machines, costly mics, these digital recordings. *High-tech* recording is happening. Now when a folk artist comes to the *high tech*, he gets scared. He is from the village, so to ask him to alter his pitch [doesn't work;] . . . whatever pitch he gets, he sticks to that. He is not *technical*, [but] he has to be these days; and he is not singing alone, he has to sing with other musicians in the team. Everyone has their instruments tuned in one way so you can't go beyond that pitch; so for today's folk artists it is important that they learn music. If they learn then they can perform well. Today there is so much competition that when people sing, the audience [can] discern when someone is off-pitch [*besoor*]. Even children identify someone who is off-pitch, even a grandmother says it. The quality has improved through listening—so when you have such an audience you have to be prepared and cannot perform carelessly.[13]

Negi's statement reveals a set of expectations for studio practice that corresponds with cosmopolitan values more generally. His point was not that

Shilpkar performers are unable to sing on pitch but that the village-based musical environments in which they are trained do not prepare them for the pitch precision and technical knowledge of studio recording. In rural settings where songs are generally used to accompany dance or ritual, the timbral and rhythmic parameters of a melody generally became more important than pitch. When singing a single melodic line to percussion accompaniment, subtle rises in absolute pitch are frequent and may intensify key moments of a narrative performance. In the studio context, however, pitch and rhythmic precision are valued at least on a par with, if not more than, other musical parameters.

Negi acknowledged the Shilpkar musician's susceptibility to financial exploitation and caste discrimination in the music industry, but he laid much of the blame on the Shilpkar's lack of professionalism and technical knowledge. Instead of negotiating a contract and recording an album with one music company, Negi noted, several Shilpkar musicians had recorded the same material for multiple labels, thereby violating copyright laws and compromising future opportunities to record. He attributed this behavior to the financial insecurity of many performers, who have sought to maximize their profit on visits to Delhi by recording as quickly and frequently as opportunities arose. I was somewhat surprised to learn that Sohan Lal had recorded sections of the Pandavalila (a local performance of the Mahabharata epic) for both the Rama Cassettes Company and T-Series Company.[14] When I asked him about this, he did not understand how this could be considered problematic because he had performed distinct portions of the narrative in each of the recordings. Moreover, even if he had performed exactly the same sections, the performances would differ from one another in a number of ways, because he would be elaborating on different parts of the narrative. Negi's and Lal's contrasting interpretations of this practice reveal two different orientations toward intellectual property. Sohan Lal's is rooted in an oral performance tradition that places a value on memory, virtuosity, and flexibility; Negi's, in contrast, values originality, literacy, and salability within the context of capitalist production.

Sohan Lal's experiences with studio recording further illuminate these conflicting value systems. In 1997, prior to attending his first recording session at the T-Series studio in Delhi, he was told to prepare a script of his heroic ballad (*panwara*) text so that the producer could review it before the recording session. Although Lal is a literate man, he balked at the idea of preparing a script for something that he had always performed as an oral tradition:

Some Garhwali people were there in the studio, and they wanted to see the script, but what do they understand about when to play from where? Then the music director [*adyaks*] said, "Sohan Lal-ji, we need you to record but you should practice first." I said, "What is there to practice?" I played and in one hour we recorded and came out, smoked a beedi, and did the second side for one hour. The *machine* guy [*mashin-wallah*] became confused. He was wondering whether we had caught the rhythm correctly [in one place]. He opened the machine [*mashin khula*] and asked me to sing again. So I sang and then the director came to me and said, "Please help us." I said, "Do you want me to sing again?" He said, "No, but open the machine and see where it is wrong." I said, "If I have to do this why are you sitting here!" But then we heard it again and there was no gap and it was perfect the first time. And they asked me, "How is this so perfect?" Because this is our music, this is what we do every day.[15]

As we spoke about this experience in his village home, Lal revealed that he was keenly aware of the different set of social and musical values in the studio environment. He became self-conscious as he described this process to me, perhaps feeling that his use of nontechnical speech ("open the machine") exposed him to the stereotype of the mountain musician in the urban studio. And yet his narrative was assertive: he was able to laugh at the ineptness of the "machine guy" and dismiss requests for notation or rehearsal before recording. Lal exuded a confidence that he could sing and play perfectly in *any* environment. He was proud of the fact that the recording sounded just as it would have sounded in a rural performance context and that there was no need to edit even one word. Later in our conversation he remarked to me that from a musical standpoint, studio recordings were less challenging than ritual performances, where he had to be able to respond to the audience by manipulating the rhythm to match the stepping patterns of dancers, for example, or by raising the absolute pitch of a singing song to heighten the intensity of a narrative.

Sohan Lal was proud of his work in the recording studio and acknowledged that his cassettes and video albums had brought him recognition within migrant communities outside Uttarakhand, where recordings are a marker of high cultural capital. On one occasion, while negotiating a fee with a potential client on the phone, I heard him mention that he was a recording artist with T-Series, presumably as a way to elevate his status. At the same time, he was not eager to repeat the experience of studio recording, which required long travel, a challenging work environment, and potential exposure to discrimination. Recordings were an important source of advertising, but they were not nearly as lucrative as performances at weddings, festivals, and healing ceremonies.

Dhol Rhizophonia

The dhol and damaun are ubiquitous in outdoor public performance in the Uttarakhand Himalayas; as instruments bequeathed by Lord Shiva, they are considered sacred and auspicious at all ritual occasions. Despite their centrality in the region, the dhol and damaun are seldom used for multi-track studio recordings; the commercial recordings of Bajgi drummers such as Sohan Lal make up a very small percentage of the total output of Uttarakhandi geet. The tabla, dholak, and octopad are the preferred percussion instruments in regional recordings. This preference is not surprising given the aforementioned challenges facing Bajgi musicians. The casteism and cosmopolitan musical values enmeshed within urban studio environments, along with the cultural and geographic distance of the recording industry, have driven away hereditary performers and with them the dhol itself. Very few performers from non-Bajgi families have become proficient dhol players, and to my knowledge none have played the dhol on studio recordings. The notion of pollution connected to the body of the lower-caste performer has carried over to the body and sound of the drum.

When asked about the relative absence of the dhol on vernacular recordings, however, studio insiders emphasized acoustic rather than social reasons. Compared to the tabla and the dholak, the dhol could not be tuned as precisely, its open strokes (*khula bol*) and closed strokes (*band bol*)—produced by damping the vibrating membrane of the drum—were less distinct, and its frequencies were considered too low and resonant to balance with other studio instruments.[16] Studio professionals thus rejected the *sound* of the dhol-damaun, but they nonetheless emphasized the importance of maintaining its rhythmic identity and thus its folk essence. Beginning in the late 1990s, Surtam Bhartwan (the brother of Pritam Bhartwan, discussed in chapter 6) and Subhash Pande began adapting the rhythmic patterns of the dhol-damaun and hurka-thali to the dholak and tabla. These patterns have subsequently become de rigueur on commercial recordings. Indeed, aside from the use of the vernacular language, I found that rhythmic patterns were the single most important sonic feature used to identify the authenticity of Uttarakhandi geet. Engineers foregrounded rhythm in the overall mix. In most recordings no fewer than two percussion parts, and often as many as five, are simultaneously layered on Uttarakhandi recordings to produce a full, "wet" sound. According to one Garhwali recording artist,

> The musicians should be from the hills [pahari]. The music director who plays Casio may or may not be from the hills, but the accompanist definitely [should]

be, because the *pattern* must be taken from the hills. The flute also will be played by a hill person. The Casio doesn't give that *feel* like the flute and rhythm do. The Casio you might want to play in a "Hindi" style, or an outside style, but the best rhythm will be Uttarakhandi. The proper Uttarakhandi *feeling* should come; if instead of the Uttarakhandi person some foreign one is used, the album will be a failure because the folk [sound] doesn't come.[17]

In the opinion of this singer, rhythm is the most critical element in generating the folk feeling. Rhythmic aptitude comes not from training but from an essentialized, biological inheritance; this inheritance is limited not by caste background but by regional provenance. People who are born in Uttarakhand can reproduce these rhythms because they are carried in the blood. Melodic aptitude, in contrast, is less integral to the folk sound and is mainly acquired through musical education (cf. Meintjes 2003: 116–117). Of all the melodic instruments used in studio recording, only the bamboo flute is singled out for producing a folk feeling; consequently, this director articulates a desire for the flutist and the percussionist to be Uttarakhandi. In my experience, however, many seasoned studio accompanists come from other North Indian regions, such as Bihar or Haryana, and have become adept at learning a wide range of vernacular melodic and rhythmic styles.

Subhash Pande is one of the few lower-caste hereditary musicians from Uttarakhand who have gained employment as a studio accompanist. Raised in a family of Bajgi drummers in Pauri Garhwal, he settled in Delhi at a young age and began training on dholak and classical tabla. When I asked him about his role in adapting dhol-damaun rhythms for regional recordings, he noted,

> There's a swing [*lasak*] and a ringing sound [*jhoomne*] in the sound of the dhol. What we did was to take things from that and put them into the dholak repertoire. We replicated what was performed on the dhol and nothing more. This was about ten years ago. No, six, seven years ago. Since all this *folk* thing started. There were no artists from the hills here in Delhi, they were all from Delhi. So they didn't understand [what pahari rhythm is]. And when these people came from the hills and listened, we thought, we can improve this. . . . And today when we play on stage, we perform Punjabi, Haryani, Bhojpuri, we work in different fields. Everything isn't the same to us, we are concerned with [matching] the tune, the composition. When we play folk we have to give it a certain *style*.[18]

Pande described the task of adapting the rhythms of the hurka-thali and dhol-damaun to the dholak and tabla as a challenging one. As discussed above, dhol-damaun rhythms are produced by two performers playing as an interlocking and synchronous unit. Pande selected some of the most commonly performed rhythmic patterns from the regional repertory and created standard versions of these patterns by converting them into conventional drum syllables (bols) that could be performed on the tabla and dholak. During a break in one recording session, I asked Subhash Pande (SP, on dholak) and two other studio accompanists, Satendra (on tabla) and Tanoj Dixit (TD, on dholak) to demonstrate the rhythmic patterns that they regularly perform on vernacular recordings:[19]

sp: The pattern for the "Pandava nritya" is like this:

Ex. 4.1

This [is played] in Garhwal. And in Kumaon . . .
td: This is the hurka style:

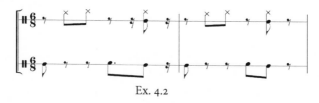

Ex. 4.2

sp: And this is the Jaunsari [pattern from western Garhwal]:

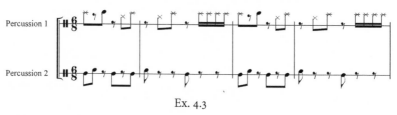

Ex. 4.3

sp: It's also in six beats, only the pattern is different.
sf: It seems like two instruments are playing together in this one, no? It appears that the damaun and the dhol are being played.
sp: Yes, we have taken this rhythm from the dhol and put it here.
td: And a very common tala in six beats is used in Bhojpuri and every language [vernacular musical style]:

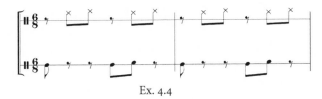

Ex. 4.4

TD: This happens in Bhojpuri [music] and in every kind, even in Garhwal. And it comes from the six-beat rhythm *dadra*, which is used in classical music [also]. And then there [is] *kaherva,* which is also found everywhere:

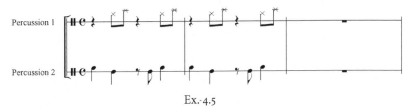

Ex. 4.5

TD: This is also played everywhere.

SF: And kaherva also has many different [subregional] forms.

TD: Oh, yes, you can make so many forms out of this.

SP: In Jaunsar the kaherva tala has another form:

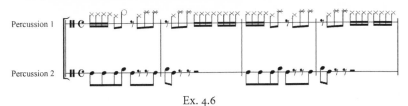

Ex. 4.6

SP: It's also eight-beat like the other kaherva, but the form is different.

SF: And in Garhwal, what's the kaherva tala?

SP: In [Garhwal] it becomes a little different:

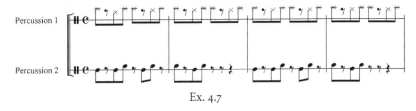

Ex. 4.7

SF: This sounds very Punjabi, no?

TD: It sounds Punjabi to you?

SP: There are slightly different versions of [kaherva]. But these are all of the beats.

SF: And the kaherva pattern in Kumaon?

SP: In Kumaon it's about like this, not very different.

TD: This is found in Rajasthan and Haryana, too.

SP: But if you go to Ladakh you'll hear [something else].

TD: Ladakh, and also in Nepal. We do work on Nepal recordings as well.

SP: [To Satendar, playing tabla]: Play the "side" [the tun bol on the tabla]:

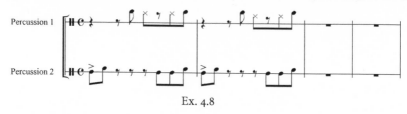

Ex. 4.8

Within the space of a few minutes, these percussionists cycled through more than a dozen stock rhythmic patterns (largely in eight- and six-beat cycles) that they regularly use on vernacular albums. Some of the patterns, such as the ones they labeled "standard folk" (music examples 4.4 and 4.5), index a pan-regional idea of folk music; these patterns are used interchangeably on vernacular albums marketed and sold across a number of North Indian regions, where the use of dholak and tabla is prevalent. Other patterns, such as the denser Jaunsari rhythms from western Garhwal (musical examples 4.3 and 4.6), and the "hurka" pattern from Kumaon (music example 4.2), clearly derive from indigenous musical practice and index specific subregional styles within Uttarakhand; these patterns would commonly be used in a setting where other subregional linguistic and musical signs were present.

The process described above must be understood as much more than a mere substitution of one set of instruments for another. Studio accompanists like Subhash Pande have adapted rhythms that have iconic and indexical significance for many Uttarakhandi listeners. The rhythms of the tabla and dholak resemble the interlocking patterns of the dhol and damaun, potentially producing an emotional interpretant of joy or recognition in the listener. At the same time, these rhythmic patterns are indexical of heightened ritual states and diverse performance settings; there is a "reality component" in that many listeners would have associations with hearing these rhythms performed in interactive social contexts (Turino 1999: 232). It is also likely that the redundancy of these rhythmic patterns on albums of Uttarakhandi geet over the course of the past several decades has created more general associations for listeners; rather than signifying a connection with the dhol and damaun specifically, these studio rhythms have come to stand for genres, subregions, or the idea of folk more generally. The semiotics of rhythm in commercial music are directly linked to a broad social transformation in the drumming profession. As so-called folk rhythms have been modified by hereditary drummers and passed on to nonhereditary and non-Uttarakhandi performers, and as dhol and damaun have been supplanted by tabla and dholak, there has been little need to call Shilpkar performers into the studio.

The arrival of the video compact disc format near the turn of the century has added another twist to the rhizophonic relation between sound and source. The video footage for these albums typically is captured after the audio tracks have been mastered and commercially released on cassette or mp3. In order to market the albums as regional folk, plains-based music companies send their production teams to locations in the mountains to capture footage that subsequently is edited to match the prerecorded audio tracks. The resulting VCD albums typically include footage of costumed dancers in front of temples interspersed with stock images of natural surroundings. As tokens of Garhwali folk, Bajgi drummers are regularly depicted playing dhol and damaun as part of the background of these scenes, even for songs that have little formal relation to village-based music or dance. There is considerable irony in the visual presentation of Bajgi drummers on VCD productions because they are forced to visually mimic rhythmic patterns that have been prerecorded on the tabla and dholak, though the studio percussionists learned these simplified and codified rhythms by imitating the dhol-damaun.

If, on the cassette depicted in figure 4.3, the drummer was heard but not seen, on the VCD album, the drummer's body is often seen (albeit in the background), but his dhol and damaun are not heard but are replaced by the tabla and dholak. In both cases, the discontinuity between the sounds and bodies of Bajgi musicians is symptomatic of the more widespread rhizophonic ambiguity concerning the desirability of folk music and the undesirability of the folk musician.

Between Two Indias

In the summer of 2011, I made plans for Sohan Lal and Sukaru Das to tour a number of universities in the United States and help me direct a student ensemble for Himalayan music at the University of Cincinnati. I had spent the previous summer in their village as an apprentice while they made six sets of dhol-damaun and continued teaching me to perform some of the repertory. By the end of the summer we shipped six pairs of dhol-damaun and hurka-thali to Cincinnati so that I could begin teaching the students in anticipation of their visit. Seemingly all of Garhwal was buzzing with the news of this tour, and Lal had become a minor celebrity, appearing in press conferences and festivals and featured in no fewer than twenty different regional and national newspaper articles. A group of filmmakers from Dehradun approached us about making a full-length documentary about our relationship and his upcoming trip to the United States, and they spent several days in Lal's village filming our music lessons.

During the last week of preparations we made our way to the U.S. consulate in Delhi for the final step of procuring visas. In the car we practiced interview questions and answers, and they were both visibly nervous. I assured them that things should go smoothly: they were both married, professional musicians with children attending school; they had proof of land ownership and tax documents; they had impressive résumés as performers at national and regional festivals and as recording artists with T-Series; they had a round-trip ticket and letters of invitation from five universities in America; and they had ample documentation of their proposed tour from articles in the *Hindustan Times* and the *Times of India*. I assumed that my presence at the consulate would help their case, but I was not allowed to accompany them to the interview. After several excruciatingly long hours they emerged from the consulate bewildered, saying that their applications had been rejected after a two-minute interview in which they were asked only a couple of questions: How did they support themselves in India? How long were they intending to go to the United States? What did they expect to do there, and who exactly was going to be interested in the dhol and damaun in the United States? Despite being handed a file with all of their documentation, the interviewer never once looked at it; all she apparently needed for this assessment were their responses to her questions. All of my attempts to overturn this decision were summarily dismissed, and I was told by a senior consular official that though I may be a very qualified person, Sohan and Sukaru were definitely not qualified to travel to the United States. But they were welcome to pay $380 again and reapply.

This story is not unique. The callousness and arbitrariness of the U.S. immigration system have been a major source of frustration for Indian musicians for decades.[20] Yet this experience tapped into something exceedingly familiar for Sohan Lal. In the days after this interview our conversations returned several times to the theme of "two Indias," about which many others have written:[21] a largely rural, "backward" India that continues to fight poverty, illiteracy, and casteism, and an urban, enlightened, neoliberal India that has embraced global capitalism with captivating speed. Social identities understood to be too firmly entrenched in the "backward India" face obstacles to admission into the more modern India. How else can Sohan Lal and many other Shilpkar artists interpret the reasons why they are denied visas to perform abroad when higher-class and higher-caste musicians are not? How else can they explain why they are not afforded the same degree of respect accorded to other artists when they enter the urban studio? How else can they articulate why their musical styles are not represented on commercial albums without being modified and purged of their local identity?

Bajgi performers have borne the brunt of systematized caste discrimination for so long that it has become thoroughly internalized and embodied; it is part of what William Sax describes as a "hexis of Harijans" (2009) reinforced by a lifetime of habits and dispositions signifying inferiority. Most Bajgi performers would never think of challenging the status quo by entering the food line in a wedding reception or by walking uninvited into the home of a higher-caste person. Sohan Lal is exceptional in his outspokenness about these forms of discrimination, but as the director of an ensemble that supports more than two dozen performers, he must pick his battles carefully.

A number of activists and reformers, including Narendra Singh Negi, have attempted to improve the status of Shilpkar performers by producing recordings and professional folk orchestras, by teaching music literacy and stage decorum, or by creating visiting lecturer positions in the university. These efforts have directly benefited Sohan Lal in some ways, but they also expose him to the risks of erasure, reform, and exploitation. Sohan Lal's experiences underline the social and musical barriers that many hereditary performers continue to face in both rural and urban spaces. The discrimination that they deal with in the urban studio is less overt, but no less pervasive. The recording studio continues to be a site of authenticity for cosmopolitan musicians who value musical literacy, originality, technological mediation, pitch precision, and performance as an end product; there is little accommodation for musicians who have honed a different set of musical and narrative skills in ritual and festival settings. Other barriers to equal participation in studio recordings include the hierarchical roles of producer, music director, engineer, studio accompanist, and soloist, the fragmented process of multi-track recording, and the conventions of verse-refrain form, song lengths of six to eight minutes, and diverse instrumentation. Negi's comments that Shilpkar musicians are too inflexible, backward, and impervious to change in the studio context stands in striking contrast to the dynamic flexibility that they demonstrate in village-based performance contexts.

This chapter has highlighted a dual process of incorporation and expurgation resulting from the vernacular music industry's fixation on folk culture. Sounds that are indexically linked to folk are valued as long as they are decoupled from the Shilpkar bodies that historically produced those sounds. One prominent example of this is the simultaneous erasure of the dhol and damaun (indices of Bajgi drummers) and the codification of dhol-derived rhythmic patterns played on tabla and dholak. Digital production values directly facilitate such rhizophonic processes, capturing sonic and visual elements in isolation before reaggregating them via technological interventions. The consequences of rhizophonia are not straightforward, but they are exacerbated by the geographic and cultural distance between rural Uttarakhand and the urbanized south, by the lack of economic stability within Shilpkar communities, by the hegemony of cosmopolitan values over the field of commercial recording, and by the caste discrimination that continues to interpenetrate the two Indias.

5 Professional Female Singers and the Gendering of Folk

Women's music has assumed an important position in scholarship concerning South Asian folklore and folk music of the past several decades (Capila 2002; Flueckiger 1991; Jassal 2012; Narayan 1993, 1997; Raheja and Gold 1994; Ramaswamy 1994; Srivastava 1991; Tyagi 1993). The scholarly focus on women's music in studies of "folk culture" is in part a corrective to late colonial and early nationalist research paradigms that focused almost exclusively on male performers and performance genres. The attention to women's expressive practices is also a feminist response to the broad social disempowerment of women; emphasizing female performance is a way of demonstrating female agency even in oppressive circumstances (Varma 1997). William Sax focused on ritual songs that women and lower-caste communities performed for the goddess Nanda, and he juxtaposed them with a parallel and more hegemonic repertory of songs maintained by men and priestly classes (Sax 1991: 23–25). Some scholars have also focused on women's songs because of a belief that their songs are older, better preserved, or more concealed than the male repertoire.[1]

I, too, am motivated to write about the experiences of female musicians because of a feminist inclination to counterbalance, at least in part, the emphasis on male experiences and viewpoints in the rest of this book. As part of the book's larger goal of deconstructing the discourse of folk in South Asia, however, I also want to interrogate the ways in which scholars—and many cultural entrepreneurs in Uttarakhand—have drawn equivalences between "women's music" and "folk culture." The idea that women are the repositories of folk culture is a familiar trope in studies of the Himalayas, South Asia, and, indeed, in many regions of the world. In her book *Images of Women in the Folk Songs of Garhwal Himalayas,* Anjali Capila writes, "In Garhwal it is difficult to think of a folk song without the woman. She is the life of the song. . . . Women are the carriers of oral tradition" in Garhwal (2002: 56–57). At the beginning of a chapter titled "Life Cycle Rituals and Folk Songs" in her book *Central Himalayan Folklore,* the scholar Helle Primdahl writes, "It may be proper to call these songs as songs of women, because these songs are primarily sung by women folk, women either of the house or of the neighborhood, or invited relatives" (1993: 13). The subject of Edward Henry's *Chant the Names of God* is the "true folk music [of the Bhojpuri region] thriving in its natural environment, little affected by self-consciousness of tradition or the ravages of mass media" (1988: 2), and the vast majority of the book focuses on women's songs.

Behind such statements is an assumption that women from rural India—because of a connection to the earth, to nature, to tradition, to agrarian forms of labor—are the primordial sources of folk music. In academic writing, women and folk culture frequently serve as symbols that are redundantly grouped together to create the impression that they are organically or naturally connected. Turino, interpreting Peircian semiotics, refers to this as an indexical cluster, arguing that through repetition, "the connections among the signs become facts in our experience and begin to be taken for granted, ultimately going unnoticed" (2008: 197). "Woman" and "folk culture" form an indexical cluster because each of these symbols shares an indexical connection to other signs such as the ideas of locality, home, nature, and tradition (Ortner 1972). Folk culture is discursively valued as a space of femininity, interiority, intimacy, and anonymity; it is implicitly or explicitly juxtaposed with the concept of popular culture that is framed as a male, external, and public domain. Oppression and marginalization are other symbols that are indexically linked to women and folk culture in academic writing. Women, understood as a general type of sign (legisign), are frequently and not incorrectly depicted as being marginalized and oppressed by various forms of misogyny and patriarchy; a parallel notion pervades writings about folk culture, another general sign that is understood to be marginalized and oppressed by the onslaught of popular culture.

As I have indicated above, these understandings are not altogether inconsistent with social reality. There are many styles that are exclusively performed by women and for women, and thus the focus on women's music to the exclusion of men's music in studies of folk culture may be understandable. This approach can usefully highlight women's performance as a unique space for sustaining cultural ways of knowing and exercising agency. I do not seek to challenge the idea that women's music is folk music, nor do I seek to undermine specific women's claims to being folk singers. My concern is that this indexical cluster has become so naturalized that folk culture and women's music are mapped onto one another as hermetically sealed categories of social analysis.

What is at stake in making such claims? What are the potential consequences of assuming that women are the repositories of folk culture? Recall the opening anecdote of the book in which the director of the music video asked several village women to clean up and change their clothes before appearing onscreen. Recall also the bitter response of an elderly woman who claimed that such production teams come to the village frequently, demanding much and offering little in return. Assuming that village women are the repositories of folk culture may obscure an understanding of women as dynamic and modern subjects; it may also place a burden on women to perform pastness or tradition at the expense of being innovative or independently creative.

Ethnomusicologists studying recording industries around the world have noted the challenges that women face within male-dominated spaces of musical production and consumption.[2] In Uttarakhand, women's participation in commercial recording is highly circumscribed. Men almost exclusively perform the roles of songwriter, producer, music director, accompanist, and lead singer. The high ratio of men among the migrant population in the urban plains, where the vast majority of commercial recording takes place, also factors into the dominant position of men in the music industry. Where women have found success, they have done so after overcoming significant gender-based obstacles, and usually with the backing of one or more male supporters within the industry.

Although the music industry permits female participation only in limited roles, it is worth considering how it may have opened new domains for women's expressive culture, particularly as this dovetails with the folk concept. Most commercial albums include women's voices and are marketed with images of women bearing markers of tradition such as skirts (*ghaghra*), nose rings (*nathuli*), and a variety of other ornaments (see figure 5.1). Genres of women's song such as *bajuband, ritu geet, mangal geet, khuder geet,* and many dance-songs have become widely available on commercial recordings, even if they are frequently performed and produced by men. The industry has also provided space for the emergence of several female stars, although their fame and status are attenuated in several ways that I examine below. With regard to female empowerment, the male-dominated music industry is an ambiguous space, but it has contributed significantly to the discourse connecting women to folk culture.

Fig. 5.1. Cover of *Bedu Pako Baramasa* (K-Series VCD, 2005)

My intention in this chapter is to further expose the multiple and contradictory meanings of the folk concept by looking at the experiences and representations of two female musicians. Meena Rana (b. 1975) is an urban middle-class singer who was raised in a migrant family in Delhi; she is one of the stars of the vernacular music industry. Bachan Dei (1947–2013) was a rural hereditary performer who worked outside the music industry but profoundly influenced it. Prior to her death after a protracted battle with tuberculosis, Bachan Dei lived in a village in Tehri Garhwal and had an active career as a lecturer, stage performer, and recording artist; she was, along with her husband, the foremost representative of the Baddi caste of performers.

By comparing and contrasting the life experiences of these two women, I seek to balance a focus on the shared experiences of female performers with a focus on the diverse and at times contradictory experiences of individual women. Although Meena Rana and Bachan Dei both faced the challenge of representing regional folk culture through their performances, each responded differently to this challenge because of her unique caste and class position and because of her unique personal relation to the folk concept. Before examining the experiences of these women in greater detail, it is necessary to take stock of some of the ways gender identities inhere in Uttarakhandi geet.

Gendered Representations in Song

In the music video for the song "Ghughuti Na Basa," sung by the late Kumaoni singer Gopal Babu Goswami,[3] a woman is shown cutting grass in the fields with tears streaming down her cheeks. She is flooded with memories of her native village and thinks of her husband, who has enlisted in the army and has been posted in the plains. The scene shifts to the husband, who reclines on the porch at the army barracks and thinks wistfully about his wife back in the village. The pain of their separation is indexed by the sound of the *ghughuti* bird, and the chorus of the song is a plea for the bird to stop calling in order to relieve them of this heartache. The ghughuti's onomatopoeic "ghur-ghur" call is a pervasive sign in many *khuder geet*, a genre of women's song that may be best translated as "songs of anguish or longing." The bird's call is heard especially often in the month of Chait (March–April), the time of year when married women are often invited back to their native villages to attend festivals; the bird's call thus becomes a sonic index of women's longing for home and family.

The ghughuti bird doesn't call.	Ghughuti na basa (x3)
On my branch the bird doesn't call.	Aame ki daai ma ghughuti na basa (x2)
When I hear the *"ghur-ghur"* sound I feel sad.	Teri ghuru ghuru suni main laago udasa (x2)
My husband has been sent away to Ladakh.	Swami myara pardesha barfilo Laddakha
The pleasant month of Chait has returned.	Ritu aige bhangi bhangi garmi chaltai ki
My memories of him have flooded back.	Yaad main kai bhautai aaige aapanai pati ki
Fly away to Ladakh	Udi jao ghughuti nahai ha Laddakha (x2)
And tell me how my husband is doing.	Haal myar batai diye myara swami paasa.

In comparison to the khuder geet that I heard performed in several village contexts, Goswami's lyrics and melodic phrases are pared down and less ornamented, and they are altered to fit the standard verse-chorus form used on the majority of commercial recordings. In spite of the stylistic shifts resulting from the commercial context of this recording, this song reinforces conventional gender norms in several interesting ways. Most obviously, the emotional content of the song typifies the feelings of separation and longing of the outmarried daughter who struggles in her affinal residence and pines for her husband's return from the battlefield, or, in more recent adaptations, the urban plains. "Ghughuti Na Basa" is but one example of many khuder geet expressing male and female experiences of dislocation. Such songs stereotypically express, from a female point of view, feelings of separation that result from gendered patterns of movement, specifically male out-migration and female outmarriage.[4]

Since the mid-nineteenth century, large numbers of Uttarakhandi men have traveled to the urban plains for education and employment, leaving their wives, children, and extended families in the village. In recent decades, the trends of migration have shifted as entire families have relocated to the plains, leaving largely empty villages in many parts of Uttarakhand. Yet this change is not reflected in commercial songs, which continue to represent migration as a quintessentially male experience (compare Narayan 1997: 30). Uttarakhandi geet frequently describe the struggle that Garhwali and Kumaoni men experience to adapt to an unfamiliar urban center. For migrant laborers in the plains, social adjustment was and continues to be a difficult process, and many people conceal overt signs of their Pahari identities from neighbors and co-workers. At the same time, the male migrant usually had a *choice* of whether to leave home, and he demonstrated considerable freedom of mobility. Migrants working in one of the North Indian plains cities often could return to their villages multiple times each year.

Women experience their own sense of loss and social adjustment after marriage, when they permanently leave their home village for that of their husband's family. The practice of patrivirilocality often means that women move across caste and subregional boundaries after marriage, so their songs can be an important source of information about cultural difference and emotional adjustment (Henry 1988: 107). Khuder geet explore many of the possible reasons why so many women struggle to adapt in their new homes, including the frequent absence of the husband, the acrimonious relationship with the mother-in-law, and the ongoing negotiations of status between wife-givers and wife-takers. Yet in contrast to male migration, a woman's departure to her new husband's residence is an obligatory rite of passage; village exogamy and patrivirilocality are built into the fabric of society, structuring economic and social relations. A newly married woman may be permitted to visit her natal home, but these visits are frequently negotiated with the members of her new household (compare Jassal 2012: 101–105; Polit 2012).

The experiences of female out-marriage and male migration also differ in terms of the permissible degree of mobility. The anthropologist Gerald Berreman emphasized the social freedoms that women in Uttarakhand enjoy in comparison to women in the Indian plains. He found "no seclusion of women and freer participation of women in most aspects of life than on the plains, including their participation in singing and dancing at festivals. Relatively free informal contact between the sexes is usual" (1960: 777). That Berreman highlights women's participation in singing and dancing at festivals is notable because it was suppressed and discouraged in many parts of South Asia by social reform movements (see Gupta 2002; Jassal 2012). Nonetheless, in comparison to the male migrant, who moves relatively unencumbered in the urban plains and between rural and urban spaces, a married woman is confined to the vicinity of the village forests, fields, and homes where she labors (Gaul 2002). This gendered contrast is also reinforced through popular representations in numerous Hindi films in which men from the plains come to the mountains to escape the pressures of modernity and to find tradition-bound, sexually available women.[5]

At a more focused level, the video for "Ghughuti Na Basa" depicts the husband emoting while reclining on the porch in a position of leisure; the wife, in contrast, emotes while toiling in the fields. This conforms to stereotypically gendered representations of labor and leisure in the central Himalayas. For men in contemporary Uttarakhand, laboring close to home is stigmatized, particularly if it involves any kind of menial or physical labor. Most men prefer to seek opportunities to study or work in the urban plains or to enlist in the army. Women are expected to carry out the vast majority of agricultural and domestic work (P. N. Pande 1996). In Uttarakhand, as elsewhere in South Asia, economists and sociologists are only beginning to rethink longstanding models of productivity to include a measure for female labor (Jassal 2012: 72).

The disparities in labor between men and women are a long-running theme in scholarship concerning the central Himalayas. Berreman writes that "one of the most striking features of Pahari life is how hard the women, in particular, work. Even a person who has been accustomed to plains villages, where women, especially those of the lower castes, are far from idle, cannot help being struck by this feature of Pahari life" (1963: 76). Descriptions of women as veritable beasts of burden date back to the early colonial period, when some civil servants sought to underline the oppressive working conditions of local women as a means of justifying colonial rule. Reginald Heber's 1824 statement in may be taken as representative: "A wife is regarded by the Khasiya peasant as one of the most laborious and valuable of his domestic animals" (cited in Viyogi and Ansari 2010: 49). In recent postcolonial scholarship, attitudes towards female labor in Uttarakhand are informed by a broader context of female disempowerment that includes strict patriarchal laws, female infanticide, bonded labor, prostitution, kidnapping, and enslavement.

As mentioned above, the gendered division of physical labor is replicated in the field of musical labor. A relatively small population of male specialists—predominantly but not exclusively belonging to the lower end of the caste hierarchy—perform and maintain the drumming, ballad, and song repertories performed during weddings and religious rituals; a much smaller repertoire of songs might be performed by nonspecialist men in participatory village settings such as seasonal festivals. In contrast, women have distinct song repertories to accompany different forms of labor and a variety of calendrical and life-cycle rituals. Jassal's characterization of gendered repertoires in rural Bihar and Uttar Pradesh applies well to Uttarakhand. She writes: "Unlike women's traditions, male *gatha* (ballad) traditions retain their vitality not only because they are remembered by village bards but also because they are periodically renewed through all-night celebrations. In contrast, women's songs, while also integral to ceremonies and rites of passage, tend to accompany agricultural works or other forms of productive activity" (2012: 6). Jassal describes not only the distinct temporal and spatial existence of women's songs but also their social devaluation as the forms of labor that the songs accompany are rendered invisible or obsolete.

Turning to the music industry, however, this division of musical labor is reversed. Women rarely perform any roles other than those of supporting singers or dancers in the video albums, and their stereotypical position as culture bearers is evident by the traditional dress they are expected to wear on album covers and in the music videos. The emotional experiences of women—primarily their experiences of loss and longing—are central to many, if not most, of the song lyrics on commercial recordings. Yet even when a large proportion of songs depict the woman's point of view, the singer is often a male. In "Ghughuti Na Basa," for example, Gopal Babu Goswami sings from the perspective of the woman. In many of Narendra Singh Negi's best-known compositions, he sings from a female perspective and attempts to convey the emotional life of Uttarakhandi women. Manuel notes that the practice of men relating to women's positions through song dates to the *bhakti* tradition of male poet-singers describing their erotic love for Krishna or Shiva from a female perspective (1993: 205). Yet the male appropriation of women's performance genres over the past century is a widespread and troubling phenomenon that can be linked to growing chauvinism and a censure of female expressive culture in public spaces (Allen 1998; Jassal 2012).

Bachan Dei

Her mouth was barely open, and her face was expressionless, but Bachan Dei's strident tone cut through the auditorium like a knife. There was little need for microphones. Her voice, suited to the open-air courtyards of Garhwali villages, carried easily to the back of the auditorium. Although powerful, her voice could also be subtle and graceful, evoking the sounds of *thumri* and *ghazal* singers of the gramophone era. The audience of academics and journalists at this folklore festival in Pauri sat rapt, overwhelmed by the power and depth of the singing. Bachan Dei's husband, Shiv Charan, accompanied her on harmonium, while a brother-in-law accompanied her on the dholak. In the middle of the opening phrase, Shiv Charan began singing, matching Dei's pitch with an even more strident and straining tone. For a few seconds the two sang in unison; then Dei dropped out, leaving Charan to complete the phrase and begin the next one. In the middle of the next phrase she entered again, overlapping with and eventually overwhelming his singing until the end of the next phrase. In the characteristic style of Baddi singing, the song ebbed and flowed between these two singers, prompting each of them to embellish melodic lines and compose semi-improvised texts. With a well-honed anticipation of each other's tendencies, they manipulated tempi, dynamics, and vocal ranges to build intensity. Halfway through the song their ten-year-old granddaughter Nidhi got up from her seat on stage and began to dance, eliciting enthusiastic applause from the audience. Her movements were hesitant but graceful, with swaying hip movements, hand gestures (*mudra*), and footwork evocative of the North Indian Kathak dance style.

When they finished the performance, a series of folklorists and writers took the stage in turn, each describing the challenges facing regional dialects and traditional musical practice with the onslaught of commercial recordings, Hindi-language media, and consumerist excess. The eminent folklorist Datta Ram Purohit gave a presentation in which he described Bachan Dei and Shiv Charan as one of the last remaining families of Baddi entertainers in Garhwal (see figure 5.2). At first, I wondered whether this was a hyperbolic statement meant to bring attention to the declining opportunities for performers within this community. Shortly after this performance Purohit invited me to join a team research project at Garhwal University to survey and begin documenting the remaining Baddi performance traditions in the Rudraprayag and Tehri districts of Garhwal. After several weeks of mostly dead-end searches, the team was able to locate only five couples; all were over the age of fifty, and musical performance offered them a supplemental form of income at best. Although our survey was hardly exhaustive, it was clear that Purohit's assessment was not far off; few if any Baddi were actively perform-

Fig. 5.2. Bachan Dei and Shiv Charan, 2007 (courtesy S. Fiol)

ing in Garhwal. Even Dei and Charan no longer supported themselves with traditional village performances; over the course of the past two decades, they had become increasingly reliant on state and academic patronage at folklore festivals and conferences. They had a brief stint as visiting professors at the Centre for Folk Performing Arts and Culture at Garhwal University in Srinagar. When Bachan Dei passed away in November 2013, there was a feeling among cultural activists that a great store of expressive culture was forever lost. One obituary was titled, "She was illiterate, but a teacher" (*anpar thi, lekin padhati thi*).

Bachan Dei was born to Mollu Ram and Shivi Devi in the village of Asena, Tehri Garhwal, in 1947. As a child she learned to sing varieties of seasonal songs (*chaiti geet*), ballads (panwara), and auspicious festival songs (mangal geet) from her grandfather Sevadhari and her grandmother Bijna Devi. Her grandparents also taught her royal ballads (*gatha*) that maintained the gene-alogy of the royal line and recounted the divine powers of the Maharaja of Tehri, who is regarded as a living incarnation of Lord Vishnu. Until the dis-solution of the princely state of Tehri following national independence, Dei's relatives performed these ballads for the royalty and the vassals (*jagirdar*) of the region and reportedly received a monthly pension of fifteen rupees.

According to an origin story, the Baddi were born from the flesh of Shiva, and thus Baddi families are not merely devotees but are in fact part of Shiva and Parvati's form and thus literally embody their divine qualities.[6] At the age of fifteen Dei was married to Charan and went to live in the village of Duni. Aside from his name, Charan's connection to Shiva in his ascetic form is manifested externally in the maintenance of uncut hair,[7] the use of hashish (*bhang*), the wearing of a silver bracelet (*dhagula*)—which also indicates mediumship in possession ceremonies—and the presence of the trident in the family shrine (*dev sthan*). In addition, he sings to the accompaniment of the *dholki*, a smaller version of the double-headed dholak drum found throughout North India. The dholki is understood to be a substitution for the *damaru*, the double-headed, hourglass-shaped drum associated with Shiva, and its shoulder strap iconically stands for the cobra around Shiva's neck. By convention, Bachan Dei also adopted a surname that communicates her divine origin; while there is no visible sign of connection to Parvati, she embodies the goddess when she dances and sings.

As is common in Baddi families, Dei and Charan's marriage was also a musical partnership, and they began accompanying older relatives in performances during the wedding season and during the month of Chait. Twice a year during Asoj–Mangseer (October–December) and Baisakh–Jeth (April–July), both coinciding with the harvest times, the family traversed an inherited territory of nine villages called the *birti*. They stayed a few days or a few weeks in each village, depending on the welcome, and in the evening they performed a range of secular and sacred songs in the village square. During one of the occasions when I visited Dei in her village, she and her female relatives wistfully shared memories from her childhood, when they traveled with great prestige within their *birti*:

> When we would visit people's villages, they would know that we were coming. And they would say, "What a wonderful thing, our Baddi have come." All the villagers would greet us and offer sandalwood paste on the forehead [*pithai*] alongside a cash offering and then we would visit all the homes in the village. At the end we would give a big performance at one place in the courtyard [*maidan*] and people would leave offerings. And people used to give so much at that time, out of respect [*iman*]. We used to get twenty kilos of rice [*ath patha dan*] in offerings [*dadwar*].[8]

Dei described a wide variety of songs and dances that she and her relatives would be requested to perform during these annual visits. During times of famine or calamity, a village might invite a Baddi family to perform rope-swinging (*bedwart*) and rope-sliding (*lang*) fertility rituals.[9] These rituals were performed on the order of the raja, local rulers, and shamans (*bakhan* or *baki*) as a remedy for an accumulated curse (*dos*) affecting the region or community and manifesting as disease, famine, or an impending catastrophe (Berreman 1961). Before, during, and after these rituals, Badin, as female members of the community are called, sang ballads (*panwara*) and devotional songs (*ausar*) while performing masked dance-dramas (*pattar*) representing high gods, demigods, saints, and rishis (Purohit 2004). During wedding festivities, Dei and her female relatives sang auspicious songs (*mangal geet*), and they also danced and performed light songs on a variety of secular themes; these performances offered opportunities for ludic and sensual play with audience members. During the Holi Festival in spring, they frequently performed Radhakhandi Ras (figure 5.3), an elaborate dance form that enacts Krishna's attempts to seduce Radha and the milkmaids and shares some stylistic elements with Kathak (M. Upreti 1959).

The function of many Baddi songs, according to Charan, was to carry the news of the world—a devastating earthquake, the Uttarakhand movement for regional statehood, a recent festival—to the villagers and the royalty alike. Like the Gaine of Nepal, the Baddi, "alert at all times to the latest political events, . . . used their own medium [of song] as a kind of oral newspaper" (Hoerburger 1970: 143). Both Dei and Charan were adept at improvising lyrics

Fig. 5.3. Bachan Dei leading a workshop on Radhakhandi Ras for students at Garhwal University, undated (courtesy D. R. Purohit)

on any topic on the spot, but they also had favorite compositions that they sang frequently. During one recording session with them I heard songs on topics including the events leading up to the prohibition of animal sacrifice at the Chandrabadni temple near Tehri, the white man's magic (*gore ki jadu*) of generating electricity from the Tehri hydroelectric dam, and the landing of the first Apollo lunar module on the moon (described in the song as the "Land of Houston," presumably because of the inclusion of the reiteration of "Houston" in NASA broadcasts!).[10]

The couple have been involved in developing and diffusing a wide range of village song types found in Uttarakhand. What makes Baddi singing unique is not the repertoire per se, but the manner of performing it. Baddi geet can be easily identified by the dialogic and overlapping manner of rendering phrases between the male and the female singer, accompanied by the dholki, dance steps, and the jingling ankle bells (*ghungru*) of the Badin. Given the strict separation of gender that characterizes much musical performance in North India, Baddi geet is notable for the equal and complementary roles of male and female performers.

Silencing the Baddi-Badin

Some have explained the decline of the Baddi entertainer as a result of "upward mobility," or Sanskritization (Berreman 1960: 199; Srinivas 1989). Baddi performers are aware of their low occupational rank and wish to improve their social status. Yet this explanation is not sufficient. The social context in which Baddi earned and gained social prestige has also eroded from underneath them, and this factor requires more attention.[11]

The dissolution of princely states shortly after national independence eliminated an important source of patronage and social prestige for Baddi performers. Despite having been included in the royal entourage, they have experienced low occupational rank and caste-based discrimination for more than a century. Much of this discrimination can be linked to female public performance. As has been well documented elsewhere,[12] a series of social reform and legal campaigns across India in the early twentieth century sought to eradicate female dancing within hereditary communities. In Uttarakhand, these efforts were blended with social and religious reform movements spearheaded by the Arya Samaj, which sought to spread access to the Vedas by encouraging Shilpkar communities to discontinue low-status activities and adopt high-status activities.

The birti-dadwar patronage system described above has also decayed as a consequence of plainsward migration, the decline in agricultural productivity in many parts of Uttarakhand, and the loss of artistic and social value for

Baddi performance. Traditionally, the Baddi cultivated a relationship with patrons over the course of generations. Social decorum regulated interactions between Badin and their patrons. Audience members sat around the village courtyard and watched the performance, offering rupee notes to show appreciation. Male patrons did not approach or touch the dancers, and in the case of inappropriate behavior with a Badin, the host of the event was expected to intervene and restore order.

In recent decades, however, Baddi performers have had to rely on a contract-based (*theka*) system of payment. *Theka* refers to the prearranged hiring of a Baddi couple or family unit for a specific function such as a wedding, festival, private party, or religious *puja*. This economic arrangement significantly alters the dynamic between them and audience members. Patronage via theka means that only one individual, the host of the function, is responsible for rewarding the Baddi for their performance. Others in attendance may make offerings, but they are not socially obligated to do so. Whereas Bachan Dei remembered audiences of the past sitting and listening respectfully during performances, she complained that contemporary audiences made lewd jokes and attempted to sing and dance with Badin.

Many Badin have responded to such experiences of sexual and caste discrimination by refusing to dance publicly. In the 1960s and 1970s several prominent cultural activists, including Bihari Lal, Sravan Das, Dharmanan Nautiyal, Sunder Lal Bahuguna, Swami Manmathan, and Bhavani Datt, supported a movement to eradicate untouchability in Uttarakhand, alongside calls for separate statehood and environmental regulation. These reformists persuaded many Baddi performers to cease relations with their traditional patrons until they were treated with respect and the government passed antidiscriminatory legislation. Flueckiger (1991) describes a similar transformation of *sua natch* performances in Chattisgarh, which also focus on the interaction between female *adivasi* dancers and higher-caste patrons.

Bachan Dei stopped dancing publicly in the mid-1970s, although she continued to offer dance demonstrations at folkloric festivals. She explained that audiences no longer knew how to show respect for artists from her community. Inebriated men often treated her and her female relatives as sex workers, attempting to dance with them even with their husbands present. And now the hosts of the event rarely intervened to defend their honor. The moral degradation associated with the Badin's dancing resonates with pre-independence female dance traditions in temples, courts, and salons on the subcontinent and with contemporary *tawaif*, *nacni*, *hijra*, and *kothi* traditions in other parts of northern India (see Allen 1997; Babiracki 2004; Maciszewski 2006; Soneji 2012; Morcom 2013).

In the early twentieth century, at the same time hereditary performers came under attack, new sources of patronage emerged among the growing middle classes located primarily in urban centers. The gramophone, radio, and film industries offered female performers opportunities to sing without exposing their bodies to public scrutiny (Weidman 2006). The first gramophone recordings from Uttarakhand were made sometime in the mid-1940s by two Kumaoni sisters, Gopi Devi and Champa Devi. Little is known about their background, but several unconfirmed accounts claim that they were Badin living in Mumbai and supporting themselves in the sex trade. In the years since, many other Badin have made commercial recordings, although it is often difficult to verify their social background. A number of prominent contemporary recording artists are widely believed to be descendants of Baddi families who have rejected the caste surnames Das or Devi/Dei in favor of ambiguous or higher-status surnames.

In the early 1990s Shiv Charan and Bachan Dei recorded the album *Pingli Pithei Cha,* which was distributed locally by a small regional music company. Subsequently a few producers made them offers, but the couple decided not to make more recordings because they were disappointed with the compensation and the lack of control over the products. Dei was wary of putting any more recordings on the market because she feared that they would become fodder for further exploitation and marginalization. She explained to me that many contemporary popular singers in Uttarakhand re-record Baddi compositions but neglect to give proper credit on the album jacket.[13] The practice of labeling a song lok geet (folk song) or paramparik geet (traditional song) generally suggests that a song has been maintained through a long oral history and that its composer is unknown, but it may also be used to conceal acts of direct appropriation from the recordings of marginalized performers. Although in my experience popular recording artists rarely take entire songs from Baddi albums, some have admitted to taking ideas from these old recordings and from the scholarly publications of Baddi song texts.

As the recording industry has expanded and its prestige has grown, hereditary performers have been replaced by female singers from higher-class backgrounds. The expansion of the music industry and the popularity of cassettes, video compact discs, mp3s, and regional music television channels as formats for home entertainment have also threatened sources of patronage for the Baddi, as have the popular hill bands hired for weddings. Numerous Baddi and Bajgi performers complained to me that when they are hired to perform during wedding processions (*barat*) and post-wedding dance parties, they are forced to compete with the higher volume and greater cachet of the hill bands and DJs. In place of performing more lengthy panwara (heroic ballads) and

mangal geet at festivals and weddings, they have begun to perform versions
of popular songs and truncated versions of traditional repertoire.

Representations of Badin in commercial recordings further explain the
decline of Baddi performance. Several amateur videos of Badin performers
have been commercially released on small regional labels in Garhwal. One
of these productions, titled *Pahari Bedu Geet: Garhwali Vilupt Hoti Sanskriti*
("Songs of the Mountain Beda: The Disappearing Culture of Garhwal"),[14]
shows male spectators dancing in turn with two Badin; in one sequence, a
man takes the Badin by the hand as he dances with her. Such interference
is exactly what the Badin described as having ruined their prospects of performing in public.

A number of the images used on cassette covers of Baddi recordings also
illustrate the stigmatization of female members of the community. Rama Cassettes released a series of twelve cassette albums titled *Bedu Geet* in the 1980s
and early 1990s; the majority of the music they contained was recorded in a
Delhi studio in a couple of days by Giriraj and Darshani Devi. These artists
received a lump sum payment and left all decisions about album presentation
entirely in the hands of the music director and producer. For the covers, the
latter decided to use a series of images depicting models wearing makeup
rather than images of the performers. Figure 5.4 shows a hand-drawn image of a man and a woman dancing to dholki accompaniment; this image
contradicts Dei's statement that Badin danced solo or in a group of two or
three women, but not with men. Figure 5.5 shows an unidentified model
wearing makeup and a blouse. Her appearance and posture, while tame for
an urban cosmopolitan setting like Delhi, are sexually explicit for a rural
Uttarakhandi audience, underlining the eroticization of the Badin. Figure
5.6 shows a hand-drawn image of a woman with a nearly transparent sari;
this cover art also exploits an erotic association, and like figure 5.4, it lists
the track names but not the singers' names; whether this was because of an
oversight or in order to protect the singers' reputations is not clear.

The music industry has also negatively impacted the livelihoods of Badin performers through caricature and imitation. In the song and dance
sequences of many Garhwali films (for example, *Kauthik* [1987] and *Ghar
Jawain* [1986]) and music videos, actors frequently mimic Baddi performance
practice by showing male-female duos playing dholki and dancing in village courtyards.[15] Such representations articulate an idealized longing for
pre-industrial Himalayan village culture, but the musical and choreographic
styles of these episodes bear little resemblance to Baddi performance practice,
instead relying on the sonic and visual conventions of Hindi films. After
watching the music video of "Cham Ghungru Bajela" ("The Sound of Ankle
Bells")[16] from the film *Ghar Jawain* (1986), featuring scantily clad "Badin"

Fig. 5.4. Cover of *Bedu ke Geet*, vol. 2, by Giriraj and Darshani Devi (Rama Cassettes)

Fig. 5.5. Cover of *Bedu ke Geet*, vol. 6, by Giriraj and Darshani Devi (Rama Cassettes)

Fig. 5.6. Cover of *Bedu ke Geet*, vol. 1, by Giriraj and Darshani Devi (Rama Cassettes)

wearing heavy makeup and garish jewelry and dancing in front of a crowd of men waving rupee notes, Shiv Charan remarked, "The CD-wallahs are showing us playing dholak while our women are begging. So the government sees this and says, 'These people are already earning, what is the need to provide for them?'"[17] His comment exposes feelings of economic vulnerability when confronted with inaccurate mass-mediated caricatures.

Many insiders and outsiders regard the Baddi who continue to perform in villages as anachronistic and anonymous figures, valuable primarily as vehicles of social memory. For them the provincial function of Baddi performance, belonging to a pre-modern conception of time and place, was predestined to be replaced by the pan-regional networks of the mass media, which belong to a modern or postmodern conception of time and place. This is a problematic position primarily because performers such as Bachan Dei have not been merely replaced by contemporary representational forms but have been exoticized and disembodied through them. In the search for distinctive emblems of cultural regionalism, the Baddi have become caricatures of Uttarakhandi folk culture, representing a vanishing and irretrievable modality of village life. The process by which Baddi have become icons of folk is thus connected to the process of excluding and silencing their contemporary presence in the regional culture industry.

Meena Rana: Songbird in the Studio

If the music industry has accelerated the decline of the Baddi community, it has also offered a range of opportunities, albeit a limited one, to a select group of female singers. A handful of them have participated in nearly all Uttarakhandi geet recordings since the early 1980s. By way of contrast, hundreds of male singers have recorded Uttarakhandi geet, of whom only a dozen might be considered established singers who earn significant sums from their recordings. In order to better understand this discrepancy in gender participation, I turn to the experiences of Meena Rana, Uttarakhand's most prolific recording artist (figure 5.7).

Meena Rana's path to becoming a recording artist was more or less accidental. In contrast to Bachan Dei's, her parents were not performers, and there was no hereditary obligation to become one. Rana grew up in Delhi and attended a Christian school along with her five siblings. She never formally studied music, but friends encouraged her to record after she sang Hindi songs in a school program. She grew up listening to her parents speak Garhwali, but like many first-generation urban migrants, she never learned to speak the language herself. "While growing up [my siblings and I] only spoke and sang in Hindi to each other," she told me. "After that when we went into this line we were shocked that there were Garhwali cassettes out there. We had no idea." She noted that in the early 1990s many Garhwali musicians were ashamed to perform on Garhwali music albums, and several tried (without success) to become playback singers (that is, singers whose recorded voices are later mimed by film actors) in the Hindi film music industry.

Yet Rana found a niche in recording vernacular albums, and over the course of the ensuing two decades she became a household name in Uttarakhand. She has earned the nickname "the Lata Mangeshkar of Uttarakhand" as much for her birdlike vocal timbre and wide range as for her prolific recording career.[18] Her voice is the most ubiquitous in the history of the Uttarakhandi music industry. Given the informal organization of the music industry, it is impossible to calculate the total number of albums on which she has sung, but in an interview from 2010 she estimated that she had recorded approximately eleven thousand songs on two thousand albums. In 2010 she was recording an average of twenty to thirty albums each month, often completing multiple projects in a single day.

Although the majority of Meena's output consists of Garhwali geet, she also records in Hindi and a number of vernacular languages including Kumaoni, Jaunsari, Sirmauri, Maithali, Nepali, Bhojpuri, Haryanavi, Rajasthani, Kargali, Balti, and Ladakhi, as well as Hindi. On a visit to Ladakh in 2007, I was surprised to learn that many Ladakhis claim Meena Rana as one of their

Fig. 5.7. Meena Rana, Sanjay Kumola, and the author (courtesy S. Fiol)

own and regard her as the finest contemporary female vocalist in the region.[19] (She has recorded more than five hundred songs in Ladakhi.) When I asked her about this, she was bemused and a little mystified about her popularity in Ladakh. She recalled being received like royalty during her one and only visit there and being asked to sing many stage programs; yet because she does not speak or understand Ladakhi, she declined to perform in public.

Rana has been able to record at such a furious pace in part because her husband, Sanjay Kumola, is one of the most sought-after freelance music directors in the industry. His studio attracts a steady stream of established and novice singers, and Rana provides vocal accompaniment on nearly all of these projects. Generally, she sings duets with male singers on select tracks that have themes of romance, longing, loss, or social and environment awareness. In many cases producers or singers will request Sanjay to direct the music on an album in part because they know that Rana will also sing for the project. The participation of a top-tier female vocalist is considered essential to the commercial success of an album, particularly when the lead male vocalist is young and inexperienced. According to the producer Mayur Nichani, "What happens is that when some of these poor people come down from the hills, they have their dream, you know? To have one song with Meena Rana. It is as if I have done vocals with [Hindi playback legend] Lata Mangeshkar. 'She and me, we have done the same project together.' You know, they brag about this kind of stuff."[20]

On July 4, 2005, I was able to observe a recording session involving Rana and a young singer named Asha Lal. He was working on a duet he had composed about the budding romance of a young couple, and Rana arrived at the studio shortly after all of the instrumental parts had been dubbed. Lal, Rana, and Kumola briefly discussed the meaning of the song and the mood they wanted to create. Rana and Lal then entered a soundproof chamber, donned headphones, and sang their parts while holding up a sheet of paper containing the lyrics. Lal was visibly nervous while singing next to Rana, but everyone in the studio encouraged him. Later she commended Lal on his "folk tone", by which she meant the enunciation of the text and the nasal quality of his vocal timbre. Rana's voice, in contrast, was bright and mellifluous—a thinner version of Lata Mangeshkar's upper range. Rana sang through her part quickly, rehearsing several of the lyrics and melodic phrases where she wanted to produce vocal embellishments. All the other participants sat inside the console room, huddled around the computer monitor.[21]

Once they had finished recording their parts, the electronically generated vocal modulation effect called D-Tune (also known as Auto-Tune) was added to Lal's vocal lines. It is one of the cosmopolitan features of commercial songs that divide the musical tastes of young and old. While the D-Tune effect could be considered an imitation of Western, Indi-pop, or Bollywood musical practice, it also corresponds to an indigenous preference for nasal and strident timbres. It is significant that the D-Tune effect was not added to Rana's vocal lines on any of the album's tracks.[22] In my experience, it is rare for this effect to be used with women's voices, a reflection of the attitude that women's voices are more "natural" than men's.

In this recording, as in others I witnessed, there was a different sonic ideal for male and female voices (see Meintjes 2003: 250; Mason 2014). The ideal timbre of women's voices is thin and bright; there is an unspoken equivalence of the female voice with sonorous melody. The male voice, in contrast, is valued primarily for diction and a rustic quality sometimes referred to as the folk tone, which implies a slightly high-pitched, nasal timbre. Women's voices tend to be more dynamic and dexterous than men's, and women are expected to learn material quickly, reproducing a melody after hearing it only a couple of times. The ability to mimic with precision is the result of practice and hard work; in order to be fully employed, female singers must work constantly and must remain open to different kinds of projects including Hindi songs, ad jingles, vernacular recordings, film voiceovers, and stage programs. The singer Anuradha Nirala explained to me that the versatility required of women in the music industry gave them the upper hand over the men in terms of technique and training.

This recording session also revealed the different roles and different sets of expectations that men and women face in the studio. A male singer, even an inexperienced one, is treated as the headliner, and he is expected to bring original texts and melodies into the studio. The female singers are treated in roughly the same way as the session musicians who dub instrumental parts. Female singers almost always perform duets with male singers; solo tracks or albums are extremely rare. Meena Rana is thus justifiably proud of the fact that she released the solo album *Chandra* (2010), which included her own composition "Ham Uttarakhandyu Cha."

By convention, albums are catalogued and marketed with the male singer's name first, even if he is the less experienced or less famous artist (which is often the case); the female singer's name appears second, third, or sometimes not at all. On VCD album covers, photos of the lead male singer and the male and female actors are often significantly larger than the female singer's photo (see figure 5.8), and sometimes the latter is not included at all. There is a similar gender hierarchy in the field of live performance. Variety shows dubbed "Garhwali Nights" or "Kumaoni Nights" have become a popular form of entertainment in urban migrant communities. In these settings, female singers are asked to sing duets and, less frequently, solo numbers, but the male artists always get top billing.

The financial compensation for female singers is also significantly less than that of their male counterparts. Accomplished male singers may earn upwards of $3,000 for a recording; the amount, negotiated with the producer, is largely determined by the commercial success of the singer's previous album. (Novice male singers typically fund recording projects out of pocket.) Female singers receive a lump sum of between $5 and $50 per song. This amount is adjusted to account for the singer's reputation, but the commercial success of her previous recordings does not play a direct role in compensation. Female singers are thus compensated in much the same way as are session musicians. Rana explained to me that the discrepancies in payment were somewhat justified by the fact that men are the songwriters, while women are simply interpreters. Of the six female singers I interviewed, only one had written a song, and most did not express much interest in what is considered a singularly male domain.

The singer Anuradha Nirala was more critical of the compensation structure within the industry. Female singers "used to get a fixed payment, and the company person was not willing to increase" it, she told me. "But I feel that if you are making money off me, you also should have a duty to make me

Fig. 5.8. Cover of *Bhana*, featuring Pritam Bhartwan and Meena Rana (pictured lower left) (Rama Cassettes VCD, 2011)

happy. Sometimes an artist does really well and the company doesn't respond to them. This is especially true for female artists who sing with males. So the male artist takes his cut [*jimba*] and says, 'I will take care of the payment [to the others]' and so the companies don't bother. Now I decide my own finances."[23]

Like the voices of playback singers in the film industry, Meena Rana's voice is seemingly everywhere in Uttarakhand, and yet many people outside urban centers have never seen her perform in person. Although male singers regularly appear in the music videos that accompany their songs, Rana and other female singers rarely do. It is socially unacceptable for a married woman to dance publicly; thus, unmarried girls are selected to dance and lip-synch in the videos.

If the rhizophonic separation between the voice and the body in popular music productions offers some protection for female artists, however, it still carries considerable risk. Public performance continues to carry stigma, and many middle-class women are discouraged by their families from practicing music or dance as a profession because of a historical association with Shilpkar communities. I often heard rumors that a number of prominent female recording artists from Shilpkar backgrounds had disguised their backgrounds by marrying men of a higher caste or class and changing their surnames. I have anecdotal evidence that many male recording artists have done so as well, but this did not become the subject of conversation nearly as often. Regardless of the truth of these rumors, they demonstrate an effort on the part of many within the industry to conflate performing ability with caste identity and to devalue the social and professional standing of female singers.

All of the female singers with whom I spoke alluded to the risk of choosing a career as a public performer after marriage. Anuradha Nirala described the need to be attentive to the level of respect and security that she experienced in the recording studio. Before agreeing to sing for a project, she reads all of the lyrics carefully—or has them translated by someone she trusts—and on several occasions she has asked for words to be altered. Meena Rana similarly noted that early in her career singers sometimes asked her to sing lyrics that she deemed offensive or inappropriate. As an example, she discussed the erotically tinged double entendres that characterize songs dealing with the relationship between a woman and her husband's younger brother (*devar-bhabhi*). In Bhojpuri geet, such songs are frequently heard during the Holi season (Jassal 2012). However, she said, "That kind of lewdness is a characteristic of Haryavani- and Bhojpuri-language albums. But in Uttarakhand it doesn't happen." The lack of eroticism in Uttarakhandi geet—as compared to neighboring regional commercial genres—was a theme that arose frequently in conversations with both men and women in the industry. Such claims are difficult to sustain in light of the sexually suggestive covers of Baddi geet albums described above. They also run counter to the statements of cultural critics who decry the overt sexuality of many video productions.[24] We might interpret such statements by industry insiders as an attempt to reinforce a sense of safety and wholesomeness within a profession that is still regarded as socially risqué. These assertions also reflect a climate of benevolent patriarchy, wherein regional purity and male honor are projected onto women's bodies.

Of the approximately one dozen women active in the industry, almost all have the support of their husbands. In most cases the husband is working as a music director, producer, or promoter, and thus he directly manages his wife's career and benefits from her success. For instance, as a way of confronting the secondary role of women in "Garhwali Nights" programs, Rana's husband, Sanjay Kumola, decided he would organize a "Meena Nights" program in which she would be the featured artist. Although this did not happen during the period of my fieldwork, the producer Rajendra Chauhan organized a "Kalpana Nights" event for his wife, Kalpana Chauhan.

I interviewed only one female singer whose husband was not supportive of her choice of career; although she still pursues opportunities to record, she claims that her husband's lack of support has allowed people to routinely take advantage of her financially. Another singer admitted that although she might like to pursue opportunities elsewhere, she works exclusively with her husband, saying: "I avoid certain things, because we live in a glamorous world. If someone else works with me, tongues might wag and [my husband] is a big man himself, and sometimes men have suspicions. I may feel that my husband is cool but who knows when men can get suspicious. I have seventeen years of good understanding with him, and I don't want to ruin it."

Conclusion

As female performing artists operating in male-dominated spaces, Meena Rana and Bachan Dei faced many of the same challenges. Women's mobility is circumscribed after marriage, when they are expected to serve the affinal household. Men, in contrast, are encouraged to travel widely in search of education and employment. The physical mobility of female performers threatens patriarchical values and leaves them open to criticism for not fulfilling their obligations as mothers and daughters-in-law.[25]

Men are the gatekeepers of public performance, controlling female performers' finances and access to patrons. Despite being one of the most prolific recording artists in Uttarakhand, Meena Rana is largely confined to the role of secondary vocalist in duets and is expected to sing whatever material she is given. Early in their partnership, Bachan Dei and Shiv Charan were equal partners on stage; with the cessation of public dancing and the kirti-dadwar system of patronage supporting it, however, Dei's musical role diminished significantly. Rana and Dei both experienced a lack of control with regard to the production of their voices and images. Disembodied female voices on audio recordings are later re-embodied by other (usually unmarried) women who dance on video albums. Such rhizophonic practices reflect the multi-track studio recording environment and the separation of audio and video production processes. Nevertheless, I have shown how Badin bodies are represented and impersonated in lewd and culturally insensitive ways, contributing to a sense of shame within the community and to Dei's decision to stop dancing. Rana also has struggled with the challenge of being made into a sexual object in the male-dominated culture industry; her reaction has been to reassert her belief in the fundamental purity of Uttarakhandi geet while refusing to sing lyrics that she deems compromising.

In spite of the shared social vulnerabilities, Rana and Dei have different relationships to the folk concept stemming from their constrasting positions on the class-caste spectrum. Rana, despite having lived her entire life in urban areas and having almost no musical training or knowledge of Garhwali as a child, has nonetheless been successful at learning and reproducing a variety of so-called folk musical styles. For her, *folk* usually signifies as a set of genres or stylistic conventions that may be selectively added to a performance.

Bachan Dei, in contrast, grew up steeped in the secular and sacred repertories of village music, but she gradually became marginalized within her own social milieu, even as her caste came to represent an idealized community of folk performers. From her perspective, *folk* signified not only a particular manner of singing or a set of genres but a *liminal social position* that is incommensurable with regional modernity. The anachronistic construction of the Baddi as an itinerant hereditary caste from the feudal past has effectively written them out of the present. Whenever Shiv Charan and Bachan Dei performed at folkloric festivals or recorded in the studio, they did so not as creative artists but as representatives of a dying caste of performers. Their identity as folk artists evokes temporal "in-betweeness," as the community's historical importance is juxtaposed with its contemporary absence and its projected extinction.

To conclude I draw on the sentiments of Chakori Devi, a Badin in her late fifties who, like Dei, stopped dancing sometime in the 1980s. As we discussed the marginalization of her community of performers, she became increasingly upset. Her statement acknowledged the Baddi's divinely sanctioned artistic inheritance as well as their position of vulnerability vis-à-vis the music industry. She accused a small number of well-known commercial singers, including Meena Rana, of appropriating the role of public entertainers from the Baddi. Given the economic and cultural decline of the Baddi in recent decades, her anger is understandable, and it underlines the radically different social positions of Shilpkar performers, on one hand, and middle-class or middle-caste artists, on the other.

> Our story is that we are Shivji's people for dancing and singing. Now others have started presenting these ballads [*gatha*]. Like who? Kishan Singh Panwar, Jagdish Bakrola, Babu Gosain [Gopal Babu Goswami], Narendra Singh Negi, Pritam Bhartwan, Meena Rana—they have started doing all this. And we've been left out! They took this from us and used it. And they made fuckers out of us! [*Hame banaye chuthiya.*] Why did we leave our crops for this? The people I'm talking about behave like this. Whether we end up fuckers or barristers, our circumstances [*aukat*] will remain. And if you take this [music] away from us, then Shivji will take care of you. I'll say that quite clearly, [because] we do service for Shivji. . . . We don't play around; we do god's play. And they do film-wallah drama, right?[26]

6 The Goddess Plugged In

*Pritam Bhartwan and the Commodification
of Possession Rituals*

A conch (*shankh*) and temple bells ring out as the dholak and tabla begin to sound an elaborate *dhunyal* pattern. Standing in front of the Sirkanda Devi temple near Mussoorie in a white and red kurta-pajama and red scarf, Pritam Bhartwan lip-synchs to his own audio recording while smiling and gesticulating to the cameras. On one side of Bhartwan stand two Bajgi drummers simulating strokes on the dhol and damaun, and on the other side stand two vocalists. An audience of around twenty devotees sits in two sections facing each other, swaying to and fro. As Bhartwan recites the physical attributes of Devi, the Mother Goddess, five individuals seated among this group begin to tremble, showing signs of possession. The rhythm shifts to a fast six-beat pattern as Bhartwan begins a well-known story from the Devi Puranas in which the great demons Madh and Kaitabh establish their tyrannical rule over heaven, earth, and hell (*triloka*). As he describes Devi's wrath and inevitable destruction of the demons, the video cuts away to corresponding scenes from previously televised mythological serials about Devi. At this point the mediums become fully possessed and rise, dancing furiously. Some stoop and place their heads against the dhol, while others throw rice in four directions, spreading fertility and blessings. Bhartwan trades phrases with his accompanists in a call-and-response format, describing Devi's various insignia (*nishan*) and all of the different godlings and castes that serve her. As he recites the name of each of Devi's regional avatars—Jwala, Dhari, Chandrabadni—a picture of her corresponding temple appears onscreen. The tempo increases at the conclusion, and Bhartwan sings the final refrain, "Jai Jwala Tero Dhyan Jagolo" (Victory to Jwala, I Remember You), applying sandalwood paste to the mediums' foreheads as a means of calming Devi and releasing them from her possession.

This twenty-two-minute performance of "Jai Jwala Tero Dhyan Jagolo" (2006) is one example of a flourishing genre of commercially produced possession rituals called *jagar* (figure 6.1).[1] Although my collection is surely incomplete, I have reviewed more than seventy cassette, video compact disc, and online recordings since 1990 that include representations of jagar.[2] Once disparaged in the public imagination and neglected in published texts and recordings, jagar have been documented in a body of commercial recordings in recent decades, complemented by a plethora of ethnographic and journalistic studies.[3] Assessing this body of work, this chapter demonstrates that, contrary to some scholarly predictions (see Fanger 1990: 174), jagar has become an increasingly visible and acceptable form of devotional expression in Uttarakhand. The public emergence of jagar is part of a broader mobilization of vernacular devotional forms across South Asia facilitated by the growing economic clout of urban migrants, the growth of vernacular music industries, the latent connections between divine and secular authority, and

Fig. 6.1. Cover of Pritam Bhartwan's jagar album *Naraini Ma Bhavani* (T-Series, 2006)

the democratization of religious authority after independence (Fiol 2010; Meyer and Moors 2006; S. H. Clark and Schofield 2002; Gellner 1994). Local factors, including an impetus to support regional cultural forms in the context of the new regional state and the rise of the charismatic hereditary healer Pritam Bhartwan, also have contributed to the dramatic rise of jagar.

Jagar possession rituals have been a pervasive part of religious life in the central Himalayas for centuries. Garhwalis and Kumaonis worship their goddesses and gods (*devi-devtao*) by dancing with them. The term *jagar* encompasses a range of performance contexts, but I am using it to refer to collective rituals in which devi-devtao are "awakened" (from the Sanskrit root *jag-*) by means of drumming and narrative performance, resulting in their dancing in the bodies of human mediums. *Panwara* is a closely related style of ritual performance focused on deified heroes who may or may not possess participants. Such rituals are organized in response to a range of motivating circumstances, including protecting one's community from maladies seen and unseen, alleviating the curse (*dos*) of a neglected deity, honoring one's ancestors and confirming their place in a spiritual lineage, calming the anger of a ghost (*bhoot*) or wandering spirit (*hauntiya*), and ensuring the blessings of a range of devi-devtao (some pan-regional, others connected to the earth, village, clan, family, or individual). Possession rituals that address some combination of these issues are common throughout the central Himalayas and in many parts of South Asia.[4] The underlying function of jagar is to heal the individual and the family, and often all family members must be present in order for the ritual to be efficacious.

My argument about the changing representation of jagar is predicated on the shifting significance of folk that I have explored throughout this book. Jagar rituals demonstrate many of the quintessential characteristics of what scholars have termed "popular religion" or "folk religion" in Indian contexts (Berlinerblau 2001; Weber 1967; Crooke 1896): animal sacrifice, corporeal and ecstatic possession by a range of left-handed Tantric divinities, and the participation of large numbers of nonprivileged social groups. These attributes are frequently juxtaposed with orthodox Brahmanical expressions of religiosity, reinforcing the binary models of Great traditions/Little traditions and Sanskritization/vernacularization that have long dominated discussions of South Asian cultural and religious life. Jagar rituals disturb such binary characterizations, however, because they regularly incorporate text-based narratives and pan-Indian divinities associated with Brahmanical Hinduism. Moreover, the vast majority of people in the central Himalayas participate in jagar ceremonies, irrespective of caste or class background. Jagar is a ritual form that enables the transaction of high and low ritual and social elements.

The habit of categorizing jagar as a form of folk Hinduism stems not from an assessment of the ritual practice per se but, rather, from the ambivalent and disdainful attitudes about jagar that have circulated in public discourse and in published scholarship. In recent decades, however, these attitudes have shifted. Government officials, commercial recording artists, and academics have begun converting jagar (and the category "folk" itself) into a positive marker of regional cultural identification for local residents as well as migrants living outside Uttarakhand. The new conditions created by state formation, mass migration, spiritual tourism, economic liberalization, and technological innovation have all contributed to an environment in which jagar has been positively reconstituted in the public imagination. If jagar was once a source of embarrassment for many Uttarakhandis, it is now appreciated as a distinctive and highly marketable form of music, dance, and ritual spectacle. In this sense, the reimagination of jagar rituals is part of a much broader pattern of rebranding and revalorizing "folk"—conceived as lok sangeet, lok dharm, lok sanskriti, and so on—in regions across post-liberalization South Asia.

The hereditary drummer and healer Pritam Bhartwan has been pivotal to the transformation of the public image of jagar. Though at first hesitant to perform it on All India Radio, his commercial recordings and stage performances of jagar have established him as one of the leading musicians of the Uttarakhandi recording industry. As I describe below, in the early 1990s Bhartwan and several others engineered a new style of presenting jagar that made mass-mediation and mass consumption easier. As might be expected, Bhartwan's transition to more commercial performance contexts has been accompanied by a shift from local to pan-regional aesthetic preferences and narrative structures. At the same time, this new mode of presenting jagar has resulted in a surge of large-scale public rituals that affirm the devotional sentiments of Uttarakhandis. In light of the longstanding discrimination that Shilpkar performers have faced, Bhartwan's becoming one of the most successful recording artists in Uttarakhand is truly remarkable, and it stands in contrast to the experiences of Sohan Lal, Bachan Dei, and other Shilpkar musicians discussed in previous chapters.

Encountering the Dancing Devtas

The public invisibility and inaudibility of jagar was a symptom of the deep ambivalence with which it has been regarded in Uttarakhand. In conversations with high-status individuals, I frequently heard jagar described as a backward and shameful practice. For most of the twentieth century it persisted but received little attention in scholarly or journalistic sources. The Garhwali and Kumaoni feature films made during the 1980s and early 1990s avoid representations of jagar, although they are replete with references to many obscure musical and ritual practices such as Baddi geet and bajuband-nyauli.

The stigma attached to jagar stems from the ambiguous status of corporeal possession vis-à-vis orthodox interpretations of Hinduism. As Fred Smith reminds us, it is important to distinguish Brahmins from Brahmanism: the former frequently participate in possession rituals, but the latter relies on the authority of a set of doctrines espoused by a literary elite of three thousand years who did not sanction possession as a legitimate form of religious expression (2006: 9). Hindus in many parts of South Asia practice corporeal possession as a method of ritual healing, but it is frequently bracketed by scholars as an element of "folk Hinduism" that attracts predominantly women, Shilpkars, and other subaltern groups (Blackburn 1985). For instance, Oakley wrote that jagar rites "are fervently believed in by the women of all castes, by the rustics generally, and especially the Doms. . . . As a general rule, the Brahmins, traders, and townspeople take no part in such cults, *and would disclaim all knowledge of them*" (1990 [1905]: 208–209, emphasis mine). In my experience, the majority of mediums in jagar rituals are women, and the majority of gurus are Shilpkar men. Yet the vast majority of Brahmins and Rajputs in Uttarakhand also participate in jagar as sponsors, mediums, gurus, accompanists, or devotees even if many hold reservations about making this participation publicly known. What is notable is not that high-castes participate but that they have done so *in secret*; this reaffirms the low status of the activity more generally (Gellner 1994: 37).

The social stigma of jagar is particularly evident within high-caste migrant communities, where ritual participation can be linked to feelings of shame for belonging to a region associated with economic underdevelopment and large-scale migration. I frequently heard stories about migrants in the plains attempting to conceal their regional background from neighbors and work associates. In urban settings, jagar are organized clandestinely within the home; the form is truncated and the volume is muted. The guru Satyeshwar Himalaya described a jagar he conducted for a Kumaoni family in Delhi as follows:

> SH: Jagar doesn't really happen in Delhi. It's like this, inside a closed room, just quietly, "tum tum tum," and the devi-devtao come quickly, and a little rice is offered, and it's done. That's how Bhairav's *puja* [that is, ritual] is done.
> SF: Do the hosts say not to make it long, to keep the puja brief?
> SH: That's right, they say [to the guru,] keep it brief. There's a lot of shame around this in these places. They are afraid that the plains people around them will think that they are crazy.

sf: Is there not as much devotion [*bhakti*] in the city?

sh: No, there's devotion. But there's shame [*sharam*] as well. There has to be devotion for them to do all the preparation that they need to have the puja. But the people around them will say, "Hey, asshole [*sala*], don't disturb us."[5]

More than any other cultural practice, jagar disturbs the anonymity of urban life because of its blend of distinctive timbres; the sustained ringing of the thali, the undulating voice of the hurka, the sustained vocal accompaniment (*baunr*), and the unbounded, ecstatic cries of devta possession easily spill over the boundaries of a domestic space, signaling to all within earshot that a possession ritual is taking place.

Uttarakhandis have long been made aware of the differences between "Great traditions" and the "Little traditions," to use the concepts popularized by Robert Redfield, McKim Marriott, and Milton Singer. As discussed in chapter 2, the conceptual bifurcation of great and little, *shastric* and *laukik*, classical and folk were useful insofar as they legitimized some of the earliest ethnographic research concerning rural societies. They also parallel the ways in which religious scholars have classified central Himalayan divinities into binary categories of high and low, orthodox and unorthodox, pure and impure, benevolent and malevolent. Hindu reformers and Christian missionaries generally saw the possession ritual as an expression of folk religion or popular religion because of the prevalence of worship of a wide range of divinities that fall outside (and below) the conventional Hindu pantheon. William Crooke advocated studying "popular Hinduism" separately from representations of Brahmanical Hinduism read through Sanskrit sources (1896: 2). Oakley (1990 [1905]: 205) and Atkinson (1973 [1882]: 840), writing from a distinctly Christian worldview, lumped all local, non-Brahmanical figures of worship into the category of demonolatry. As Atkinson described it, the rituals' "montane and non-Brahmanical origin is sufficiently shown by the names of the deities worshipped by them: Ganganath, Bholanath, Masan, Khabish, Goril, Kshetrapal, Saim, Airi, Kalbisht or Kalua . . . most of these gods and goddesses and deified mortals are known under the generic name *bhoot-pret*. These too possess their followers and cause them to dance and leap and cry out and throw ashes on their heads and beat themselves with nettles. They eat greedily of uncooked rice and split pulse and altogether appear demented. Their relatives then call in the aid of the Dholi or Badi as an exorcist and offer at the nearest shrine of the demon said to possess the patient" (ibid.: 446–447).

Contemporary practitioners of jagar stress the hierarchical organization of deities, many of which protect and serve the interests of particular caste communities. William Sax (2009) has conducted extensive research on jagar ceremonies centered on the worship of ghosts (bhoot-pret), wandering spirits (hauntiya), and varieties of Aghori spirits and devtao who incorporate hetero-dox or "left-handed" Tantric practices and live in cremation grounds and who are particularly concerned with the protection of low-status communities. Yet jagar also incorporates a wide range of local and regional deities associated with high-status communities (for example, Narsingh and Pandavas) and that often are interpreted as avatars of pan-Indic gods such as Vishnu, Shiva, and Devi. In the context of jagar, these low- and high-status deities frequently interact, mirroring the behavior of their low- and high-status devotees. As much as jagar has become a vehicle for intra-caste solidarity, then, it is also a means by which power is negotiated between different caste communities and their gods (Lecomte-Tilouine 2009).

The marginalization of possession within the study of Hinduism has a parallel in mainstream medicine. Sax (2014) has argued that the state health-care system in India has been "structurally blind" to the existence of healing rituals, despite the demonstrated health benefits that healing ceremonies offer participants. He poses a number of explanations for this omission, argu-ing that mainstream medicine is predicated on a Cartesian mind-body split and privileges a notion of the individual that is at odds with the concept of personhood in South Asian ritual settings. The methods of standardization and verification required in modern medicine are incompatible with ritual systems that have developed to serve and adapt to local settings. Medicine fragments the body into parts that need to be treated separately, whereas jagar rituals attempt to heal the whole person in relation to his or her family and broader community. Sax points, above all, to the particular worldview that informs participation in modern medicine, one rooted in cosmopolitan modernism and rational secularism, and one that dismisses any practice that can be deemed backward or non-modern.

Animal sacrifice (*balidan*) is one practice within jagar that is considered non-modern or irrational by many Uttarakhandis. Many devi-devtao require one or more animals (typically goats or water buffalo) to be offered during the course of a ritual. Campaigns against animal sacrifice in Uttarakhand have a long history (Oakley 1990 [1905]: 193; Sax 1991; Govindrajan 2013), but in recent decades religious and animal rights groups, predominantly but not entirely based in the plains, have stepped up efforts to eradicate the practice. Their efforts have been effective in replacing animal sacrifices with vegetar-ian offerings (in the form of coconuts, lemons, or butter) at widely known temples such as the Chandrabadni Devi temple near Tehri and the Mahasu Devta temple in Hanol (Chakknatt 2002). Although animal sacrifices are still prevalent in village-level rituals and large-scale festivals such as the famous

Bhunkal mela in Pauri Garhwal, frequently some faction of attendees resist the practice. On several occasions I was asked not to videotape the balidan portion of jagar rituals, and on one occasion at the Bhagnaol festival, two devtas had a dispute about whether the balidan should be nonvegetarian. Eventually the devotees simply ignored the devta who forbade them to kill the goat. The man who killed the animal was self-conscious afterward, claiming, "These things should not be done, but what to do? Uttarakhand is very backward."[6]

The desire to eradicate animal sacrifice as well as the consumption of meat or alcohol during jagar might be interpreted as an attempt to alter ritual practice in the direction of high-caste religious ideals. Srinivas defined Sanskritization as "the process by which a 'low' Hindu caste, or tribal or other group, changes its customs, ritual, ideology and way of life in the direction of a high caste" (1967: 6). While the concept of Sanskritization has heuristic value in particular cases, it is important to reiterate that jagar cannot be regarded as a low religious or cultural practice, despite the stigma to which it has been subjected; more accurately, it is a ritual form through which elements of "highness" and "lowness" interact and transact. Taylor (2011), for instance, describes a *saptah* (seven-day) ritual in Garhwal in which devta possession was blended with the recitation of the *Bhagavata Purana*. Although the latter is a high-status activity performed exclusively by Brahmins, Taylor rejects this as an illustration of Sanskritization because members of three caste communities (Brahmins, Rajputs, and Shilpkars) were collectively involved in the ritual.

The Public Face of Jagar

Despite being a preeminent form of ritual expression in homes and villages across Uttarakhand, jagar's status as an emblem of regional spirituality has been regarded with some ambiguity. Atkinson relates an apocryphal story about Sudarshan Shah (1784–1859), the Maharaja of Tehri Garhwal. He summarily bound and killed so-called sorcerers practicing possession rituals in his kingdom, and he beat a woman who was said to be possessed by Goril devta. Following this campaign of violence, Atkinson writes, the mere mention of the name Sudarshan Shah could drive away the gods (Atkinson 1973 [1882]: 833; Crooke 1896: 157). Rather than illustrating antagonism between the ruler and the gods, however, this story highlights the rajah's displeasure with particular gods or with the religious authority of the gurus. After all, as the Maharaja of Tehri, Sudarshan Shah and all of his successors are given the title Bolanda Badrinath, signaling their own mediumship as the "mouthpiece" of Lord Badrinath, an avatar of Vishnu (Galey 1991–1992).

Jagar rituals are not only ceremonies for healing; they are spaces where supplicants can appeal to the devtas for justice, particularly when there are disputes or failures of confidence in the local judicial and penal system. Colonial administrators accommodated possession rituals as a form of customary law in which locals administered their own form of justice subject to the decision of the devta. In Kumaon there is long tradition of dispensing justice through appeals to Golu devta, an incarnation of Gaur Bhairav (Shiva). The Chitai temple just outside Almora is considered Golu devta's "Supreme Court," and it remains common for residents to seek justice from him by means of pujas, jagar rituals, vows (*mannat*) written on paper, and offerings of bells attached to the outside of the temple ("Kin of 'Maoists'" 2014; Agarwal 2005; Fanger 1990; Leavitt 1997; Malik 2009).

As one might expect, the public face of jagar extends to the political sphere as well. In post-independence India, politicians have occasionally sponsored jagar as a means of attracting publicity through spectacle. When Member of the Legislative Assembly Ganesh Godiyal sponsored a jagar in his village in 2007, he and other members of his entourage regaled the audience with propaganda speeches for three hours before the ritual started. He was shrewd enough to recognize that a ritual performance by an esteemed guru would draw a large crowd and that he would be able to leverage the benefits of such a performance.

When sponsored by the state, jagar tend to be staged at rallies or festivals. With attention given to costumes, makeup, and amplification, they resemble any other folkloric or theatrical performances. Basanti Bisht has been invited to perform jagar for numerous state-funded programs; though she eschews possession, is not a healer, and only began performing in her forties, she has capitalized on the novelty of being one of the first women to publicly perform jagar and was even awarded one of the Indian state's highest civilian awards, the Padma Shree, in 2017 (Chatterjee 2011). Vidyadhar Sricala, a folk theater ensemble directed by Datta Ram Purohit and based in Srinagar, Garhwal, has been mounting large-scale, scripted performances that draw on jagar and other local ritual practices. Early in their performance of Chakravyuh, an episode from the Mahabharata, a group of musicians plays a series of rhythms on the dhol-damaun while the actors simulate possession by their respective deities. Watching this spectacle from afar, audience members often become possessed, forcing the musicians to continue playing until the possession has subsided and blurring the boundary between theater and ritual. Polit (2010) has described such performances as forging a space in which heritage and culture appear concrete to regional inhabitants.

Jagar has also been exploited as a platform for political satire. One remarkable example from the late 1970s involved Hemvati N. Bahuguna, the former chief minister of Uttar Pradesh and a native of Uttarakhand. As the anthropologist Claus Peter Zoller (1985) describes it, Bahuguna staged a jagar on the national independence day in the middle of Old Delhi's popular shopping area, Chandni Chowk, as a means of protesting the Emergency rule of Prime Minister Indira Gandhi. Several months earlier, Bahuguna had resigned from his post as general secretary of the Congress Party in order to make way for the prime minister's son, Sanjay Gandhi. His protest, therefore, likely was driven as much by personal animosity as it was by a sense of loyalty to those whom he felt were being oppressed under Emergency rule.

Bahuguna's staged jagar drew on the duality of temporal and divine rule manifested in the figure of Indira Gandhi, who was, on one hand, praised for bestowing fertility on the nation as the avatar of Indira Bhavani (a title for "goddess"), and, on the other, critiqued for generating sterility in the nation as the avatar of Indira the prime minister.[7] Demonstrating the adaptability of ritual signs within jagar, Bahuguna's text replaced ritual invocations of the Ashta Bhairav, guardians of the goddess who protect the eight cardinal points of the village, with an invocation of four leaders protecting the four corners of Hindustan. He subtly chastised the "flatterers of the mistress"—appropriating a vernacular phrase used in jagar to signify the subservient deities' flattery of Devi—to call attention to the passive obedience of Congress ministers and opposition leaders to the prime minister. Finally, instead of "sending the goddess home" (*gharbaun*) as would be appropriate during the concluding section of a jagar, Bahuguna read a text invoking the presence of all the gods and goddesses and praised Devi for allowing Hindustan to exist.

Bahuguna's public endorsement of jagar on a national stage was an exceptional event. In what could be considered a radical act at the time, Bahuguna played the role of a hereditary drummer during the performance, holding and playing the dhol despite his being a Brahmin. Jagar offered Bahuguna a quintessentially regional vehicle through which to critique the prime minister. His performance may have been interpreted as a challenge to the legitimacy of the ruler, but it did not carry the risk of political backlash because only the migrant Uttarakhandi community would have been able to interpret its underlying layers of irony and protest.[8]

In 2010 Uttarakhand became the first Indian state to adopt Sanskrit as an official language; this move has resulted in the promotion of Sanskrit across the region, including an effort to make the language a compulsory subject in schools. For local activists who have unsuccessfully campaigned for decades for recognition of Garhwali and Kumaoni as official state languages or to have them added to the Eighth Schedule of the Indian Constitution, this decision was accepted with bitter irony. The Uttarakhand government's advocacy of Sanskrit before Garhwali and Kumaoni is similar to its advocacy of pan-Indian forms of Hindu spirituality instead of pan-regional forms such as jagar. The state has promoted tourism under the motto "Dev Bhumi" (Land of the Gods) and has marketed the spiritual qualities of the region through the sponsorship of pilgrimages and festivals at major shrines and temples (for example, Nanda Devi Raj Jat and Char Dham Yatra). These efforts demonstrate the goal of attracting spiritual tourists from other parts of South Asia rather than promoting regional religious forms and practices.

Recent developments point to a shift in regionalist discourse. In 2013 Uttarakhand's tourism minister, Amrita Rawat discussed the need for a "revival" of jagar in a television interview, invoking the ritual form as one of the quintessential varieties of regional folk music.[9] Her use of the English term *revival* is striking, because only the public perception of jagar appears to have suffered; there is no evidence that the practice has suffered. As Turino (2000) and Livingston (1999) have argued, nationalists and cosmopolitans often invoke the concept of revival to bring attention to practices and forms that conjure up an idealized past and to offer an alternative to the supposedly harmful effects of mainstream culture. It is difficult to know Minister Rawat's personal motivations for invoking a jagar revival, but it was almost certainly a way for her to affirm her identification with Uttarakhandi village life, while also promoting the development of eco-tourism projects tied to indigenous lifeways in Uttarakhand.

The experience of Manohar Lal, the former deputy secretary of the National Congress Party, also points to a broader acceptance of jagar in the early twenty-first century. Lal learned to play hurka from his father, but he never played for rituals, preferring to play privately next to the family shrine in his home. In 2003, however, he was encouraged by Dehradun-based cultural activist Swami S. Chandra to perform a Devi jagar at a folkloric event alongside an actress who danced and performed the role of Devi's medium. After the positive response to this performance, Lal later made two commercial recordings of jagar[10] and published a book about the sociocultural context of jagar performance. His shift from performing jagar for his private enjoyment to embracing it as part of his public identity speaks to the more general transformation of jagar into a publicly accepted musical and ritual form. Pritam Bhartwan has been a key instigator of this transformation, and it is to his story that I now return.

Pritam Bhartwan: The Making of a Ritual Healer

Pritam Bhartwan was born in 1970 in the village of Silla, twenty kilometers from the hill station of Mussoorie (figure 6.2). Because he belonged to a family of hereditary (Auji or Bajgi) drummers, Bhartwan's childhood was suffused with the sounds of dhol-damaun and hurka-thali. He used to accompany his relatives during the month of Chait (mid-March to mid-April) to sing seasonal ballads and to play dhol-damaun. His father, Hem Das Bhartwan, and his two paternal uncles were esteemed musicians and healers (gurus) who were regularly invited to villages near and far to perform jagar.

In most jagar rituals there are six distinct types of participants: the medium, or *paswa* (lit. "beast," also called the *mali* or *dangariya* [lit. "little horse"] in some areas); the ceremonial specialist, or guru (also called the *jagariya*); one or more vocal and instrumental accompanists; the host; the gods and goddesses (devi-devtao); and the invited attendees. These roles frequently become blurred during the course of the ritual. For instance, attendees may rise and sit in front of the guru, thereby acknowledging their identity as a medium, or attendees may become unexpectedly possessed by a devta while

Fig. 6.2. Pritam Bhartwan with a photo of his late uncle, 2005 (courtesy S. Fiol)

seated far from the music. In order to summon and communicate with the gods, a guru may use astrology and divination in combination with percussive rhythms, sung narrative, and spoken mantras.

In his youth, Bhartwan never performed with his father because he was afraid of making a mistake in front of him. But beginning at the age of seven, he began accompanying his paternal uncle Kalam Das. The young Bhartwan would provide vocal support (*baunr*) and play thali, the bronze plate that accompanies indoor ceremonies, while his uncle performed rituals for regional divinities including Goril, Hauntiya, Devi, Pari, Pandau, and Narsingh. In Uttarakhand, divinity manifests in a plethora of forms—ghosts (*bhoot-pret*), fairies (*pari*), demons (*raksha*), Muslim saints (*pir*), ancestral spirits (*pitr*), godlings, gods, goddesses, and wandering, unappeased spirits (hauntiya)—some of which are harmful and unwanted and others of which are well-meaning and benevolent. Insiders use the generic terms *devta* (god) and *devi* (goddess) or the plural form, *devi-devtao* to signify this range of entities. Bhartwan's family members perform jagar for a range of devi-devtao, but their family god (*kul devta*) is Goril, a great Katyuri king from Champawat (Kumaon) who became a god. Goril is one of a number of devi-devtao whose influence has expanded westward from Kumaon, where he is known as Golu devta, and settled in Garhwal.

Accompanying his relatives on these journeys, Bhartwan learned a number of rhythmic patterns and sacred mantras that his uncle used to invoke and appease the devi-devtao, to exorcise unwanted spirits, and to heal individuals. At the age of twelve Bhartwan was invited to lead his first jagar ritual when his father and uncle had been called to perform rituals elsewhere. Although he was initially nervous, the villagers had complete faith that he could successfully call the devta because he was Hem Das's son, and the spiritual power (*siddhi*) of a guru is understood as an inherited trait.

All jagar rituals incorporate elements that assist in the arrival and departure of the devi-devtao, including incense (*agarbati*), the sacralized cloth of the devi-devtao, offerings of food and money, sandalwood paste, and the fragrant smoke of *ghee* poured on a lamp of coals (*dhoopana*). Many devi-devtao require the sacrifice of goats, chickens, or buffalo as offerings or as a fulfillment of a devotee's vows. Perhaps the most powerful element in attracting the devi-devtao is the spoken formula (mantra), the knowledge of which is carefully protected by the guru in both its oral and written forms. A guru's claim to possessing unique spiritual power (*siddhi prapt*) is bolstered by blood inheritance, but it must be proven via the performance of Tantric rites at cremation grounds and by the possession of sacred mantras recorded in books handed down through the family.

Bhartwan insists on the centrality of proper drumming and singing technique to the success of a jagar ritual. Central Himalayan drumming is based on interlocking, often asymmetrical rhythmic patterns. In performance, rhythmic patterns become indices of particular devi-devtao or particular functional sections of the ritual such as summoning the devta, dancing the devta, or calming and sending off the devta. Some rhythmic patterns, such as the basic *dhunyal*, are played in more or less the same way by gurus across Uttarakhand, whereas others have evolved in unique and unpredictable ways as they have spread across the region.

Three pairs of instruments are generally used to perform jagar: hurka and thali or daunr and thali are commonly played indoors, whereas dhol and damaun are usually played outdoors. Each instrumental pairing reveals a contrast of high and low frequency and high and low density of strokes; when played in fast, tightly interlocking combinations, these contrasts appear to emerge from a single part (Chandola 1977). The playing strokes of hurka, daunr, and dhol (the "lead" instruments in each of the pairs) are more variable and forceful than their accompanying rhythmic counterparts, but they also decay faster in comparison to the regular undercurrent of pulsation provided by the thali and damaun. An important aesthetic of jagar rituals is the continuous, unbroken sound maintained by the interweaving of strokes produced by one pair of instruments. Continuous sound is also ensured by the extended male vocal accompaniment at each phrase caesura (called *baunr* in Garhwali, *hebar* in Kumaoni) during sections of pitched recitation and dance-song, as well as by repeated strokes on the hurka between lines of text in sections of pitched recitation and unpitched recitation.[11]

The medium's contact with all of these contextual elements reinforces the synesthetic experience of jagar, in which smell, touch, sound, taste, and sight are all essential to the efficacy of the ritual. By orchestrating when and how these elements should enter the ritual, Bhartwan learned to control when and how healing occurs. Depending on the needs of the participants, he moves between textures of heightened narrative recitation, dance-songs, and conversation with the devi-devtao.

The performance of jagar can create a sense of communal solidarity that cuts across hierarchies of gender and caste, even as the practice of jagar also illuminates these social hierarchies. For example, participation as a medium is not limited by gender or caste. As with the situation described by Kapadia (1996) in South India, however, many devi-devtao only possess members of a particular caste, though they may be worshipped by all castes. Moreover, a larger percentage of mediums are women, but the well-established mediums for the most powerful devi-devtao are generally men.

Unlike most specialist musical traditions in Uttarakhand (such as Baddi geet and Chaiti geet), jagar is not performed by one hereditary community for the benefit of others. Rather, individuals from different families collaborate in order to successfully bring and communicate with the devi-devtao. Bhartwan is frequently invited to lead jagar rituals for Rajput or Brahmin families, and Brahmin or Rajput gurus are sometimes, if infrequently, called to lead jagar for Shilpkar families.[12] The cultural historian M. P. Joshi writes,

> In jagara rituals the Shilpkars participate as freely as non-Shilpkars. In fact on many occasions the Shilpkars in Kumaon also act as diviners and ritual singers of various hymns. It is significant to note that during the Nanda Devi festival (which belongs to the "great tradition") the Nanda Devi jagara is sung by certain Shilpkars who sit *at the doorstep* of the Nanda Devi temple, Almora. In local traditions of Garhwal, Kaliya Lohara figures as the progenitor of the Loharas (ironworkers) and the creator of the Pandavas weapons. . . . It follows then that the Shilpkars are not only associated with the folk deities (belonging to the "little tradition") but also with pan Indic cult deities. *During jagar they are as much respected as non-Shilpkar participants.* (1992–1993: 315–316, emphasis added)

Joshi reiterates the familiar trope of the Great tradition/Little tradition and folk/pan-Indian binaries, but he also points to the ways in which ritual practices have brought communities together, reducing caste discrimination. Indeed, during rituals, Shilpkar gurus are generally treated with a great deal of respect, in striking contrast to the Bajgi or Baddi performers discussed in previous chapters. Bhartwan explained that the respect he received from a young age was a legacy of his father's and uncle's stellar reputations for musical and ritual knowledge. Bhartwan remembers his father as a very proud man: "He used to tell me, 'Pritam, never be ashamed of your hereditary work'" (*khandani kam se kabhi sharm nahi honi chaindi*). On one occasion Bhartwan's uncle received garlands at the outskirts of a village and was given a horse to escort him to the village. The relatively high status of the guru is also reflected in his form of compensation. Again in contrast to the Bajgi or Baddi performer, who received a fixed or pre-arranged payment (*dan*) for his musical services, the guru rarely stipulated any amount, preferring to be compensated in the form of an offering (*dakshina*) from the hosts.

Nonetheless, Joshi's statement that "Shilpkars participate as freely as non-Shilpkars" requires qualification. Bhartwan and other gurus I interviewed describe several ways in which caste politics influenced the performance of jagar. For instance, Shilpkar gurus are sometimes made to play hurka or daunr in the stone courtyard outside the temple or Brahmin family's home, rather than inside as is the custom.[13] The boundaries of the home and the temple are viewed as particularly susceptible to pollution among orthodox Hindus, and Shilpkar performers are frequently prevented from entering these spaces. Joshi's last qualification is an important one: during the ritual, the identity of the guru as one who calls and intercedes in the affairs of the gods temporarily supersedes his identity as a lower-caste person. In their temporary position of authority as ritual healers, Shilpkar gurus may even feel empowered to challenge discriminatory practices. One related a story in which he was invited to perform a jagar but was seated outside the temple; after performing the invocatory rhythms, he stopped playing and refused to call the devi-devtao until he was given permission to seat himself within the temple.

Bringing Jagar into the Studio

After entering secondary school in Mussoorie, Bhartwan had fewer occasions to practice jagar, and he was careful not to reveal his background to classmates from Haryana, Panjab, or Delhi. Jagar was a regular part of life in Garhwali villages, but in the cosmopolitan environment of Mussoorie—famous for its Christian schools and bazaars—it was not openly accepted. On one occasion, however, his Garhwali friends encouraged him to perform a Chaiti geet and an excerpt of a jagar during a school program. The performance was well received, and a progressive school principal commended him and encouraged him to continue performing.

Tracing the well-worn path of Mohan Upreti, Narendra Singh Negi, and many other artists, Bhartwan turned to the medium of radio as a platform to launch an independent recording career. In 1987 he went to Najibabad with his maternal and paternal uncles and auditioned at All India Radio in front of a panel including Madhuri Barthwal (see chapter 3). After Bhartwan sang several Garhwali folk songs, Barthwal asked for something even more traditional, and he decided to perform one section of a jagar for Goril, his family's main god. His uncle's name was added to the audition sheet so that he would be allowed to provide vocal accompaniment. Bhartwan passed the audition with a B grade, and he began to sing regularly on radio request programs.

In 1991 Bhartwan arrived in Delhi to record his first cassette album with Rama Cassettes. In one day, he recorded eight of his own compositions, but he later learned that the studio misplaced a twelve-inch reel containing four of his tracks. He was called back to re-record those four songs, but he did not have the money to hire the studio and the session musicians for a full day. In a pinch, he decided to sing several sections of a jagar for Nagraja devta, which he extended to fifteen minutes, and in the remaining fifteen minutes he sang an excerpt of the epic ballad (panwara) of Bima Katheit. His uncle Kalam Das provided vocal support and accompaniment on the thali. These two tracks were almost afterthoughts, but they were by far the biggest hits on Bhartwan's first album, *Rangili Bauji* (1993). He claims that from the time of the release of this album people started referring to him as the "jagar-wallah" (one who does jagar), and one shopkeeper in Mussoorie displayed a hand-painted sign advertising the "Bima Katheit cassette," ignoring the official title of the album.

Many critics have praised Bhartwan's singing for its folk tone, an unteachable quality of the voice that can be described as nasal and rich in overtones. He has a wide range, and his vocal style is mellifluous, characterized by highly improvisatory runs and a succession of quick mordents at phrase endings. According to Bhartwan, performing jagar and panwara in all-night rituals for so many years imparted the physical stamina needed to perform on tour and prepared his voice to produce complex melismas over a broad melodic range; indeed, he explained that singing other folk genres came to him easily after training in the more rigorous and musically complex jagar tradition.

Bhartwan was not the first to commercially record jagar and panwara; he was following in the footsteps of several other hereditary gurus such as Dev Singh Jagari, Devaraj Rangila, and Kunanand Juyal, all of whom recorded full-length cassettes of jagar in the 1980s. Yet Bhartwan pioneered a unique style of presenting jagar that can be contrasted with those of the earlier singers. Instead of recording an album consisting of just one or two lengthy jagar or panwara, Bhartwan selects five- to ten-minute excerpts from several different jagar and panwara narratives and presents these as independent tracks. He has also "modernized" the instrumentation on his recordings: while maintaining the use of hurka and thali on many recordings, the percussion mix is dominated by tabla and dholak.

For Bhartwan, the specific instruments used to accompany jagar is less important than the rhythmic patterns that they play. He claims that when he first used to go to Delhi, no one knew how to play Pahari rhythms; percussionists laughed at him when he attempted to teach them these rhythms. Later he decided to bring accompanists from the hills because classically trained accompanists were not able to reproduce these rhythms.

As we've seen, producers of Uttarakhandi geet seek to offer topical and musical variety on their albums, blending tracks containing sacred traditional repertoire with original compositions on themes of love (*sringar geet*) and nature (ritu geet). In this sense the format of Bhartwan's cassette albums conformed to the industry standard (see Bhartwan 2010). His inclusion of jagar excerpts alongside secular love songs and topical village songs both facilitated and reflected the gradual transformation of jagar from something marginal and sold separately as a novelty item to an accepted part of the folk heritage of Uttarakhand.

Almost all of Bhartwan's video and cassette albums have followed a similar pattern of including one or more jagar or panwara excerpts, usually featured as the first or last track on the album. The jagar tracks follow a fairly consistent structure, beginning with the dhunyal (or *vrid-bane*) portion of the jagar, in which Bhartwan summons various devi-devtao in a heightened form of recitation accompanied by a looping rhythm on the hurka and thali. After thirty to sixty seconds he transitions to the *leheri* rhythm, in which he tells the central narrative of the devta. The climax of the track is the *mannan* section, which often includes a call-and-response section involving a male chorus.

Bhartwan's jagar recordings differ from his performances of jagar in live ritual settings in a number of predictable ways. Village rituals generally focus on one or more devi-devtao whose mediums have been invited to the ceremony, but there is no way to predict which devi-devtao might appear during the course of the ritual, and the guru must alter his performance to accommodate the new arrivals. Recordings of jagar, in contrast, nearly always focus on a single devi or devta's narrative from start to finish. Moreover, the recordings tend to focus on such pan-Indic and popular devi-devtao as Narsingh, Bhairav, Durga, Goril, Bhimsen, and Draupadi.[14] Bhartwan admitted to me that only in rare cases has he recorded jagar for Aghori or for hauntiya spirits because the latter are performed in intimate and personal rituals following the death of a family member.

When recording jagar in the studio, Bhartwan prepares a script with careful consideration of each line of text. While emphasizing only a small section of the longer ballad narrative, he often alludes to other parts of the story that have been cut out of the performance, thereby reminding the listener of the broader narrative context. One guru I interviewed was critical of Bhartwan's recordings for tending to follow versions of the narratives derived from the Sanskrit Puranas rather than more local oral variants. In comparison with ritual contexts, his recordings offer a more polished performance, a more predictable linear structure, a truncated narrative with less internal repetition, a more embellished and variable approach to melody, clearer enunciation of the text, and an expanded use of electronic and acoustic studio instruments.[15]

The Reception of Commodified Jagar

On the night of April 16, 2006, the first Uttarakhandi jagran was held in R. K. Puram, the suburb of Delhi with one of the largest Uttarakhandi migrant populations. This performance was recorded live in front of several thousand people and was released by T-Series on the 2-VCD set titled *Jagar*.[16] Over the course of an all-night, seven-hour extravaganza, Kumaoni and Garh-wali singers took the stage in turn to perform bhajan, devotional songs, and jagar renditions. Behind the stage was an enormous façade made of plaster and plastic depicting various devi-devtao and scenes from Puranic tales. At the rear of the hall, Uttarakhandi food and chai were served to the crowd. Accompanists sat at the back of the stage with a full array of studio and indigenous instruments: tabla, dholak, hurka, daunr, synthesizer, octopad, flute, and mandolin.

Pritam Bhartwan concluded the program by singing a Devi jagar. A few minutes into his performance of the leheri section, his voice became more animated, and between vocal phrases he added spoken mantras describing the physical appearance of Devi. Mass possessions began to occur in the audience, and approximately twelve mediums gathered in front of the stage to dance. Eventually they were sprinkled with water and gradually came out of their trance. Bhartwan himself became momentarily possessed while singing and holding the microphone. In the middle of singing a phrase, he fell dramatically onto his back. He was helped up within seconds, and with only a brief hesitation he continued singing the rest of the phrase. This was the climax of the performance; the VCD was edited to have the credits roll just after Bhartwan's possession.

Perhaps no event better represents the transformation of jagar in the twenty-first century. Once a ritual performed discreetly by Uttarakhandi families in their Delhi homes, jagar is today the banner under which the distinctive spirituality of Uttarakhand is being marketed. Bhartwan noted that during all-night jagar rituals in rural settings, it was not uncommon for many people to show up after dark and to sit in the back so that they would not be visible to other attendees. In the brightly lit venues where jagar rituals are being staged in urban areas, concealing one's identity is not an option; these events are indicative of a new pride in expressing regional belonging through the medium of communal devotion.

This event also demonstrates the ways in which elements of jagar have been coopted and modified in the process of commercialization. Conforming to a more general trend within the music industry, the stage performances at this jagran were modeled on existing recordings. Much of Bhartwan's stage performance of the Devi jagar closely resembled his recording of "Jai Jwala Tero Dhyan Jagolo" (2006). The vocal style, choice of instrumentation, and formal structure of the performance closely replicated those of the earlier recording; in fact, several instrumental accompanists at the jagran had been on the recording. Although the predictability of this presentation disrupted the spontaneity that is the norm in ritual performances of jagar, it did not appear to compromise the effectiveness of the performance for audience members. Although I did not study this aspect, it would be interesting to know whether audience familiarity with the VCD recording contributed to the ecstatic response to Bhartwan's performance.

The use of the word *jagran* to describe this event stems from the desire of the organizers to imitate the large-scale rituals sponsored by Panjabis living in Delhi and Chandigarh. Panjabi jagran have evolved into all-night variety shows featuring high-paid devotional singers like Narendra Chanchal and conspicuous displays of wealth (Erndl 1991). The commercial success of Panjabi jagran led the primary organizer of this event, Rajender Chauhan, to invent a parallel tradition for Uttarakhandi migrants in Delhi. He billed it as the "first annual" Uttarakhandi jagran, and the trend of staging jagran has indeed continued in Dehradun, Kotdwar, Delhi, and other parts of Uttarakhand.[17] Chauhan sold tickets to audience members, sold the copyright for the video recording to T-Series, and designed a faux-devotional set similar to those used in Hindu theme parks in Haridwar, for example, or televised productions of the Ramayana (Lutgendorf 1990). Drawing on pan-Hindu iconography, he created a variety show of the biggest names in Uttarakhandi popular music, using popular Hinduism and devta possession as the common denominators.

Since 2000 the rise of recorded jagar has been most notable in the VCD format. Nearly all of Bhartwan's cassette recordings have been re-released on VCD, and his corpus now totals more than fifty albums. His jagar videos visually simulate a ritual setting, with mediums sitting opposite the guru and accompanists and a crowd of spectators watching from a distance, as in the opening example of the chapter. According to one producer, video recordings of jagar were not produced for the purpose of entertainment but rather to bring about "a feeling of devotion" (*bhakti*) in the listeners and to remind them of the qualities and omnipotence of the devi-devtao. Bhartwan also credits these videos with showing Uttarakhandis living in the urban plains what real jagar should sound like and look like. Another producer opined that jagar on VCD sell well not only because of the religious sentiments they conveyed but also because the music is danceable and the rituals are visually interesting. He noted that purely devotional genres like Garhwali bhajan are musically slower and therefore have not sold as well.

Visually depicting possession dances can be a palpable sign of the devta's power as well as Bhartwan's potency as a guru, but it also exposes Bhartwan to public scrutiny.[18] Several viewers were critical of the dancers' control of their bodies in the video, claiming that they must be actors and not mediums. Such claims can be harmful for Bhartwan's reputation, because a guru is understood to always be able to successfully call the devi-devtao and verify their presence. Another critique leveled at the visuals of jagar on VCD is that many contain excessive violence. Many of the narratives describe battles between gods and demons in gory detail, but video producers have accentuated these details by inserting graphic scenes drawn from television serials.

I also heard criticism of jagar's new visibility in commercial spaces; some expressed the view that the commercialization of jagar trivializes communal ritual practice. It is important to emphasize, however, that ritual performances of jagar nearly always involve commercial transactions in some form. I have met gurus who refuse to accept cash payment for their performances, preferring the traditional manner of payment in the form of ritual offerings in kind, but many gurus do accept cash payments. The difference between them and other Shilpkar performers (such as Bagji or Baddi) is that gurus do not ask for this compensation; it is conceived as a form of offering rather than a prearranged payment.

Jean and John Comaroff (2009: 19–21) have written that cultural commodification contradicts the law of economics such that greater supply can lead to greater demand. The rise of mass-mediated productions of jagar does not appear to have resulted in diminishing participation in rituals; according to Bhartwan, the effect is nearly the opposite. The wide dispersal and consumption of these albums on VCDs and cable television networks has allowed jagar to become the representative genre of regional spirituality in Uttarakhand. It has also aided the diffusion of knowledge about localized traditions involving possessed dancing (such as Pandavlila, Ramman, and Nanda Devi Jat).

Some have also accused Bhartwan of being reluctant to play hurka or dhol on his albums. One producer pointed out that there were almost no photographs of Bhartwan performing on these instruments; this individual attributed this to an "inferiority complex," arguing that Bhartwan chose not to call attention to his background as a low-caste hereditary performer in commercial productions. Indeed, none of the album covers from the first twenty years of his career show him holding the dhol or the hurka (for an example, see figure 6.3).[19]

It is revealing to contrast Bhartwan's jagar production of *Naraini Ma Bhavani* (2006) with the jagar production *Nau Durga Naraini* (2006) by Narendra Singh Negi, the non-hereditary, upper-caste singer featured in chapter 3.[20] Both albums were produced by T-Series in praise of Devi, and they emerged in the marketplace within a week of each other. In Bhartwan's production, he is depicted standing in front of the temple wearing a kurta and vest while two other musicians stand off to the side playing dhol and

देवी, नरसिंग, भैरों
(जागर)
गायक : प्रतिम भरतवाण

Fig. 6.3. Cover of Pritam Bhartwan's jagar album *Devi, Narsingh, Bhairav* (Rama Cassettes, 1999)

damaun, instruments that Bhartwan is adept at playing. Negi's video shows him wearing the Nehru-style cap worn by traditional gurus while singing and playing the dhol—or more accurately, miming the playing of the dhol, as it is not used in the audio tracks of the recording, and Negi does not play this instrument. Negi's video moves through the same stages of the ritual as Bhartwan's video, and "possessed" actors begin to dance at roughly the same point in the narrative. Yet Negi's vocal phrasing is more melodically and rhythmically square than Bhartwan's, and he sings in a low register with little in the way of ornamentation. In places, Negi's performance sounds more like a bhajan (devotional song) than like jagar.

Why does Negi simulate the role of a guru, while Bhartwan, a real guru, stands without his instrument? Nearly everyone in Uttarakhand knows the two men's backgrounds. Yet in the VCDs they switch positions: Negi appears as a guru and champion of the dhol, while Bhartwan resembles a high-caste *pandit* standing in front of a sacred temple, the inner sanctum of which, ironically, Shilpkars cannot enter. Negi's adoption is reminiscent of Mohan Upreti's adoption of the hurka in stage performances during the 1950s and Bahuguna's adoption of the dhol during the politicized ritual described above; these were all acts of provocation that enabled the performer to make a political statement by identifying with a stigmatized element of local cultural practice.

Bhartwan has begun to consciously embrace the dhol and hurka as part of his public identity. He teaches and offers workshops in hurka and dhol performance through his registered NGO, Hem Lok Kalakendra, as well as through the NGO Shri Bhuvaneshwari Mahila Ashram, headquartered in Gairsain. Since 2011 he has begun playing dhol and hurka on recordings and in stage programs and mass rituals across India, Dubai, Oman, New Zealand, Germany, England, and the United States (figure 6.4). I believe his adoption of these instruments has become possible in part because of the growing prestige and visibility of jagar, and in part because of Bhartwan's upward social mobility. As someone who lives in Mussoorie and Dehradun but maintains a residence in his village, Bhartwan has chosen a lifestyle that resembles that of his upwardly mobile fan base. He eschews alcohol, maintains an immaculate wardrobe, speaks some English, and has authored several texts—all attributes that set him apart from most village-based healers. It is relatively safe for him to now adopt the markers of a traditional healer because he occupies a different social position than most ritual healers.

Fig. 6.4. Promotional photograph of Pritam Bhartwan with dhol, undated

In October 2011, I had the opportunity to host Bhartwan for a month-long residency at the University of Cincinnati and a performance tour of six universities. Before our first performance, I introduced him as a prominent commercial singer and recording artist. After the performance, he asked that I instead introduce him as a folk artist. Bhartwan's openness to embracing public performance on the dhol and hurka and his preference for the "folk artist" label are all part of a broader shift in the imagination of jagar as a prestigious and unique part of regional cultural heritage.

The Shifting Ground of Folk Religion

In some respects, the recent commodification of jagar is hardly surprising, given the importance of religiosity in public and private discourse across South Asia and the centrality of jagar ritual in the lives of the majority of Uttarakhand's population. The commodification of jagar can be understood as part of a much more widespread effort to incorporate popular religious beliefs and ritual practices into the Indian public sphere.[21]

In other respects, however, the commercialization of jagar is surprising given the secrecy and ambiguity with which many practitioners have long engaged with this ritual form. Many gurus acknowledge the danger of exposing ritual knowledge to those who are untrained, and they worry about inaccurate representations of the ritual propagated by commercial recordings. Many ritual participants are wary of marketing or publicly endorsing what they see as a backward practice that conflicts with an ideal of religiosity rooted in Brahmanical orthodoxy. The association of jagar with Shilpkar healers, female mediums, and taboo practices such as animal sacrifice has been the biggest obstacle to its being accepted as a legitimate and representative religious practice.

It is instructive to compare the recent commercialization of jagar with the commercialization of ritual practices involving possession in other parts of the world, such as Sanghyang in Bali (Picard 1990) and the complex of African diasporic religious forms including Santeria (Hagedorn 2001), Candomble (Van de Port 2006), and Vodun (Landry 2013). Each of the last three is a regional conglomeration of localized ritual practices that has come to international prominence through a combination of factors, including the world music industry, academic scholarship, and spiritual tourism. At various points in their histories, each of these possession-based ritual systems has been driven underground, their practitioners persecuted, because of the perceived threat they posed to systems of authority in colonial governments and established religious orders. These histories of persecution and perseverance have been integrated into the narratives of ritual practitioners, and they have become part of what attracts international devotees and scholars to the study of these practices.

In contrast to practitioners of African diasporic religions, jagar participants have not been persecuted en masse. Though many integral aspects of jagar such as corporeal possession and animal sacrifice have been challenged by cultural elites and by Brahmanical orthodoxy, the practice of jagar has not been systemically attacked by the state. During the colonial period, jagar was a little-understood ritual phenomenon that was accommodated even as Orientalist scholars of the late nineteenth and early twentieth centuries found it to be evidence of a lower evolutionary stage of religious consciousness.

In comparison to Santeria and Candomble, which have attracted large numbers of non-local practitioners, jagar has remained a provincial ritual practice that is firmly ensconced in family- and village-based social structures. The current wave of commercial recordings of jagar, however, is an indication of the cultural capital that has accrued to this form. It is difficult to assess whether the frequency of village-level and family-level jagar rituals has increased within Uttarakhand generally, but it is certain that jagar has become a more visible and acceptable manifestation of what has alternately been called popular Hinduism or folk Hinduism. Gellner (1994) stresses that the spread of new and more powerful mediums in Nepal has corresponded with the spread of democratic values after 1951; because religious authority is no longer vested in the priests, who wield less political power, there is more opportunity for the laity to assert their religious authority. This explanation is not sufficient in the context of Uttarakhand, because the regional government has continued to bolster the authority of Brahmin priests who preside over rituals in the major pilgrimage sites.

As I have reiterated throughout the book, folk is a dynamic concept that has shaped the way scholars have approached and interpreted such phenomena as jagar rituals. The concept of folk religion in India initially emerged to encompass any village-based ritual activity that did not conform to Brahmanical and Sanskrit-based religious practice. I join several scholars in pointing out the inadequacy of studying ritual such as jagar in a binary "classical/folk" framework (Sinha 2006; Taylor 2011; Sontheimer 1995). Although the performance of jagar can facilitate the expression of subaltern religiosity and can promote intra-caste solidarity, it also facilitates the movement across and between "higher" and "lower" registers of divinity, caste and class hierarchies, and oral and textual idioms. Sanskritization has become a useful heuristic for understanding how and why some ritual practitioners attempt to elevate their practices to achieve a higher, more legitimate status (Hiltebeitel 1993; Sinha

2006; Sontheimer 1989). Nevertheless, this idea cannot explain the processes of change influencing the new wave of jagar performances. Bhartwan has incorporated elements of orthodox Hinduism into his productions, to be sure, but he has also emphasized qualities that have long been considered taboo within orthodox Hinduism: bloodthirsty goddesses, mass possession, and ecstatic dancing and drumming.

In order to understand the meaning of the term *folk religion* today, we need to turn away from the binary models offered by social scientists of South Asia. Instead of searching for "folk" expressions that can be juxtaposed with classical, Brahmanical Hinduism, we might think of folk religion as a site for particular kinds of fluid interactions and transactions in status and rank. The inclusiveness and fluidity of jagar rituals grant them a unique polysemous power, signifying a connection to various communities and to the region as a whole. Moreover, if the label "folk religion" once signified alterity and cultural provincialism in academic discourse, it has been rebranded and revalorized to signify an inclusive form of regional devotional expression. This transformation has been precipitated by the growth of the vernacular music industry and the increased spending power of migrant Uttarakhandis living in plains cities in India and in the transnational diaspora. That these communities of migrants seek to consume the sounds and images of their villages through commercial productions demonstrates a profound shift in their self-conception, a pride in regional belonging.

As someone who embodies the desires for upward mobility within migrant communities, Pritam Bhartwan has been a catalyst for the resignification of folk religion and for the transformation of jagar. Early in his career, Bhartwan maintained separation between his hereditary occupation as a ritual drummer and healer and his professional occupation as a commercial singer. With the emergence of a folk culture industry that places value on village-based forms of authority, filtered through the reformist ideals of competition and mass-mediated presentation, Bhartwan has begun integrating the two sides of his professional identity.

Conclusion

This book has offered a series of historical and ethnographic perspectives about the concept of folk music in the Indian Himalayas. After exploring a range of performers and performances, it should be evident why I have not offered a single definition of folk music. Folk music is best understood as a multidimensional concept that has been instrumentalized by a range of individuals and communities for various political and economic ends. I have examined a century's worth of engagements with the folk concept as the outcome of two intertwined processes, one revivalist (turning dying folk into living folk) and the other rhizophonic (separating the folk sound from the folk body). Although each of these processes has been discussed to some extent in scholarship concerning invented traditions, music revivals, and modernist reformism, they have not previously been theorized as processes inherent to folklorization.

By juxtaposing performance contexts and historical settings over the course of the previous century, *Recasting Folk* has sought to illuminate many of the general features and consequences of folklorization. In late-nineteenth and early-twentieth-century Uttarakhand, native scholars such as Ganga Datt Upreti and Tara Dutt Gairola and nonnative scholars like E. S. Oakley began inscribing cultural difference onto the Khasa, Dom, and Adivasi communities (tribals) and describing their practices as backward and vanishing. At the same time, these scholars reclaimed folklore as a constitutive part of Kumaoni and Garhwali collective identity, which could then be used to make the case for a distinct political identity. This articulation was presented as pan-ethnic and pan-regional, but it was dominated by the values of the much more numerous and higher-status Rajput and Brahmin communities.

Another process of folklorization unfolded in the post-independence period of the mid-twentieth century as the numbers of migrant classes from peripheral rural areas swelled in urban centers. Through publications, radio broadcasts, gramophone recordings, and stage performances, Mohan Upreti and other upper-caste urban migrants and their patrons established the discursive terms and premises by which folk culture would become essentialized and valued. Lower-caste artisans from rural areas were celebrated as the source of the artistic heritage of the nation, but upper-caste artists were required to reform these raw materials and transform them into folklore.

The growth of regional (sub-national) politics and vernacular recording industries in the 1980s and 1990s paved the way for the branding and marketing of folk culture that continues to accelerate today. In this phase, the processes of folklorization have been less beholden to the goals of cultural nationalism than they have been to those of economic regionalism. Most participants in the culture industry—including inhabitants of Uttarakhandi villages as well as migrant and diasporic communities—have instrumentalized the discourse of folk as a means of selling products that stand for regional belonging. As in the two earlier historical periods, high-caste individuals from non-hereditary backgrounds such as Narendra Singh Negi have been at the center of folklorization efforts. Many Shilpkar artists cannot or do not package their artistry as "folk art," and those who do frequently feel the need to conceal their caste identity. Yet select individuals such as Pritam Bhartwan and Bachan Dei have been able to command a position of respect within the culture industry by emphasizing their unique and hereditary embodiment of the cultural patrimony of the region.

My emphasis on commercial and mass-mediated spaces of musical production and consumption may seem curious in a book that interrogates the concept of folk music. After all, in South Asian studies, the term *folk* has commonly denoted fields of cultural production that are explicitly village-based and noncommercial in nature. Folk music's Other has tended to be cast as classical music or popular music, both contentious and ideologically loaded terms in their own right. But this understanding of *folk* sets up a series of false binaries. It has been written elsewhere that the folk do not generally recognize themselves as the folk. The articulation of lok sanskriti as a distinct domain of cultural expression has only become possible with modernist conceptions of the world and new subjectivities enabled by new financial and political regimes, new systems of (post)colonial education, and new modes of intra- and intercontinental travel. In the progression from a feudal economy to a Nehruvian socialist economy, a post-liberalization economy, and finally what many have called a neoliberal market economy, the idea of "folk culture" has become wedded to the creation and marketing of unique regional brands within India that are as essential to attracting international capital as they are to articulating the interests of local elites (Oakes 2000; Wigen 1999: 1188). Urban and rural cosmopolitans in colonial India initially looked toward Europe (and Scotland in particular) to articulate the folk concept, but they also looked to Sanskrit models and local indigenous models. It is crucial to recognize that the folk concept has been predominantly shaped and disseminated through the channels of print and recorded media, and it is precisely by an examination of these media that we can better understand why and how this concept continues to be relevant in contemporary society.

There are some in Uttarakhand who feel that vernacular commercial music has moved further and further away from folk culture, increasingly absorbing influences from Hindi film music and international styles of popular music. Yet even in recent recordings we can find references to village-based musical styles in the rhythmic articulation, instrumentation, and melodic embellishment, to say nothing of the visual markers of regional culture on video albums. Part of what this book traces is a shift in the way commercial recordings have come to represent "folk culture" over the course of the past four decades: as entire albums or songs founded on village-based forms of music or dance have become less common, *folk elements* have become integrated into the textural, timbral, melodic, and rhythmic fabric of otherwise modern-sounding Uttarakhandi geet.

The shift in the sonic representation of folk culture is directly linked to issues of social status and mobility. The expansion of the folk culture industry across literary, sonic, and visual performance domains throughout the twentieth century was only possible with the reconfiguration of cultural authority and ownership in Uttarakhand and in South Asia more broadly. Although some people operating in the music industry refute the idea of caste privilege, it is an irrefutable fact. As Grandin notes in the context of the Nepali music industry, "One might say that medialization among other things has implied that music has moved upwards in the social hierarchy, this being a result not from social upward mobility by the traditional musical specialists, but from the recruitment among new people to music: ascribed low-caste specialists have given way to achieved middle- or high-caste specialists" (1989: 188). This statement accurately describes the social transformations within the Uttarakhandi music industry and probably a range of other vernacular industries across South Asia. Nonetheless, I am struck by the dearth of scholarly attention to the contributions of Shilpkars or Dalits in histories of Indian recorded music. This lack of attention is derived in part from the reluctance of music producers to acknowledge the influence of caste-based ideologies within commercialized urban spaces; popular music has become an essential part of creating the myth that modernized India has become casteless.

A related factor is that the dominant position of high-status individuals from migrant classes has necessitated a shift in the way hereditary musicians can claim ownership of the folk. Once positioned as *the* quintessential folk artists, hereditary musicians are largely ignored within the industry or are cast as part of a backward community of dying traditions. That there has not been a complete disappearance of Shilpkar artists in Uttarakhand speaks to the resilience of customary practices and ritual structures in village life and the perseverance of particular individuals who have sought to break through caste and gender barriers.

As discussed in chapter 5, female performers have been underrepresented in the music industry despite their abundance in village areas. A small group of female singers has emerged as the do-it-all archetypes of feminine subjectivity in the Uttarakhandi music industry, paralleling the dominance of a small group of female playback singers in the Hindi film music industry in the second half of the twentieth century. I have argued that these female singers have been accommodated in the vernacular music industry in part because of a persistent discourse about the centrality of women as repositories of folk culture. Perhaps not surprisingly, female recording artists, to a much greater extent than their male counterparts, tend to come from lower-status, hereditary families. In spite of the importance of a hereditary background to claims of cultural authenticity, however, most female singers have chosen to conceal their caste identities. Facing gender discrimination on numerous levels, many are vulnerable to social appraisal on the basis of their purity in a way men are not. Female singers face continual pressure to embody regional folk culture in their recordings and stage performances, and success in a competitive music industry necessitates the construction of a neutral public persona with a normative (that is, high-status) social identity.

To be clear, I am not suggesting that the term *folk* be banished from scholarship, nor am I advocating that it be replaced with some other word. There is little possibility of this happening in any case, because the folk concept has become an entrenched part of academic and everyday discourse in India, as in many other parts of the world. Ethnographic and journalistic writings tend to articulate the anxieties of loss and decay within so-called folk music traditions without also examining the political, economic, and cultural repercussions of their discourse. Ethnomusicological studies also have contributed to the uncritical acceptance of the folk concept across South Asia. This book has attempted to trace the roots and routes of the folk concept in one corner of the Indian Himalayas as a means of demonstrating the wide range of ideological objectives to which this concept has been linked. The concept of folk carries a certain ambivalence, signifying both the backward, primitive, and shameful aspects of culture and the exalted, timeless, national, regional, or ethnolinguistic heritage under threat from modernity. In Uttarakhand, as in many other settings, *folk* may stand for a decaying cultural tradition or community of artists, a sign of social status, a slogan for regional political mobilization, or a commercial brand within the culture industry. An identification with folk culture has become central to the way Uttarakhandis articulate their relation to the nation, the region, and their own locality. This is probably true in any part of India, but it is especially salient in border zones or areas that are removed from the economic and cultural center of the nation.

Yet it is worth asking why "folk" continues to be used as a de facto analytical category in the scholarship concerning South Asian musical and cultural life to a much greater extent than in scholarship in African, European, or American contexts. I have suggested that the uncritical acceptance of the term *folk music* is part of a legacy of binary structuralist models (Srinivas's Sanskritization/vernacularization, Redfield's Great tradition/Little tradition) that attempt to holistically account for all cultural production in South Asia while implicitly privileging text-based, pan-regional, "classical" traditions. The recent post-structural turn in South Asian ethnomusicology has perpetuated this legacy by deconstructing the idea of classical music while leaving folk music as an unmarked and essentialized category. This book has endeavored to draw out the intellectual genealogies of the folk concept, to expose its historical legacies and inherent contradictions. As folk has become part of the discourse through which artists identify themselves and their artistic expressions—and the way the culture industry markets them—we need to remain cognizant of the risks and potentialities carried by this discursive construct.

Notes

Introduction

1. It did not come as a surprise when, after we returned to Dehradun, the producer told me that the sequences recorded in this village would not be used in the final version of the VCD despite the efforts of the crew and the villagers. His decision was a reminder that authority over the presentation of tradition ultimately rests with producers and performers in plains-based studios.

2. The term *vernacular* has a number of distinct associations in the fields of literature, history, and architecture. In this study I use *vernacular* to indicate the shared cultural forms and practices of a particular period or locality. I also use it in the sense described by Filene, "to suggest songs employing a musical language that is current, familiar, and manipulable by ordinary people" (2000: 4). Although the term is not without problems, it is not loaded with the ideologies of purity, simplicity, rurality, and timelessness that tend to accompany the term *folk*.

3. See Bigenho (2007), Feldman (2006), Hagedorn (2001), Mendoza (2008), Rios (2012), and Turino (2000).

4. Throughout the book I use the local term *Shilpkar* ("artisan") to gloss hereditary members of lower-caste artisan communities (e.g., blacksmiths, barber-musicians, potters, and tanners). There are a plethora of other ascriptive and descriptive labels for subaltern communities in Uttarakhand, including *Harijan, Mirasi, Untouchable, Scheduled Caste, Das, Dom,* and *Dalit.* As Lybarger notes (2011), we lack historical and ethnographic evidence to demonstrate the longevity of most terms or the degree to which performers use these terms to self-identify. Dalit is not a prevalent identity category in Uttarakhand, as it is in many other parts of India. Das ("servant") is a common surname for musician castes, as it is for many Mirasi communities of the North Indian plains, but it also carries pejorative associations, as does the now-obsolete category Dom (see chapter 1).

5. Alter confirms this interpretation of *folk artist* in Garhwal (2000: 99–101). The interpretation of folk *artist* may depend heavily on local demographics. In a survey-based study conducted in three districts of Uttarakhand (Pandey 2012), those identifying as artists (the term *folk* was left out but implied) in Almora District included predominantly high-caste, educated, non-hereditary performers supported by governmental and nongovernmental agencies. In Pauri and Dehradun Districts, in contrast, those identifying as artists were predominantly lower-caste, less well-educated hereditary performers who rely on large extended families and individual patrons for support.

6. See, e.g., Berreman (1963), Hardgrave (1969), Sanwal (1976), Singer (1972: 260–269), and Srinivas (1989). McKim Marriott (1976) expanded the focus on attributes to include social transactions between caste groups.

7. Scholars including Carroll (1977) have critiqued these models for being ethnocentric, arguing that modernization is used synonymously with Westernization and Sanskritization with Brahmanization. For a defense against such critiques, see Berreman (1971).

8. A video of this performance from October 2011 can be accessed at the following link: https://vimeo.com/41522876.

9. See, e.g., Keil (1978) and Harker (1985).

10. See, e.g., Feldman (2006), Filene (2000), Gelbart (2007), Mendoza (2008), Miller (2010), Nicholls (2000), and Rios (2012).

11. A fuller discussion of these debates within folklore studies can be found in Bendix (1997), Dorson (1978), Filene (2000) and McLucas (1994).

12. Chatterji (2003) offers an incisive critique of the folk concept in India in the realms of art and religion, and Babiracki (1991), Allen (1998), Greene (2001), and Paige (2009) problematize the history of the folk concept in India, but all of these authors ultimately fall back on folk as an analytical category. Likewise, a number of historians of South Asia criticize the ideologies underpinning academic folklore studies—see Blackburn and Ramanujan (1986), Korom (1989, 2006), Naithani (2006b), Narayan (1993), Pande (1965), and Ramanujan (1993)—but most continue to employ "folk" as a descriptive category.

13. See, e.g., Feldman (2006), Filene (2000), Gelbart (2007), Mendoza (2008), and Miller (2010).

14. Scholars who address the relation between folk and classical include Babulkar (1964), Blackburn and Ramanujan (1986), Hansen (2014), Manuel (2015), Ramanujan (1993), Sinha (1970), and Verma (1987).

15. One methodology has been to explore the folk concept as one element in a larger evaluative and categorical dialectic, usually encompassing popular or classical musics. Matthew Gelbart offers a lucid historiography of the folk concept as it gradually was articulated in dialectical counterpoint with the concept of the classical in Western Europe (2007). He shows that these concepts became dichotomized only in the late eighteenth century as folk music was increasingly identified by origins rather than function and classical was increasingly identified by the notion of individual genius mediating between science and nature.

16. Sherinian (2014) asserts that Western scholars are at least partly to blame for the overvaluation of "classical arts"; in an effort to have legitimacy, Western scholars have gravitated to high classical Asian musics rather than nonclassical musics, thereby reiterating and reinforcing the views of their gurus.

Chapter 1. Genealogies of the Folk Concept in Colonial Uttarakhand

1. I am sensitive to the critique of Briggs and Naithani (2012) that folkloristics, contrary to the genealogies of Dorson (1968) and Chakrabarty (2000), should not be understood as having been invented in Europe and then exported wholesale to the colonies; rather, folkloristics as a discipline and folk as a concept were constituted through the asymmetrical and power-laden relationships forged by colonial empire. Nonetheless, the "infrastructure of the study of folklore" was developed in metropoles and then imposed in the colonies in the form of Eurocentric categories, theories, and methods (Briggs and Naithani 2012: 247).

2. My approach in this chapter owes much to Matthew Gelbart's (2007) research on the ideological roots of the folk concept across Europe, both preceding and following the first attempt to define the word *folk* by William John Thoms in 1846.

3. For a detailed historical account of the development of folklore studies in India, see Blackburn and Ramanujan (1986), Narayan (1993), and Vidyarthi (1973).

4. See, e.g., Bendix (1997), Bohlman (1988), Dorson (1968), Gelbart (2007), Harker (1985), McLucas (1994), and Wiora (1971).

5. See, e.g., Blackburn and Ramanujan (1986), Hauser (2002), Korom (1989, 2006), Narayan (1993), and Pande (1965).

6. My framing of the genealogy of the folk concept in these terms is indebted to Amanda Weidman's explication of the dual legacy of "classical music" ideology as rooted in both Euro-American concepts and an essential Indianness (2006). Also relevant to this discussion are Allen (1998), Bakhle (2005), Farrell (1997), Schofield (2010), and Subramanian (2006).

7. T. Pande (1965) reviews the various attempts by Indian folklorists to come up with an indigenous (national) term that would be equivalent to *folklore*.

8. For discussions of the changing significance of marga and desi, see Allen (1998: 24), Babiracki (1991), Coomaraswamy (1937), Parmar (1977), Narayan (1993: 185), and Schofield (2010).

9. Coomaraswamy elaborates, writing that *desi* and *lok-a* "are not merely terms that could be derogatively employed by city people or courtiers to countrymen in general, but [are terms] that could be employed by dwellers in the city of God or in any holy land with reference to those beyond the pale. . . . From the Brahmans' point of view (who are 'gods on earth'), whatever is geographically and/or qualitatively removed from an orthodox centre, from a Holy Land (such as Aryavarts) where the heavenly pattern is accurately imitated, will be at the same time geographically and spiritually 'provincial'; those are pre-eminently *desi* who are outer barbarians beyond the pale; and in this sense *desi is the equivalent of 'heathen'* or *'pagan'* in the primary sense of 'pertaining to the heaths or wastes,' as well as 'pagan' in the secondary sense of worldly or sentimental (materialistic)" (1937: 78–79, emphasis added). The musicologist P. Sambamoorthy was notably dismissive of the value of folk music (see Sherinian 2014: 44) and maintained that it was neither marga, which signified Vedic music, nor desi, which signified so-called art music.

10. For other descriptions of the animal-like qualities of those inhabiting the Himalayas and the popular field of zoocryptology, see Bishop (1988), "Folklore from India" (1914), and Williams (1992 [1874]: 31).

11. Much has been written about the perceived backwardness of Himalayan subjects in colonial and postcolonial contexts. See especially Berreman (1963: 322), Bharati (1978) and Moller (2003: 255).

12. See, e.g., Cumming (1884), Fraser (1982 [1820]: 67, 204, 209), and Walton (1989 [1910]: 80).

13. It is striking that the most distinctive musical legacy of the British army in the Indian Himalayas is the highland bagpipe, which was introduced by the former military men and is now a regular feature of hill bands performing at weddings and in festival contexts across Uttarakhand. See A. Alter (1998a).

14. Research by Bryant and Bryant expertly teases apart the various strands of the Aryan migration theory in the nineteenth and twentieth centuries. Taking us back to the roots of the folk concept, the authors remind us that J. G. Herder was one of the most prominent supporters of the theory that "the central point of the largest quarter of the Globe, the primitive mountains of Asia, prepared the first abode of the human race" (Bryant and Bryant 2001: 19).

15. The term *tribe* (translated in Hindi as *adivasi*) was initially used more or less synonymously with *nation* or *caste* to mark small communities living at the margins of Himalayan society, but by the late nineteenth century *tribe* had appeared on census forms to identify small groups evidencing some combination of "[distinct] cultural practices, geographic isolation, uniqueness of language and the nature of interaction between the 'tribal' community in question and outsiders" (Wolf 2001: 8).

16. See, e.g., Oakley's comments in G. D. Upreti (2003 [1894]: v–vii).

17. These reversals did little to dislodge a habitus rooted in centuries of state-enforced discrimination. In the 1970s Fanger noted that several Dom families, although they owned agricultural land, were reluctant to take up the plow because of the persistence of discriminatory attitudes (1980: 224).

18. See also Atkinson (1973 [1882]: 700) and a summary of such perspectives in Leavitt 1992. In South India, colonial administrators occasionally counterbalanced Brahmanical biases with pro-Dravidian, subaltern perspectives; see Gover (2002 [1871]).

19. Blunt wrote in 1931 that Dom castes from the mountains bore no relation to the "tribal" Doms found in the plains; nevertheless, the former so feared association with the latter that they repudiated the label (2010 [1931]: 143).

20. See also Strachey (1851: 83), who wrote that the Khasa "were a race of Hindus very lax in the practice of their faith."

21. See L. D. Joshi (1929, 1984 [1856]) and M. C. Joshi (1990).

22. Polyandry was a topic of a great deal of speculation for colonial ethnographers. See Berreman (1983), Ibbetson (1883), Mann (1996: 59–70), D. N. Majumdar (1960), and Saklani (1998).

23. These social evolutionary theories remained popular into the middle of the twentieth century. See Foster (1953) and Redfield (1947).

24. This parallels the experience of peasant populations in western Europe in the seventeenth and eighteenth centuries, who were dispossessed by new strictures on land use during the transition from dynastic monarchy to territorial nationalism. As Abrahams writes, "there are manifest ironies in this process of sentimentalizing a way of life only after those who once practiced it have been taken from the land" (1993: 4).

25. The amount of published folklore originating in Garhwal and Kumaon appears to be much less than that found in many other Himalayan regions. Fisher (1985) attributes this dearth of scholarship in the central Himalayas to the Orientalist fascination with more remote, nonliterate, and inaccessible populations living in the eastern or western Himalayas.

26. See Fiol (2011b) and Berreman (1961) for an overview of these rituals, as well as Ahmed (1891, 1:128), Cockburn (1894, 3:205–206), Fraser (1982 [1820]), Grierson (1968 [1916]: 1), Harcourt (1871: 318), Moorcroft and Trebeck (1841, 1:17), "Mountaineer" (1860: 41), Rose (1894: 4:55–57), Russell (1975 [1916]: 289), Traill (1991–1992 [1828]: 45), and Woodruff (1947: 50).

27. See Powell (1914) and Oddie (1995).

28. See Naithani (2006b) for a parallel example of collaboration between the British folklorist William Crooke and his Indian "assistant" Pandit Ram Gharib Chaube.

Chapter 2. Mohan Upreti and the Assimilation of Folk Music in Nehruvian India

1. Himanshu Joshi, Mohan Upreti's nephew and a singer in the popular band Indian Ocean, has published comprehensive resources about the Kumaoni Ramlila under the name OpeRama. Performed excerpts are available on his website: http://www.himanshu joshi.me/operama/audiogallery.html#sthash.Hs8P74Ma.6b4sqSMr.dpbs.

2. For a variety of reasons, including poor financial management, the center closed in 1943. The Uttarakhand State Directorate of Culture is now planning to reopen the Uday Shankar Academy in Falsima, about seven kilometers from Almora.

3. Ramanujan (1993) offers one of the earliest and most influential discussions of a dialectical relation between folk and classical traditions in India. Matthew Gelbart (2007) documents the process whereby ideas about folk culture in eighteenth- and nineteenth-century Europe emerged in dialectical relation to the "classical" within the realms of literature, music, and art.

4. See, e.g., Bakhle (2005), Kippen (2006), Kobayashi (2003), and Powers (1992).

5. Blackburn and Ramanujan (1986: 20), Subramanian (2006: 362), Paige (2009: 58), and Shernian (2014) all provide examples of negative assessments of folk music.

6. The term *folk culture* has frequently (and confusingly) been used to encompass both tribal and low-status, nontribal communities in India. As Babiracki notes, distinguishing tribal from nontribal communities has long been a highly politicized and dynamic process, not least because such labels give community members different levels of access to employment and educational benefits from the state. She nonetheless points out that "regional folk musics tend to unite diverse populations over a large geographic area, while indigenous tribal musics are confined to one linguistic and cultural group" (1991: 75).

7. Gelbart documents a similar process occurring in Great Britain with the Scots, whose folk style was eventually celebrated as a national model after many decades of being described as backwards (2007).

8. It is interesting that this dual motivation to identify with the local while rejecting the foreign was shared by many early-twentieth-century folklorists in Britain. As Ralph

Vaughn Williams remarked, "[T]he knowledge of our folk-songs did not so much discover for us something new, but uncovered for us something which had been hidden by foreign matter" (quoted in Van der Linden 2013: 5).

9. An interesting parallel for this kind of identification through musical impersonation is Rabindranath Tagore's play *Phalguni* (1916), in which he cast himself as a Baul singer.

10. Bhagwat Upreti, personal communication, May 29, 2014, New Delhi.

11. Today there are more than four thousand registered Uttarakhandi organizations in Delhi alone. This number is an indication of the continuing growth of urban migrant classes and the desire for state and nongovernmental institutional support to fund cultural activities.

12. In all, thirty or so Garhwal and Kumaoni gramophone records were produced in the late 1940s and 1950s; sadly, I have not been able to locate any that are in playable condition.

13. In an article about the development of *adhunik geet* ("modern song") in Nepal in the 1970s and 1980s, Grandin primarily credits the patronage of state-funded radio with "opening up the possibility [for] artists [to] make their music for the artistically most qualified 'audience' possible—their own peers—whereas the national audience [became] no more than eavesdroppers" (2005: 240). Uttarakhandi radio programs on AIR from the 1950s to the 1970s functioned in a similar way, allowing folk forms to evolve in a protected environment in which songwriters and folk enthusiasts essentially performed for each other (see Fiol 2012a).

14. Representative folkloric publications from this period include Govind Chatak's *Garhwali Lok Gathae* [Garhwali Folk Epics] (1958), Mohan Upreti's "Folk-Dances of Kumaon and Garhwal" (1959), D. N. Majumdar's *Himalayan Polyandry* (1960), M. L. Babulkar's *Garhwali Lok-Sahitya ka Bibechanatmak Adhyayan* [A Critical Study of Garhwali Folk Literature] (1964), and Anoop Chandola's *Folk Drumming in the Himalayas* (1977); see also Upadhyaya (1954).

15. For cross-cultural examples of state-supported folkloric ensembles, see Buchanan (1995: 392), Shay (1999), and Rios (2012).

Chapter 3. Turning Dying Folk into Living Folk

1. Narendra Singh Negi, personal interview, August 11, 2005, Pauri Garhwal.

2. Hughes notes with irony that songs of labor were thus transformed into songs of leisure for the wealthier middle class and that "the folk" were the ones being parodied in folk music recordings (2002: 466). There would have been little reason for middle-class Indians to identify as the folk prior to the nationalist movement; the folk were more significant as ideal types that reminded middle-class Indians of their moral and cultural superiority.

3. Stephen Alter's book *Sacred Waters* (2001) eloquently describes the transitions in the pilgrimage experience and economy caused by road building.

4. For a more detailed investigation of All India Radio and the discourse of folk music in Uttarakhand, see Fiol (2012a).

5. Negi interview, August 11, 2005.

6. Unfortunately, few of Anuragi's writings (1961, 1983–1984) about Garhwali music have ever been published. His authoritative manuscript *Nand Nandini*, about the enigmatic

Dhol Sagar treatise, was never published, although it purportedly became the basis of Shivanand Nautiyal's published account (1981).

7. Anuragi was a source of inspiration to a number of upper-caste musicians and folklorists with whom I interacted. Tragically, he passed away in his late thirties.

8. Madhuri Barthwal, personal interview, June 2, 2005, Najibabad, Uttar Pradesh.

9. Negi, interview, April 11, 2005.

10. Ibid.

11. Ibid.

12. Bhol jab phir rat khoolali, dharti ma nai paudh jamali, puranu dali thangra hweki, nai lagulyun saru dyala. Mi ta niraulu mera bhoolaon, tum dagiri mera geet rala (N. S. Negi 2002: 22).

13. Negi interview, April 11, 2005.

14. Narendra Singh Negi, personal interview, June 25, 2010, Pauri Garhwal.

15. Ibid.

16. These were *Ghar Jawain* (1986), *Kauthig* (1987), *Bantwaru* (1992), *Beti-Bwari* (1996), *Chakrachal* (1997), *Aunsi ki Rat* (2004), and *Meri Ganga Holi Te Memu Ali* (2006).

17. Narendra Singh Negi, *Cali Bhai Motor Cali: Uttaranchali Chitrageet*. T-Series VCD (CDVNF-01/3893). This video may be accessed online: https://www.youtube.com/watch?v=OyNnQI1bCzg.

18. *Nyoli*, the name of a Kumaoni folk song genre and verse form, takes its name from a female bird who sings when alone, offering the appearance of searching for her mate. It is no coincidence that such songs, like *khuder geet* (see chapter 5), deal mainly with themes of longing and separation.

19. In addition to cassettes, several books of Negi's song lyrics have been published (N. S. Negi 1999, 2002, 2009), and his lyrics have also been widely distributed in small pamphlets. *Akshat*, a Festschrift on Negi's music and life compiled by Kirti Navani and Ganesh Kughshal (2000), contains a sample of articles about and testimonials to Negi's contribution to Uttarakhandi music.

20. Shepherds in Himachal Pradesh often play small bamboo flutes (murli) on extended, high-altitude treks. The cousin of the bansuri, the twin-flute (algoja) was once frequently played by Baddi performers in Uttarakhand (Petshali 2002), but in my experience it has become largely obsolete. Some of the reasons for the decline of flute varieties in the central Himalayas have been examined by A. Alter (2014: 65–79). In some cases, live flute performance may have decreased as a result of the incursion of other kinds of popular music in the region; in other cases, popular ballads (e.g., *Jeetu Bagdwal*) linking flute playing to dangerous organ-stealing fairies (*pari, ancheri*) located in high-elevation meadows and forests may have played a role in dissuading live performance.

21. P. Kumar (2000) and Husain (1995) offer two of the most nuanced accounts of the Uttarakhand movement.

22. I gratefully acknowledge the assistance of Dr. Datta Ram Purohit for helping me translate a number of Garhwali idioms used in this song.

23. Narendra Singh Negi, *Utha Jaga Uttarakhandyu* (in Garhwali and Kumaoni): Rama, 1994.

24. Narendra Singh Negi, personal interview, August 13, 2005, Pauri Garhwal.

25. Well-known examples of Indian artists-turned-politicians include Bhupen Hazarika in Assam, Kabir Suman in Bengal, M. G. Ramachandran and Jayalalithaa Jayaram in Tamil Nadu, and Chiranjeevi in Andhra Pradesh.

26. See Fiol (2011a) for a musical analysis of this album and a discussion of the feedback loop connecting village-based and urban performances of songs associated with the goddess Nandadevi.

27. This not-so-subtle allusion to Tiwari's notorious womanizing foreshadowed his eventual downfall as a politician. After losing the election in Uttarakhand, Tiwari became governor of Andhra Pradesh in 2007 but was sacked in 2010 following the release of a sex video showing the eighty-six-year old in a sex romp with three young women. This scandal rejuvenated the popularity of "Nauchami Narayana," which has sold more than nine hundred thousand copies (Gusain 2010), and at the time of writing has been viewed nearly three hundred thousand times on Youtube.

28. For a more detailed analysis of "Nauchami Narayana" and its political repercussions, see Fiol (2012b).

29. Negi interview, April 11, 2005.

30. Such criticisms have been echoed by the folklorist Anoop Chandola (1977: 16–17).

31. Negi interview, August 11, 2005.

32. Negi interview, April 11, 2005.

33. Narendra Singh Negi, *Nau Durga Naraini (Uttarakhandi Devi Bhajan)*. T-Series VCD (CDVNF 01/5563), 2006.

34. One of many recent songs rooted in a traditional dhol-damaun rhythm is "Hay Ambika" by Sahab Singh Ramola and Akanksha Ramola (SDe Productions, 2016): https://www.youtube.com/watch?v=JKeRLGcOhmA&spfreload=10.

Chapter 4. *The Folk Sound without the Folk Body*

1. As mentioned in chapter 1, many Shilpkar artists in Uttarakhand have dropped the caste surname Das and replaced it with a generic surname such as Lal. This trend was encouraged within reformist and anti-untouchability movements popular in the 1930s and later in the 1970s and 1980s.

2. I am indebted to Datta Ram Purohit for initially connecting me to Sohan Lal, who was also an informant for the ethnomusicologist Andrew Alter (2008: 100).

3. Sohan Lal, personal interview, March 2, 2007, Srinagar, Garhwal.

4. *Disabhent* is a custom whereby a drummer is expected to visit each outmarried woman originally from his village, bringing her gifts and news of her family and friends.

5. Anuragi (1983–1984) and Shiv Prasad Dabral (1989) are particularly insistent about the authority of this elusive text. Andrew Alter is more skeptical, noting that the *Dhol Sagar* may in fact have existed as an "oral tradition of knowledge—memorized texts and/or drum patterns—that was always fragmentary" (2014: 104).

6. One precedent for this kind of folk orchestra is the Choliya ensemble found in some parts of Kumaon, which includes dancer-acrobats and a range of indigenous horns, drums, and bagpipes.

7. Narendra Singh Negi, personal interview, April 11, 2005, Pauri Garhwal.

8. Mayur Nichani, personal interview (in English), March 1, 2005, Dehradun.

9. For example, Sohan Lal and Bharat Lal, *Kalnath Bhairaun: Mandan* (Garhwali): Noida: T-Series, Super Cassettes Industries Ltd., SGHNC 01/33 (1997); Sohan Lal and Bharat Lal, *Naurata Mandan: Garhwali Chitrageet*. T-Series VCD CDVNF 01/5071 (2006).

10. Vikram Rawat, personal interview, July 15, 2005, Delhi.

11. Unnamed recording engineer, personal interview, February 7, 2005, Delhi.

12. Subhash Pande, personal interview, July 14, 2005, East Delhi.

13. Negi interview, April 11, 2005.

14. Sohan Lal and Bharat Lal et al., *Mandan-Barta-Jagar*. T-Series mp3 album (138), 2003.

15. Sohan Lal, personal interview, March 3, 2007, Tehri Garhwal.

16. These limitations prompted Narendra Singh Negi and Chander Singh Rahi to independently experiment with the dhol's design by adding nut-adjustable clamps that allow for more precise tuning. To date, however, these modified instruments have been infrequently used for recordings.

17. Gajendra Rana, personal interview, July 14, 2005, East Delhi.

18. Pande interview, July 14, 2005.

19. Musical examples 4.1–4.8 are representations of the patterns played simultaneously by the tabla and the dholak during a recording session on July 14, 2005. The bottom and top staves correspond to the left-hand (Percussion 2) and right-hand patterns (Percussion 1) of the two drums, respectively. I have simplified the tonal variations of the left-hand parts (*duggi*) as either high or low; the right-hand parts are simplified into combinations of four signs: ♪ represents the *tun*, or open and resonant sound of the tabla; the ♪ represents the *kat*, or closed sound produced on the dholak or tabla; and the ♪♪ represents the *ti ta* sound produced by striking the center of the drum and then the outer rim.

20. After the formation of the Department of Homeland Security in 2002, U.S. visas for international artists of most backgrounds were subject to increased scrutiny and profiling. See Rohter (2012).

21. Examples are Ramesh (2006) and Toyama (2012).

Chapter 5. Professional Female Singers and the Gendering of Folk

1. Benjamin Filene notes a similar tendency in Appalachian music research (2000: 20).

2. These studies include Bradby (1993), Diamond (2010), Impey (1992), Jassal (2007), Meintjes (2003), and Scales (2012).

3. *Ghughuti Na Basa* (Kumaoni), 1975–1980, K-Series 7005, vol. 1 (cassette); 2005, K-Series 7005, vol. 1 (VCD). This video may be accessed at https://www.youtube.com/watch?v=S6WMiNLanNw.

4. In her ethnography of *pakharu* songs from Kangra, Kirin Narayan (1997) shows how male absence is not simply an ethnographic fact but a multivocal sign in women's songs that may stand for a range of emotional and contextual factors. In the few performances of khuder geet that I have observed in rural Garhwal, women similarly express a range of emotions. Here I am primarily interested in exploring the stereotypical interpretations of khuder geet that circulate in mass-mediated representations.

5. The narrative of the plains-based hero entering the mountains and being seduced by the tribal girl is an oft-repeated narrative strategy in many Hindi films, including *Barsaat*

(1949), *Madhumati* (1958), *Junglee* (1961), *Kashmir Ki Kali* (1964), *Jaanwar* (1965), *Jab Jab Phool Khile* (1965), *Phir Wohi Dil Laya Hoon* (1963), *Aarzoo* (1965), *Himalaya ki God Main* (1965), *Road to Sikkim* (1969), *Ram Teri Ganga Maili* (1985), *Dil Se* (1998), *Gharwali Baharwali* (1998), and *Taal* (1999). See Fiol (2016), Kabir (2005), and Lutgendorf (2005) for analyses of filmic representations of the Himalayas.

6. The literature concerning North Indian music and communities of hereditary musicians is replete with references to Shiva and Parvati. See, e.g., Bakx (1998), Divekar and Tribhuwan (2001), Merchant (2003), and Reck (1972).

7. This individual will never complete the hair-cutting ceremony (*mundan*), one of the central life-cycle ceremonies of a Hindu, and will only shave his head up to the height of the temples following the death of a family member.

8. Darshani Devi, personal communication, June 22, 2007, Duni village, Tehri Garhwal.

9. See Fiol (2011a) for a more detailed description of these fertility rituals.

10. A number of my field recordings of Baddi songs can be accessed through the Smithsonian Folkways website: http://www.folkways.si.edu/baddi-geet-songs-of-the-community-of-garhwal/india-world/music/album/smithsonian.

11. Elsewhere I have written extensively about the Baddi community and their experience of different forms of liminality (Fiol 2011b). Other scholarship concerning Baddi musical and social life includes Berreman (1961), Cox (1993), Gairola and Oakley (1977 [1935]), Purohit (2004), and Shukla and Purohit (2012).

12. See Allen (1997), Babiracki (2004), Gupta (2002), Maciszewski (2001), Morcom (2013), Soneji (2012), Tewari (1974), and Weidman (2003).

13. One example she offered was Narendrs Singh Negi's song "Teru Macholi," from the album *Naucami Narayana* (2006), https://www.youtube.com/watch?v=BjXh5c15Nhc.

14. *Pahari Bedu Geet: Garhwali Vilupt Hoti Sanskriti* [Songs of the Mountain Beda: The Disappearing Culture of Garhwal], 2006. Srinagar, Garhwal: Nirula Traders (Park Label), 2006 (VCD).

15. One example is Mamta Dildaar's song "Meri Ringmati" (2012) on the T-Series Regional YouTube channel, https://www.youtube.com/watch?v=ySOrdcoCHBk.

16. This clip can be accessed at https://www.youtube.com/watch?v=QfWCD2rEE08.

17. Shiv Charan, personal communication, August 15, 2005, Duni village, Tehri Garhwal.

18. Lata Mangeshkar is the best-known Hindi-language playback singer; the *Guinness Book of World Records* for 1974 credited her with recording twenty-five thousand songs since the late 1940s. Although this figure is in dispute, it is a reasonable estimate. Her high-pitched vocal aesthetic became the dominant sound of Hindi film music, and by extension, many vernacular styles as well.

19. This observation was confirmed by the ethnomusicologist Noe Dinnerstein, a specialist in Ladakhi music. Personal communication, November 11, 2015.

20. Mayur Nichani, personal communication, March 1, 2005, Dehradun.

21. See Fiol (2013a) for a lengthier ethnographic description of gender dynamics within the acoustic and social relations of studio production.

22. For an example, see the recent song "Khudeni Na Rayee" by Rakesh Panwar and Meena Rana, https://www.youtube.com/watch?v=oDjz9U4hIyM (Riwaz Music, 2016).

23. Anuradha Nirala, personal interview, August 31, 2011, East Delhi.

24. Sexually suggestive Uttarakhandi geet abound on YouTube, including sexually explicit videos that have been made to accompany traditional folk songs like "Runjun Barkha"; see, e.g., https://www.youtube.com/watch?v=QjJES6OHHns.

25. Karen Gaul (2002) has offered a helpful analysis of the different types of mobility in the central Himalayas (local mobility for work and leisure, intraregional transhumance, and interregional education or job-related mobility), arguing that women's social positions and the spaces they occupy are mutually constitutive.

26. Chakori Devi, personal interview, June 18, 2007, Tehri Garhwal.

Chapter 6. *The Goddess Plugged In*

1. Pritam Bhartwan, *Naraini Ma Bhavani: Jagar ev. Bhajan* (Uttarakhandi), T-Series VCD (CDVNF 01/5601), 2006. This video can be accessed at the following link: https://www.youtube.com/watch?v=reJUJHLbPSc.

2. Cassette recordings of jagar by hereditary gurus Dilawar Singh Jagari (father of Chander Singh Rahi) and Devraj Rangila began appearing in the late 1980s. Gurus who recorded commercially in the 1990s included the Garhwhalis Daulat Ram, Devendra Kumar, Sohan Lal, Sudama Lal, Sanu Sanam, and Kulanand Juyal and the Kumaonis Sundar Lal, Ramesh Lal, and Gopal Das. After 2000, Nain Singh Rawal, Daulat Ram, and Pritam Bhartwan led the effort to record jagar on VCD and online streaming sites.

3. Published accounts of jagar include Agarwal (2005), A. Alter (2008), Chatak (2000), Fanger (1990), Fiol (2010), Leavitt (1997), K. Majumdar (1996), Mazumdar (1998), Nautiyal (1991), B. Rao (1992–1993), Sax (2009), and K. L. Upreti (1990).

4. Possession rituals having similar musical and social features in other parts of South Asia have been described by Gellner (1994), Gold (1988), Holmberg (1984), Kapferer (1991), Ortner (1978), Roche (2001), and Wadley (1976), among others.

5. Sateshwar Himalaya, personal interview, April 17, 2007, Chamoli, Garhwal.

6. Sax (1991: 182–195) describes a dispute concerning the form of sacrifice during the Nanda Devi Raj Jat of 1987.

7. The charge of bringing sterility has particular significance in the context of Gandhi's Emergency campaign (1975–1977), which was widely criticized for a program of forcibly sterilizing the poor.

8. Another instance of invoking jagar as a form of political protest is Narendra Singh Negi's best-selling song "Nauchami Narayana." This song is briefly discussed in chapter 3 and is analyzed in detail in Fiol 2012b.

9. See http://www.news18.com/videos/uttarakhand/uttarakhand-tourism-minister-pitches-for-revival-of-jagar-music-158997.html

10. The recordings are *Uttarakhand Sanskriti ke Svar* (TV-Giridoot, 2003) and *Uttranchal Ke Jagar Aur Dait Sanghar* (T-Series, 2006).

11. A. Alter (2008: 180–214) offers a detailed analysis of one guru's flexible use of these vocal delivery styles during the performance of a panwara. The panwara is musically indistinguishable from the jagar, but the function is to narrate the epics of ancient warriors and royal lineages, not to bring about corporeal possession.

12. In Kumaon the jagar for Bholanath, Ganganath, and Dana Golu are exclusively held indoors, and they are officiated by Brahmin or Rajput gurus and accompanied on the dholak. The worship of these devtao can be linked to their narratives of injustice. Bholanath and Ganganath, both disinherited sons of Chand kings, were cast out of the house and later murdered on the orders of their own family; their worship by Brahmin or Rajput gurus may be linked to their royal status (as well as the high-caste guilt transferred by these murders), and the performance of dholak may be linked to the pollution associated with their being killed by a Shilpkar (the killing of Ganganath, so the story goes, was carried out by a *lohar*, or blacksmith).

13. Although hurka and thali are generally played indoors, there are exceptions. In the Kaub region of Chamoli District, for example, hurka and thali are exclusively played outdoors. In fact, during my recording of a mock jagar there, one guru intentionally played hurka inside his home as a means of deterring the devi-devtao from being attracted to the music and possessing someone.

14. Generally speaking, rituals directed by Shilpkar gurus seem to draw from a greater number of spirits and devi-devtao. Chandola (1987) notes, for example, that the Narsingh myth in Garhwal as performed by a Brahmin guru strictly adheres to the Puranic version, whereas the rituals directed by Shilpkar gurus call on avatars of Devi, Narsingh (Vishnu), and Nath sectarianism without clear delineation.

15. Compare with Marcus (1995), who discusses the effects of *bhajan* commercialization in similar terms (e.g., standardization of instrumentation, Sanskritization).

16. Narendra Singh Negi et al., *Jagar: Bhag 1 & 2*. T-Series VCD (CDVNF 01/5137 and 01/5138), 2006.

17. The video at the following link is representative of the many videos of urban all-night jagran found on Youtube: https://www.youtube.com/watch?v=zKbV4nP3wH0.

18. Although I do not focus on reception in this chapter, elsewhere (Fiol 2010) I adapt Erving Goffman's frame analysis and Edward Bruner's critique of authenticity to analyze the reception of recorded jagar.

19. The first video I have identified in which Bhartwan plays hurka is "Gyanu Mala Bhima Katheit (Panwara)" on the album *Gailya Dhanuli* (T-Series, 2005). From 2009 onward most of his videos show him performing hurka ("Jagar—Goril Devta" on *Bhana* [Rama, 2009], "Jagar—Bhairau Devta" on *Hiya Parani* [Vasu Music, 2009]). The first video in which he performs on the dhol is "Jagar (Bali Vasudanta Arjun)" on the album *Saj* (T-Series, 2013).

20. Narendra Singh Negi, *Nau Durga Naraini (Uttarakhandi Devi Bhajan)*, T-Series VCD (CDVNF 01/5563), 2006. This video can be accessed at https://www.youtube.com/watch?v=xA-vp-KtFjU.

21. See Erndl (1991), Greene (1999), Lutgendorf (1990), Mankekar (2002), Marcus (1995), Qureshi (1999), Wadley and Babb (1995), and Schultz (2013).

Glossary

Hindi, Garhwali, Kumaoni, and Jaunsari words are romanized throughout the book. The translations are approximate and correspond with their widespread utilization in Uttarakhand.

Arya Samaj. Hindu reformist movement of the late nineteenth and early twentieth centuries that sought to promote social equality and the infallibility of the Vedas.

asthai-antara. The primary and secondary musical themes, respectively, in many varieties of North Indian song.

Baddi. Caste of itinerant performers who appear in pairs consisting of a man who sings and plays dholki and a woman who sings and dances.

baja. The word for instruments in general and specifically the harmonium; any rhythmic pattern played on dhol and damaun.

Bajgi. Caste of hereditary drummer-tailors in the central Himalayas who perform on the dhol-damaun; called Auji in some regions.

bajuband. Free-rhythm, improvised, and often dialogic song form in Garhwal that traditionally is performed between two people cutting fodder in the jungle.

bansuri. Transverse bamboo flute.

barat. Bridegroom's party.

barhai. Rhythm of invocation of the gods performed on the dhol and damaun.

bedwart. Rope-sliding fertility ritual performed by the Baddi.

bhajan. Hindu devotional song.

bhankora. Long natural trumpet made of copper and played in Garhwal.

bhaun. Elongated vowel that accompanists sing as a continuation of vocal phrases during performances of jagar and panwara.

Bhotiya. Group of ethnolinguistic communities found in northern borderlands of Uttarakhand that once supplied trade between Tibet and India.

binai. Kumaoni term for mouth harp.

birti. Set of inherited villages in which a Bajgi performs for his patrons.

bol. Lit., "to speak"; the mnemonic syllables used to represent drum strokes.

Brahmin. Highest-level caste group whose members are often religious officiates.

Chaiti. Referring to the season of spring; also a vocal and drumming gender associated with spring.

Chand. Medieval dynasty located in present-day Kumaon from approximately 700 to 1200 CE..

dadwar. Garhwali term for the system of ritual and economic exchanges between clients and patrons; referred to as the jajmani system more generally in North India.

damaun. Shallow kettledrum that is paired with the dhol and played throughout the central Himalayas.

daunr. Shallow hourglass-shaped drum accompanied by the thali and used in ritual contexts in Garhwal.

desi. Colloquially, "of the plains"; also a Sanskrit term for arts with a more secular, humanist, and contemporary orientation.

devi. Goddess; a feminine form of the divine in Hinduism.

devta. God; the masculine form of the divine in Hinduism.

dhol. Double-headed barrel drum that is paired with the damaun and played throughout the central Himalayas.

dholki. Small cylindrical two-headed drum played by the Baddi of the central Himalayas.

dhunyal. Set of rhythmic patterns used to propitiate and summon the gods in ritual settings.

doli. Bride's palanquin.

Dom. Derogatory term for a person of lower-caste rank.

Garhwali. The language and people belonging to the western division of Uttarakhand.

gatha. Sung epic.

geet. Song.

ghasyari. Grass cutter; genre of women's song performed while cutting grass.

Gurkha. An ethnolinguistic category in Nepal; the Nepali kingdom that ruled over a large swath of the central Himalayas from approximately 1790 to 1815; one of the quintessential martial races reified in British India through the formation of Gurkha regiments.

guru. Spiritual teacher; a healer and performer in the context of jagar rituals.

hurka. Hourglass-shaped, double-headed pressure drum; a smaller variant is known as the hurki.

Hurkiya. Caste of hereditary performers associated with the hurki.

jagar. Possession rituals in which gods are awakened (from the Hindi root "jag") in the bodies of human mediums; the song genre used in such rituals.

jagariya. The drummer, singer, and healer for jagar rituals, also referred to as the guru.

jagran. All-night ritual spectacles that have become popular since the late twentieth century across urban North India.

jajmani. System of economic and social obligations between caste groups; in Garhwal, the Brahmins' role of performing ritual duties.

jati. Occupational caste or community.

Jaunsari. A distinct linguistic and ethnic category found in the Jaunsar region in the northwestern corner of Garhwal.

kalakar. Artist.

Katyuri. Medieval dynasty in Garhwal and Kumaon from approximately 700 to 1200 CE.

kaherva. Eight-beat rhythmic pattern common to vernacular musics across North India.

Khasa. Caste designation for someone descended from one of the early Aryan "races" of Uttarakhand, who were believed to maintain ancient, pre-Brahmanical rites and customary laws; also pronounced Khasiya.

khemta. Six-beat rhythmic pattern common to vernacular musics across North India.

khuder geet. Genre of love song associated with the anguish and longing in a woman's life.

Kumaoni. The language and people belonging to the eastern division of Uttarakhand.

laman. Genre of love song from the Jaunsar and Rawain regions of Garhwal.

lang. Rope-swinging fertility ritual performed by the Baddi.

lok geet. Folk song.

lok sanskriti. Folk culture.

mait. Native or natal village.

mangal geet. Lit., "auspicious songs"; usually songs performed during weddings and other rites of passage.

marga. Sanskrit term for arts with a religious and philosophical orientation.

mashakbaja. Bagpipes.

mela. Fair or festival.

nada. Primordial sound within Hindu metaphysics.

naggara. Large kettledrum.

naubat. Set of drum rhythms that marks the auspicious time for ritual action.

nyoli. Free-rhythm improvised song form in Kumaon performed while cutting fodder in the forest or taking animals out to graze.

Pahari. Lit., "of the mountains.".

paswa. Human medium for divine possession.

panwara. Heroic epic or ballad.

puja. Worship.

raga. Melodic framework for improvisation within Hindustani (North Indian) music.

raja. King.

Rajput. Most numerous and economically dominant caste group in Uttarakhand.

Ramlila. Theatrical enactment of scenes from the Ramayana epic.

ransingha. S-shaped natural horn.

sanskara. Rite of passage in a Hindu's life.

shabd. Lit., "word"; a virtuosic and semi-improvised item in dhol-damaun repertoire.

Shiva. Member of the triumvirate of supreme Hindu deities.

Shilpkar. Lit., "artisan"; a member of lower-status, hereditary artisan caste (e.g., blacksmith, barber, drummer-tailor, or tanner).

tabla. Pair of hand drums associated with Hindustani art music.

tala. Cyclical framework for rhythmic improvisation within Hindustani (North Indian) music.

tandi. Round dance and song genre from western Garhwal.

thadya. Round dance and song genre from Garhwal.

thali. Bronze plate turned over and struck with two sticks to accompany the hurka and daunr.

Bibliography

Abrahams, R. (1993). Phantoms of Romantic Nationalism in Folkloristics. *Journal of American Folklore, 106*(419), 3–37.

Agrawal, C. M. (2005). Golu Devata's Jagar: Based on Folklore. *Journal of the Meerut University History Alumni, 5*, 150–152.

Ahmed, A. (1891.) Garhwal—Rope-Riding—Propitiation of Mahadeva. *North Indian Notes and Queries, 1*, 128.

Alavi, S. (1995). *The Sepoys and the Company: Tradition and Transition in Northern India, 1770–1830*. Delhi: Oxford University Press.

Allen, M. H. (1997). Rewriting the Script for South Indian Dance. *The Drama Review, 41*(3), 63–100.

Allen, M. H. (1998). Tales Tunes Tell: Deepening the Dialogue between "Classical" and "Non-Classical" in the Music of India. *Yearbook for Traditional Music, 30*, 22–52.

Alter, A. (1998a). Garhwali Bagpipes: Syncretic Processes in a North Indian Regional Musical Tradition. *Asian Music, 29*(1), 1–16.

Alter, A. (1998b). Negotiating Identity in the Garhwali Popular Cassette Industry. *South Asia, 21*(1), 109–122.

Alter, A. (2000). *Dancing the Gods: Power and Meaning in the Music of Garhwal, North India* (Doctoral dissertation). Monash University, Melbourne, Australia.

Alter, A. (2008). *Dancing with Devtas: Drums, Power and Possession in the Music of Garhwal, North India*. Surrey: Ashgate.

Alter, A. (2014). *Mountainous Sound Spaces: Listening to History and Music in the Uttarakhand Himalayas*. Delhi: Cambridge University Press.

Alter, S. (2011). *Sacred Waters: A Pilgrimage up the Ganges River to the Source of Hindu Culture*. San Diego, CA: Harcourt.

Anand, M. R. (1950). *The Indian Theatre* (Vol. 41). London: Dennis Dobson.

Anuragi, K. (1961). Garhwal aur Kumaon main Dhol ke Gunj [The Resonant Sound of the Dhol in Garhwal and Kumaon]. *Sangeet*, 17–20.

Anuragi, K. (1983–1984). Gorakhpanth ke Paripreksya men Dholsagar [The Gorakhpanth's View of the Dhol Sagar]. *Chhayanat, 20*, 43–45.

Archer, M. (1980). *Early Views of India: The Picturesque Journeys of Thomas and William Daniell, 1786–1794*. London: Thames and Hudson.

Atkinson, E. T. (1973 [1882]). *The Himalayan Gazeteer* (Vol. 2:1). Delhi: Cosmo.

Awasthy, G. C. (1965). *Broadcasting in India*. Bombay: Allied Publishers.

Babiracki, C. M. (1991). Tribal Music in the Study of Great and Little Traditions of Indian Music. In B. Nettl & P. Bohlman (Eds)., *Comparative Musicology and Anthropology of Music: Essays on the History of Ethnomusicology* (pp. 69–90). Chicago, IL: University of Chicago Press..

Babiracki, C. M. (2004). The Illusion of India's "Public" Dancers. In J. Bernstein (Ed.), *Women's Voices across Musical Worlds* (pp. 36–59). Boston, MA: Northeastern University Press.

Babiracki, C. M. (2008). Between Life History and Performance: Sundari Devi and the Art of Allusion. *Ethnomusicology, 52*(1), 1–30.

Babulkar, M. L. (1964). *Garhwali Lok-Sahitya ka Bibechanatmak Adhyayan* [A Critical Study of Garhwali Folk Literature]. Prayag: Hindi Sahitya Sammelan.

Bahadur, R. P. R. (1992). *Garhwal: Ancient and Modern*. Delhi: Vintage.

Bajeli, D. S. (2006). *Mohan Upreti: The Man and His Art*. New Delhi: National School of Drama.

Bakhle, J. (2005). *Two Men and Music*. New York, NY: Oxford University Press.

Bakx, P. (1998). *The Jew's Harp and the Hindu God Shiva: Into the Symbolism of Procreation*. Middelburg, The Netherlands: Stichting Antropodium.

Bausinger, H. (1990). *Folk Culture in a World of Technology*. Bloomington, IN: Indiana University Press.

Bayly, S. (1995). Caste and Race in the Colonial Ethnography of India. In P. Robb (Ed.), *The Concept of Race in South Asia* (pp. 165–218). Delhi: Oxford University Press.

Beaster-Jones, J. (2016). *Music Commodities, Markets, and Values: Music as Merchandise*. New York, NY: Routledge.

Bendix, R. (1997). *In Search of Authenticity: The Formation of Folklore Studies*. Madison, WI: University of Wisconsin Press.

Bennett, G. (1993). Folklore Studies and the English Rural Myth. *Rural History, 4*(1), 77–93.

Berlinerblau, J. (2001). Max Weber's Useful Ambiguities and the Problem of Defining "Popular Religion." *Journal of the American Academy of Religion, 69*(3), 605–626.

Berreman, G. D. (1960). Cultural Variability and Drift in the Himalayan Hills. *American Anthropologist, 62*(5), 774–794.

Berreman, G. D. (1961). Himalayan Rope-Sliding and Village Hinduism: An Analysis. *Southwest Journal of Anthropology, 17*(4), 326–342.

Berreman, G. D. (1963). *Hindus of the Himalayas: Ethnography and Change*. Oxford: Oxford University Press.

Berreman, G. D. (1971). The Brahamanical View of Caste. *Contributions to Indian Sociology, 5*, 16–23.

Berreman, G. D. (1983). The U. P. Himalaya: Culture, Cultures, and Regionalism. In O. P. Singh (Ed.), *The Himalaya: Nature, Man and Culture* (pp. 227–265). New Delhi: Rajesh Publications.

Bharati, A. (1978). Actual and Ideal Himalayas: Hindu Views of the Mountains. In J. F. Fisher (Ed.), *Himalayan Anthropology: The Indo-Tibetan Interface* (pp. 77–82). The Hague: Mouton.

Bhartwan, P. (2010). *Surj Kanthyon*. Dehradun: Winsar.

Bharucha, R. (1990). *Theatre and the World: Performance and the Politics of Culture*. London: Routledge.

Bharucha, R. (1998). *In the Name of the Secular: Contemporary Cultural Activism in India*. Calcutta: Oxford University Press.

Bhatia, N. (1997). Staging Resistance: The Indian People's Theatre Association. In L. Lowe & D. Lloyd (Eds.), *The Politics of Culture in the Shadow of Capital* (pp. 432–460). Durham, NC: Duke University Press.

Bhattacharya, A., M. Upreti, & S. Parmar (1967). Folk-Lore: Notes on the Forum on Preservation in Folk-Lore Studies. *Journal of the Sangeet Natak Akademi, 4*: 88–98.

Bigenho, Michelle. (2007). Bolivian Indigeneity in Japan: Folklorized Musical Performance. In M. de la Cadena & O. Starn (Eds.), *Indigenous Experience Today* (pp. 247–272). Oxford, UK: Berg.

Bishop, P. (1988). *The Myth of Shangri-La*. Berkeley, CA: University of California Press.

Blackburn, S. H. (1985). Death and Deification: Folk Cults in Hinduism. *History of Religions, 24*(3), 255–274.

Blackburn, S. H. (2003). *Print, Folklore, and Nationalism in Colonial South India*. Delhi: Permanent Black.

Blackburn, S. H., & A. K. Ramanujan (Eds.). (1986). *Another Harmony: New Essays on the Folklore of India*. Berkeley, CA: University of California Press.

Blunt, E. A. H. (2010 [1931]). *The Caste System of Northern India*. New Delhi: Isha Books.

Bohlman, P. (1988). *The Study of Folk Music in the Modern World*. Bloomington, IN: Indiana University Press.

Bradby, B. (1993). Sampling Sexuality: Gender, Technology and the Body in Dance Music. *Popular Music, 12*(2), 155–176.

Briggs, C. L., & S. Naithani. (2012). The Coloniality of Folklore: Towards a Multi-Genealogical Practice of Folkloristics. *Studies in History, 28*(2), 231–270.

Brown, K. (2006). The Social Liminality of Musicians: Case Studies from Mughal India and Beyond. *twentieth-century music, 3*(1): 13–49.

Bruce, C. G. (1910). *Twenty Years in the Himalaya*. London: Edward Arnold.

Bryant, E., & E. F. Bryant. (2001). *The Quest for the Origins of Vedic Culture: The Indo-Aryan Migration Debate*. New York, NY: Oxford University Press.

Buchanan, D. (1995). Metaphors of Power, Metaphors of Truth: The Politics of Music Professionalism in Bulgarian Folk Orchestras. *Ethnomusicology, 39*(30), 381–416.

Capila, A. (2002). *Images of Women in the Folk Songs of Garhwal Himalayas: A Participatory Research*. New Delhi: Concept.

Caplan, L. (1995). Marital Gurkhas: The Persistence of a British Military Discourse on "Race." In P. Robb (Ed.), *The Concept of Race in India* (pp. 260–281). Delhi: Oxford University Press.

Carroll, L. (1977). "Sanskritization," "Westernization," and "Social Mobility": A Reappraisal of the Relevance of Anthropological Concepts to the Social Historian of Modern India. *Journal of Anthropological Research 33*(4), 355–370.

Chakknatt, J. (2002). *Public Action and Religious Praxis: A Socio-religious Inquiry into Two Cases of Public Action in the Garhwal Region and Their Implications for the Self-understanding and Praxis of the Church*. New Delhi: Intercultural.

Chakrabarty, D. (2000). *Provincializing Europe: Postcolonial Thought and Historical Difference*. Princeton, NJ: Princeton University Press.

Chakraborty, S. (1999). *A Critique of Social Movements in India: Experiences of Chipko, Uttarakhand, and Fisherworker's Movement*. New Delhi: Indian Social Institute.

Chalmers, R. (2002). Pandits and Pulp Fiction: Popular Publishing and the Birth of Nepali Print Capitalism in Banaras. *Studies in Nepali History and Society, 7*(1), 35–97.

Chalmers, R. (2004). When Folk Culture Met Print Culture: Some Thoughts on the Commercialisation, Transformation and Propagation of Traditional Genres in Nepali. *Contributions to Nepalese Studies 31*(2): 243–256.

Chandola, A. (1977). *Folk Drumming in the Himalayas: A Linguistic Approach to Music*. New York, NY: AMS.

Chandola, A. (1987). Symbolism and Myth in Garhwali Religion: The Hot Ladle Licking Ritual. In M. K. Raha (Ed.), *The Himalayan Heritage* (pp. 189–199). Delhi: Gyan.

Chatak, G. (1958). *Garhwali Lok Gathaen* [Garhwali Folk Ballads]. Dehradun: Mohini Prakashan.

Chatak, G. (2000). *Garhwali Lokgeet* [Garhwali Folksongs]. New Delhi: Sahitya Akademi.

Chatterjee, M. (2011). Ethnic Folk Music Finding Echoes in Capital. *Indo Asian News Service*.

Chatterji, R. (2003). The Category of Folk. In Veena Das (Ed.), *The Oxford India Companion to Sociology and Anthropology* (pp. 567–597). New Delhi: Oxford University Press.

Clark, S. H., & L. Schofield (Eds.). (2002). *Practicing Religion in the Age of Media*. New York, NY: Columbia University Press.

Clarke, H. (1881). The English Stations in the Hill Regions of India: Their Value and Importance, with Some Statistics of Their Products and Trade. *Journal of the Statistical Society of London, 44*(3), 528–573.

Cockburn, W. (1894). Garhwal-Peculiar Ceremony. *North Indian Notes and Queries, 3*: 205–206.

Cohn, B. S. (1996). *Colonialism and Its Forms of Knowledge: The British in India*. Princeton, NJ: Princeton University Press.

Comaroff, J. & J. Comaroff. (2009). *Ethnicity, Inc*. Chicago, IL: University of Chicago Press.

Coomaraswamy, A. K. (1937). The Nature of "Folklore" and "Popular Art." *Indian Art and Letters, 11*(2), 76–84.

Cox, T. (1993). *The Badi: Prostitution as a Social Norm among an Untouchable Caste of West Nepal*. Kathmandu: Asian Ethnographer Society Press.

Crooke, W. (1896). *The Popular Religion and Folklore of Northern India* (Vol. 1). Westminster: Archibald Constable and Company.

Cumming, C. F. G. (1884). *In the Himalayas and on the Indian Plains*. London: Chatto and Windus.

Dabral, S. (1989). *Dholsagar Sangrah* [Ocean of Dhol Collection]. Dugadda, Garhwal, UP]: Veer-Gatha Prakashan.

Dalmia, V. (2006). *Poetics, Plays, and Performances: The Politics of Modern Indian Theatre*. New Delhi: Oxford University Press.

de Maaker, E. (2013). Performing the Garo Nation? Garo Wangala Dancing between Faith and Folklore. *Asian Ethnology, 72*(2), 221–240.

Dharwadker, A. B. (2005). *Theatres of Independence*. Iowa City, IA: University of Iowa Press.

Diamond, B. (2010). Native American Contemporary Music: The Women. *The World of Music, 52*(1/3), 387–414.

Dinnerstein, N. (2012). Songs, Cultural Representation and Hybridity in Ladakh. *Himalaya, 32*(1), 72–84.

Divekar, H., & R. D. Tribhuwan (2001). *Rudra Veena: An Ancient String Musical Instrument*. New Delhi: Discovery.

Dorson, R. (1968). *The British Folklorists: A History*. Chicago, IL: University of Chicago Press.

Dorson, R. (1978). Editor's Comment: We All Need the Folk. *Journal of the Folklore Institute, 15*(3): 267–269.

Edye, E. H. H. (1992–1993 [1921]). The Depressed Classes of Kumaon Hills. In A. C. Fanger, M. P. Joshi, & C. W. Brown (Eds.), *Himalaya: Past and Present* (Vol. 3, pp. 115–120). Almora: Shree Almora Book Depot.

Erndl, K. (1991). Fire and Wakefulness: The Devi Jagrata in Panjabi Hinduism. *Journal of the American Academy of Religion, 59*(2), 339–360.

Fanger, A. C. (1980). *Diachronic and Synchronic Perspectives on Kumaoni Society and Culture* (Doctoral dissertation). Syracuse University, Syracuse, NY.

Fanger, A. C. (1990). The Jagar—Spirit Possession Seance among the Rajputs and Silpakars of Kumaon. In A. C. Fanger, M. P. Joshi, & C. W. Brown (Eds.), *Himalaya: Past and Present* (Vol. 1, pp. 173–191). Almora: Shree Almora Book Depot.

Farrell, G. (1993). The Early Days of the Gramophone Industry in India: Historical, Social and Musical Perspectives. *British Journal of Ethnomusicology, 2*, 31–54.

Farrell, G. (1997). *Indian Music and the West*. Oxford: Clarendon.

Feld, S. (1996). Pygmy POP: A Genealogy of Schizophonic Mimesis. *Yearbook for Traditional Music, 28*, 1–35.

Feldman, H. (2006). *Black Rhythms of Peru: Reviving African Musical Heritage in the Black Pacific*. Middletown, CT: Wesleyan University Press.

Filene, B. (2000). *Romancing the Folk: Public Memory and American Roots Music*. Chapel Hill, NC: University of North Carolina Press.

Fiol, S. (2010). Dual Framing: Locating Authenticities in the Music Videos of Himalayan Possession Rituals. *Ethnomusicology, 54*(1), 28–53.

Fiol, S. (2011a). From Folk to Popular and Back: Assessing Feedback between Studio Recordings and Festival Dance-Songs in Uttarakhand, North India. *Asian Music, 42*(1), 24–53.

Fiol, S. (2011b). Sacred, Inferior, and Anachronous: Deconstructing Liminality among the *Baddi* of the Central Himalayas. *Ethnomusicology Forum, 19*, 191–217.

Fiol, S. (2012a). All India Radio and the Genealogies of Folk Music in Uttarakhand. *Journal of South Asian Popular Culture, 10*(3), 1–12.

Fiol, S. (2012b). Articulating Regionalism through Popular Music: The Case of *Nauchami Narayana* in the Uttarakhand Himalayas. *Journal of Asian Studies, 71*(2), 447–474.

Fiol, S. (2013a). Making Music Regional in a Delhi Studio. In G. Booth & B. Shope (Eds.), *More than Bollywood: Studies in Indian Popular Music* (pp. 179–197). New York, NY: Oxford University Press.

Fiol, S. (2013b). Of Lack and Loss: Assessing Cultural and Musical Poverty in Uttarakhand. *Yearbook for Traditional Music, 45*, 10–24.

Fiol, S. (2016). Folk Tropes: Sonic and Visual Representations of the Himalayas in Film Songs. In J. Beaster-Jones & N. Sarrazin (Eds.), *Music of Contemporary Indian Film* (pp. 133–146). New York, NY: Routledge.

Fisher, J. (1985). The Historical Development of Himalayan Anthropology. *Mountain Research and Development, 5*(1): 91–111.

Flueckiger, J. B. (1991). Genre and Community in the Folklore System of Chattisgarh. In F. J. K. Arjun Appadurai & M. A. Mills (Eds.), *Gender, Genre, and Power in South Asian Expressive Traditions* (pp. 181–200). Philadelphia, PA: University of Pennsylvania Press.

Folklore from India: A Female Mowgli Found in India. (1914). *Folklore, 27*(4): 418–419.

Foster, G. M. (1953). What Is Folk Culture? *American Anthropologist, 55*(2), 159–173.

Fox-Strangways, A. H. (1914). *The Music of Hindostan.* Oxford: Oxford University Press.

Fracchia, E. (2006). *Colonialism and Devlopment: Reinventing Tradition and Gendered Work in Kumaon, India* (master's thesis). University of Oregon, Eugene.

Fraser, J. B. (1982 [1820]). *The Himala Mountains.* Delhi: Neeraj.

Gaborieau, M. (1975). La Transe Rituelle dans l'Himalaya central: Folie, avatar, meditation. *Purusartha, 2*, 147–172.

Gairola, T. D. (1926). Folk-lore of Garhwal. *Vishva-Bharati Quarterly, 4*, 27–43.

Gairola, T. D., & E. S. Oakley. (1977 [1935]). *Himalayan Folklore: Kumaon and West Nepal* (Vol. 10). Kathmandu: Ratna Pustak Bhandar.

Galey, J.-C. (1991–1992). Hindu Kingship and Its Ritual Realm: The Garhwali Configuration. In A. C. Fanger, M. P. Joshi, & C. W. Brown (Eds.), *Himalaya: Past and Present* (Vol. 2, pp. 173–237). Almora: Shree Almora Book Depot.

Gaul, K. (2002). Traveling High and Low: Verticality, Social Position, and the Making of *Pahari* Genders. In S. Sarker [Per Worldcat] & E. N. De (Eds.), *Trans-Status Subjects: Gender in the Globalization of South and Southeast Asia* (pp. 129–146). Durham, NC: Duke University Press.

Gelbart, M. (2007). *The Invention of "Folk Music" and "Art Music": Emerging Categories from Ossian to Wagner.* Cambridge: Cambridge University Press.

Gellner, D. (1994). Priests, Healers, Mediums and Witches: The Contexts of Possession in the Kathmandu Valley, Nepal. *Man, 29*(1), 27–48.

Ghosh, M. (2004). *Folk Music of the Himalayas.* Gurgaon: Shubhi.

Gold, A. (1988.) Spirit Possession Perceived and Performed in Rural Rajasthan. *Contributions to Indian Sociology, 22*, 35–63.

Gover, C. E. (2002 [1871]). *The Folk-Songs of Southern India.* New Delhi: Rupa.

Govindrajan, R. (2013). *Beastly Intimacies: Human-Animal Relations in India's Central Himalayas* (Doctoral dissertation). Yale University, New Haven, CT.

Grandin, I. (1989). *Music and Media in Local Life.* Linkoping, Sweden: Linkoping University Press.

Grandin, I. (2005). The Soundscape of the Radio: Engineering *Modern Songs* and Superculture in Nepal. In P. Greene & T. Porcello (Eds.), *Wired for Sound* (pp. 222–244). Middletown, CT: Wesleyan University Press.

Greene, P. (1999). Sound Engineering in a Tamil Village: Playing Audio Cassettes as Devotional Performance. *Ethnomusicology, 43*(3), 459–489.

Greene, P. (2001). Authoring the Folk: The Crafting of a Rural Popular Music in South India. *Journal of Intercultural Studies, 22*(2): 161–172.

Grierson, G. (1901). An Old Kumauni Satire. *The Journal of the Royal Asiatic Society of Great Britain and Ireland, 33*(3): 475–479.

Grierson, G. (1968 [1916]). Specimens of Pahari Languages and Gujuri. *Linguistic Survey of India* (Vol. 9). Delhi: Motilal Banarsidass.

Guha, R. (2000). *The Unquiet Woods: Ecological Change and Peasant Resistance in the Himalaya.* Berkeley, CA: University of California Press.

Gupta, C. (2002.) *Sexuality, Obscenity, Community: Women, Muslims, and the Hindu Public in Colonial India.* New York: Palgrave.

Gururani, S. (2002). Forests of Pleasure and Pain: Gendered Practices of Labor and Livelihood in the Forests of the Kumaon Himalayas, India.. *Gender, Place & Culture, 9,* 229–243.

Gusain, R. (2010, January 4). Folk Song Thrives on Tiwari Sex Scandal. *India Today.*

Hagedorn, K. (2001). *Divine Utterances: The Performance of Afro-Cuban Santeria.* Washington, DC: Smithsonian Institution Press.

Hansen, K. (2014). *Grounds for Play: The Nautanki Theatre of North India.* 2nd ed. Berkeley, CA: University of California Press.

Harcourt, A. F. P. (1871). *The Himalayan Districts of Kooloo, Lahoul, and Spiti.* London: William H. Allen.

Hardgrave, R. L. (1969). *The Nadars of Tamilnad: The Political Culture of a Community in Change.* Berkeley, CA: University of California, Center for South and Southeast Asia Studies.

Harker, D. (1985). *Fakesong: The Manufacture of British "Folksong," 1700 to the Present.* Philadelphia, PA: Open University Press.

Hauser, B. (2002). From Oral Tradition to "Folk Art": Reevaluating Bengali Scroll Paintings. *Asian Folklore Studies, 61*(1), 105–122.

Heber, R. D. D. (1829). *Narrative of a Journey through the Upper Provinces of India : From Calcutta to Bombay, 1824–1825.* London: J. Murray.

Henry, E. O. (1988). *Chant the Names of God: Music and Culture in Bhojpuri-Speaking India.* San Diego, CA: San Diego State University Press.

Herzfeld, M. (2004). *Body Impolitic: Artisans and Artifice in the Global Hierarchy of Value.* Chicago, IL: University of Chicago Press.

Hiltebeitel, A. (1993). Epic Studies: Classical Hinduism in the Mahabharata and the Ramayana. *Annals of the Bhandarkar Oriental Research Institute, 74,* 1–62.

Hoerburger, F. (1970). Folk Music in the Caste System of Nepal. *International Folk Music Council Yearbook, 2,* 142–147.

Holmberg, D. (1984). Ritual Paradoxes in Nepal: Comparative Perspectives on Tamang Religion. *The Journal of Asian Studies, 43*(4): 697–722.

Holton, K. D. (2005). *Performing Folklore: Ranchos Folkloricos from Lisbon to Newark.* Bloomington, IN: Indiana University Press.

Hughes, S. P. (2002). The "Music Boom" in Tamil South India: Gramophone, Radio and the Making of Mass Culture. *Historical Journal of Film, Radio, and Television, 22*(4), 445–473.

Husain, Z. (1995). *Uttarakhand Movement: The Politics of Identity and Frustration, a Psycho-Analytical Study of the Separate State Movement, 1815–1995.* Bareilly: Prakash Book Depot.

Ibbetson, D. (1883). *Punjab District Gazeteers*. [Punjab]: Compiled and published under the authority of the Punjab government.

Impey, A. (1992). They Want Us with Salt and Onions: Women in the Zimbabwean Music Industry (Doctoral dissertation). Indiana University, Bloomington.

Jairazbhoy, N. (1977). Music in Western Rajasthan: Stability and Change. *Yearbook of the International Folk Music Council, 9*, 50–66.

Jassal, S. T. (2007). Taking Liberties in Festive Song. *Contributions to Indian Sociology, 41*(1), 5–40.

Jassal, S. T. (2012). *Unearthing Gender: Folksongs of North India*. Durham, NC: Duke University Press.

Joshi, L. D. (1929). *The Khasa Family Law in the Himalayan Districts of the United Provinces of India*. Allahabad: Government Press, United Provinces.

Joshi, L. D. (1984 [1856]). *Tribal People of the Himalayas: A Study of the Khasas*. Delhi: Mittal.

Joshi, M. C. (1990). The Khasas in the History of Uttarakhand. In A. C. Fanger, M. P. Joshi, & C. W. Brown (Eds.), *Himalaya: Past and Present* (Vol. 1, pp. 193–200). Almora: Shree Almora Book Depot.

Joshi, M. P. (1990). Kumaoni Vansavalis: Myth and Reality. In A. C. Fanger, M. P. Joshi, & C. W. Brown (Eds.), *Himalaya: Past and Present* (Vol. 1, pp. 201–244). Almora: Shree Almora Book Depot.

Joshi, M. P. (1992–1993). The Silpakaras (Artisans) of Central Himalaya: A Diachronic Study. In A. C. Fanger, M. P. Joshi, & C. W. Brown (Eds.), *Himalaya: Past and Present* (Vol. 3, pp. 301–333). Almora: Shree Almora Book Depot.

Joshi, M. P. (2011). *Sudrom ka brahmanattva: Madhya Himalayi anubhav* [The Brahmanism of Shudras: Central Himalayan Considerations]. Dehradun: Shree Yugshail Kalyan Samiti.

Joshi, P. C. (1995). *Uttarakhand: Issues and Challenges*. New Delhi: Har-Anand.

Joshi, P. C. (2000). Uttarakhand People's Artist Mohan Upreti and His Discovery of the Guru. *Mainstream*, 14–22.

Juyal, R. (2006, November 22–28). Tham Nahi Raha Aawaaz ko Rukhsat Karne ka Silsila [The Ongoing Chain of Events to Muzzle Negi's Voice]. *Samay Sakshya* (Dehradun, Uttarakhand), pp. 1, 3.

Kabir, A. J. (2005). Nipped in the Bud? Pleasures and Politics in the 1960s "Kashmir Films". *South Asian Popular Culture, 3*(2): 83–100.

Kapadia, K. (1996). Dancing the Goddess: Possession and Class in South India. *Modern Asian Studies, 30*(2), 423–445.

Kapferer, B. (1991). *Exorcism and the Aesthetics of Healing in Sri Lanka*. Oxford: Berg.

Kazmi, S. M. A. (2006, May 22). Garhwali Satire Breaks Sales Records, no Laughing Matter for Tiwari Govt. *Indian Express* (Dehradun, Uttarakhand).

Keil, C. (1978). Who Needs "the Folk"? *Journal of the Folklore Institute, 15*(3), 263–265.

Keil, C. (1987). Participatory Discrepancies and the Power of Music. *Cultural Anthropology, 2*(3): 275–283.

Kennedy, D. (1996). *The Magic Mountains: Hill Stations and the British Raj*. Los Angeles, CA: University of California Press.

Keskar, B. V. (1967). *Indian Music: Problems and Prospects*. Bombay: Popular Prakashan.

Kin of "Maoists" Plead for Justice at Golu Devta's Court. (2014, 10 May). *United News of India* (Almore, Uttarakhand).

Kinnear, M. S. (1994). *The Gramophone Company's First Indian Recordings, 1899–1908.* Bombay: Popular Prakashan.

Kippen, J. R. (2006). *Gurudev's Drumming Legacy: Music, Theory, and Nationalism in the Mrdang aur Tabla Vadanpaddhati of Gurudev Patwardhan.* Aldershot: Ashgate.

Kobayashi, E. (2003). *Hindustani Classical Music Reform Movement and the Writing of History, 1900s to 1940s* (Doctoral dissertation). University of Texas, Austin, TX.

Korom, F. (1989). Inventing Traditions: Folklore and Nationalism as Historical Process in Bengal. In M. P. Frykmane & D. Rihtman-Augustin (Eds.), *Folklore and Historical Process* (pp. 57–83). Zagreb: Institute of Folklore Research.

Korom, F. (2006). *South Asian Folklore: A Handbook.* London: Greenwood.

Krakauer, B. (2015). The Ennobling of a "Folk Tradition" and the Disempowerment of the Performers: Celebrations and Appropriations of Baul-Fakir Identity in West Bengal. *Ethnomusicology, 59*(3), 355–379.

Kumar, A. (2011). *The Making of a Small State: Populist Social Mobilisation and the Hindi Press in the Uttarakhand Movement.* Hyderabad: Orient Blackswan.

Kumar, P. (2000). *The Uttarakhand Movement: Construction of a Regional Identity.* New Delhi: Kanishka.

Lampert, V. (1982). Bartók's Choice of Theme for Folksong Arrangement: Some Lessons of the Folk-Music Sources of Bartók's Works. *Studia Musicologica Academiae Scientiarum Hungaricae, 24*(3/4), 401–409.

Landry, T. R. (2013). *When Secrecy Goes Global: Vodun, Tourism, and the Politics of Knowing in Benin, West Africa* (Doctoral dissertation). University of Illinois, Champaign-Urbana.

Leavitt, J. (1992). Cultural Holism in the Anthropology of South Asia: The Challenge of Regional Traditions. *Contributions to Indian Sociology, 26*, 3–49.

Leavitt, J. (1997). The Language of the Gods: Craft and Inspiration in Central Himalayan Ritual Discourse. In J. Leavitt (Ed.), *Poetry and Prophecy: The Anthropology of Inspiration* (pp. 129–168). Ann Arbor, MI: University of Michigan Press.

Leavitt, J. (2000). On the Complexity of Oral Tradition: A Reply to Claus Peter Zoller's Review Essay "Oral Epic Poetry in the Himalayas". *European Bulletin of Himalayan Research, 18*, 58–78.

Lecomte-Tilouine, M. (2009). The Social Dimension of Himlayan Mediumism. In M. Lecomte-Tilouine (Ed.), *Bards and Mediums* (pp. 29–54). Almora, Uttaralkand: Almora Book Depot.

Lelyveld, D. (1994). Upon the Subdominant: Administering Music on All-India Radio. *Social Text, 39*, 111–127.

Liechty, M. (2003). *Suitably Modern: Making Middle-Class Culture in a New Consumer Society.* Princeton, NJ: Princeton University Press.

Livingston, T. E. (1999). Music Revivals: Towards a General Theory. *Ethnomusicology, 43*(1), 66–85.

Lutgendorf, P. (1990). Ramayana: The Video. *The Drama Review, 34*(2), 127–176.

Lutgendorf, P. (2005). Sex in the Snow: The Himalayas as Erotic Topos in Popular Hindi Cinema. *Himalaya, 25*(1), 29–38.

Lybarger, L. (2011). Hereditary Musician Groups of Pakistani Punjab. *Journal of Punjab Studies, 18*(1–2), 97–129.

Maciszewski, A. (2001). Multiple Voices, Multiple Selves: Song Style and North Indian Women's Identity. *Asian Music, 32*(2), 1–40.

Maciszewski, A. (2006). Texts, Tunes, and Talking Heads: Discourses about Socially Marginal North Indian Musicians. *twentieth-century music, 3,* 121–144.

Mahmood, S. (2000). *The Politics of Piety.* Princeton, NJ: Princeton University Press.

Majumdar, D. N. (1960). *Himalayan Polyandry.* Bombay: Asia Publishing.

Majumdar, D. N. (Ed.). (1946). *Snowballs of Garhwal.* Lucknow: The Universal Publishers.

Majumdar, K. (1996). *Healing through the Spirits: Embodiment, Experience and Narratives of Spirit Possession among the Jaunsaris of Uttarakhand, India* (Doctoral dissertation). Michigan State University, East Lansing.

Malik, A. (2009). Dancing the Body of God: Rituals of Embodiment from the Central Himalayas. *Signs, 6*(1), 80–96.

Mankekar, P. (2002). Epic Contests: Television and Religious Identity in India. In L. A.-L. Faye Ginsburg & B. Larkin (Eds.), *Media Worlds: Anthropology on New Terrain* (pp. 134–151). Berkeley, CA: University of California Press.

Mann, K. (1996). *Tribal Women on the Threshold of Twenty-First Century.* New Delhi: M. D. Publications.

Manuel, P. (1993). *Cassette Culture: Popular Music and Technology in North India.* Chicago, IL: University of Chicago Press.

Manuel, P. (2014). The Regional North Indian Popular Music Industry in 2014: From Cassette Culture to Cyberculture. *Popular Music, 33*(3), 389–412.

Manuel, P. (2015). The Intermediary Sphere in North Indian Music Culture: Between and Beyond "Folk" and "Classical." *Ethnomusicology, 59*(1), 82–115.

Marcus, S. L. (1995). On Cassette Rather Than Live: Religious Music in India Today. In S. Wadley & L. Babb (Eds.), *Media and the Transformation of Religion in South Asia* (pp. 167–185). Philadelphia, PA: University of Pennsylvania Press.

Marriott, M. (1976). Hindu Transactions: Diversity without Dualism. In B. Kapferer (Ed.), *Transaction and Meaning: Directions in the Anthropology of Exchange and Symbolic Behavior* (pp. 109–142). Philadelphia, PA: Institute for the Study of Human Issues.

Maskiell, M. (1999). Embroidering the Past: Phulkari Textiles and Gendered Work as "Tradition" and "Heritage" in Colonial and Contemporary Punjab. *The Journal of Asian Studies, 58*(2), 361–388.

Mason, K. (2014). On Nightingales and Moonlight: Songcrafting Femininity in Malluwood. In G. Booth (Ed.), *More than Bollywood: Studies in Indian Popular Music* (pp. 75–93). New York, NY: Oxford University Press.

Mawdsley, E. (2002). Redrawing the Body Politic: Federalism, Regionalism and the Creation of New States in India. *Commonwealth and Comparative Politics, 40*(3), 34–54.

Mazumdar, L. (1998). *Sacred Confluences: Worship, History, and Politics of Change in a Himalayan Village* (Doctoral dissertation). University of Pittsburgh, Pittsburgh, PA.

McLucas, A. D. (1994). The Multi-Layered Concept of "Folk Song" in American Music: The Case of Jean Ritchie's "The Two Sisters." In R. C. Pian, B. Yung, & J. S. C. Lam (Eds.), *Themes and Variations: Writing on Music in Honor of Rulan Chao Pian* (pp. 212–230). Cambridge, MA: Harvard University Press.

Meintjes, L. (2003). *Sound of Africa! Making Music Zulu in a South African Studio*. Durham, NC: Duke University Press.

Meissner, K. (1985). *Malushahi and Rajula: A Ballad from Kumaun (India) as Sung by Gopi Das*. Wiesbaden: Harrassowitz.

Mendoza, Z. S. (2008). *Creating Our Own: Folklore, Performance, and Identity in Cuzco, Peru*. Durham, NC: Duke University Press.

Merchant, V. V. (2003). Siva: Nataraja—The Lord of Dance, Drama and Music; Siva as Transformer—Liberator. *International Journal of Humanities and Peace, 19*, 3–5.

Meyer, B., & A. Moors (Eds.). (2006). *Religion, Media and the Public Sphere*. Bloomington, IN: Indiana University Press.

Miller, K. H. (2010). *Segregating Sound: Inventing Folk and Pop Music in the Age of Jim Crow*. Durham, NC: Duke University Press.

Moller, J. (2003). Insiders and Outsiders: Community and Identity in Kumaon, North India. In M. Lecomte-Tilouine & P. Dollfus (Eds.), *Ethnic Revival and Religious Turmoil: Identities and Representations in the Himalayas* (pp. 240–276). New Delhi: Oxford University Press.

Monier-Williams, S. M. (2006). *A Sanskrit-English Dictionary*. New Delhi: Nataraj.

Moorcroft, W., & G. Trebeck. (1841). *Travels in the Himalayan Provinces of Hindustan and the Punjab*. Vol. 1. London: John Murray.

Moors, B. M., & A. Moors (Eds.). (2006). *Religion, Media and the Public Sphere*. Bloomington, IN: Indiana University Press.

Morcom, A. (2013). *Illicit Worlds of Indian Dance: Cultures of Exclusion*. New York, NY: Oxford University Press.

Mountaineer. (1860). *A Summer Ramble in the Himalayas*. London: Hurst and Blackett.

Naga, S. W. (n.d.). Facing Challenges in the Music Scenario of Nagaland: How Marketable Is Our Music? http://www.nagamusiconline.com, accessed March 30, 2009.

Naithani, S. (2006a). How about Some Artistic Recognition? Folk Performers in Post-Independence India. In L. N. Kadekar & S. R. Charsely (Eds.), *Performers and Their Arts: Folk, Popular and Classical Genres in a Changing India* (pp. 111–122). London: Routledge.

Naithani, S. (2006b). *In Quest of Indian Folktales: Pandit Ram Gharib Chaube and William Crooke*. Bloomington, IN: Indiana University Press.

Narayan, K. (1993). Banana Republics and V. I. Degrees: Rethinking Indian Folklore in a Postcolonial World. *Asian Folklore Studies, 52*(1), 177–204.

Narayan, K. (1997). Singing from Separation: Women's Voices in and about Kangra Folksongs. *Oral Tradition, 12*(1), 23–53.

Nautiyal, K., S. D. Kandpal, & D. R. Purohit. (2003). Chakravyuh: Garhwali Lok-Natya [Chakravyuh: Garhwali Folk Drama] (script).

Nautiyal, S. (1981). *Garhwal ke Lok-Nritya Geet* [Folk-Dance Songs of Garhwal]. Allahabad: Hindi Sahitya Sammelan.

Nautiyal, S. (1991). *Garhwal ka Lok Sangit ev. Vadhya* [Folk Music and Instruments of Garhwal]. Lucknow: Sulabh Prakashan.

Navani, K., & G. Kughshal. (2000). *Akshat*. Dehradun: Winsar.

Negi, N. S. (1999). *Ganyun ki Ganga Syanyun ka Samodar* [River of Motives, Ocean of Attempts]. Dehradun: Winsar.

Negi, N. S. (2002). *Mutta Botiki Rakh: Uttarakhand ke Suprasiddha Kavi-Gayak ke Kuch Geet* [Keep the Fist Clenched: Songs of Uttarakhand's Famous Poet-Singer]. Nainital: Pahar.

Negi, N. S. (2009). *Kuchkandi* [Flower Basket]. Dehradun: Winsar.

Negi, S. S., & J. S. Khatri. (2005). British Garhwal Main Shilpkar Andolan [The Shilpkar Movement in British Garhwal]. *Journal of the Meerut University History Alumni, 5,* 364–371.

Neuman, D., S. Chaudhuri, & K. Kothari. (2006). *Bards, Ballads and Boundaries: An Ethnographic Atlas of Music Traditions in West Rajasthan.* Oxford: Seagull.

Nicholls, D. G. (2000). *Conjuring the Folk: Forms of Modernity in African America.* Ann Arbor, MI: University of Michigan Press.

Nowak, F. (2014). Challenging Opportunities: When Indian Regional Music Gets Online. *First Monday, 19*(10). Retrieved from http://firstmonday.org/ojs/index.php/fm/article/view/5547.

Oakes, T. (2000). China's Provincial Identities: Reviving Regionalism and Reinventing "Chineseness." *Journal of Asian Studies, 59*(3), 667–692.

Oakley, E. S. (1990 [1905]). *Holy Himalaya.* Nainital: Gyanodaya Prakashan.

Oddie, G. A. (1995). *Popular Religion, Elites, and Reforms: Hook-Swinging and Its Prohibition in Colonial India, 1800–1894.* New Delhi: Manohar.

Ortner, S. (1972). Is Female to Male as Nature Is to Culture? *Feminist Studies, 1*(2), 5–31.

Ortner, S. (1978). *The Sherpas through Their Rituals.* Cambridge, UK: Cambridge University Press.

Osella, F. & C. Osella. (2000). *Social Mobility in Kerala: Modernity and Identity in Conflict.* London: Pluto.

Paige, A. (2009). Acoustic Entanglements: Negotiating Folk Music in Naiyanti Melam Performance. *Indian Folklore Research Journal, 6*(9), 45–66.

Pande, P. N. (1996). *Drudgery of the Hill Women.* New Delhi: Indus.

Pande, T. (1965). The Concept of Folklore: Its Befitting Indian Synonyms. *Folklore,* 7–13.

Pandey, S. P. (2012). *Incredible North India: Folk Cultural Traditions.* New Delhi: Serials Publications.

Pangtey, K. S. (2006 [1949]). *Lonely Furrows of the Borderland.* Nainital: Pahar.

Parlby, F. P., I. Ghose, & S. Mills. (2001 [1850]). *Wanderings of a Pilgrim in Search of the Picturesque.* Manchester, UK: Manchester University Press.

Parmar, S. (1977). *Folk Music and Mass Media.* New Delhi: Communication Publications.

Pathak, S. (1987). *Uttarakhand mein kuli begara pratha: Eka soshaka pratha aura usake viruddha hue jana-andolana ka adhyayana* [The Practice of Kuli Begar in Uttarakhand: A Study of an Exploitative Practice and Its Opposition through a People's Movement]. New Delhi: Radhakrishna.

Pathak, S., & H. S. Bhakuni (1998). *Sarafarosi ki tamanna: Uttarakhand mein svadhinata sangrama ka drishya itihaas* [The Desire for Sacrifice: The Independence Movement from a Historical Perspective]. Nainital: Kumaun Mandala.

Petshali, J. K. (2002). *Uttarancala ke loka vadya* [Folk Instruments of Uttaranchal]. New Delhi: Takshasila Prakasana.

Picard, M. (1990). "Cultural Tourism" in Bali: Cultural Performances as Tourist Attraction. *Indonesia, 49,* 37–74.

Polit, K. (2010). Staging Ritual Heritage: How Rituals Become Theatre in Uttarakhand, India. In C. Brosius & U. Hüsken (Eds.), *Ritual Matters: Dynamic Dimensions in Practice* (pp. 29–48). London: Routledge.

Polit, K. (2012). *Women of Honour: Gender and Agency among Dalit Women in the Central Himalayas*. New Delhi: Orient Blackswan.

Porcello, T. (1996). *Sonic Artistry: Music, Discourse and Technology in the Sound Recording Studio* (Doctoral dissertation). University of Texas, Austin.

Powell, J. H. (1914). "Hook-Swinging" in India: A Description of the Ceremony, and an Enquiry into Its Origin and Significance. *Folklore, 25*(2), 147–197.

Powers, H. S. (1992). Reinterpretations of Tradition in Hindustani Music: Omkarnath Thakur Contra Vishnu Narayan Bhatkhande. In J. Katz (Ed.), *The Traditional Indian Theory and Practice of Music and Dance* (pp. 9–51). New York, NY: Brill.

Primdahl, H. (1993). *Central Himalayan Folklore: Folk Songs in the Rituals of the Life-cycle*. Copenhagen: Nordic Institute of Asian Studies.

Purohit, D. R. (2004). Satire and Civil Society in the Mask Theatre of Garhwal. In M. D. Muthukumaraswamy (Ed.), *Folk, Public Society and Civil Society* (pp. 177–185). Delhi: Indira Gandhi National Center for the Arts.

Qureshi, R. B. (1999). His Master's Voice? Exploring Qawwali and "Gramophone Culture" in South Asia. *Popular Music, 18*(1), 63–98.

Rahaim, M. (2011). That Ban(e) of Indian Music: Hearing Politics in the Harmonium. *The Journal of Asian Studies, 70*(3): 657–682.

Raheja, G. G. (1996). Caste, Colonialism, and the Speech of the Colonized: Entextualization and Disciplinary Control in India. *American Ethnologist, 23*(3), 494–513.

Raheja, G. G. (1999). The Illusion of Consent: Language, Caste, and Colonial Rule in India. In P. Pels & O. Salemink (Eds.), *Colonial Subjects: Essays on the Practical History of Anthropology* (pp. 117–152). Ann Arbor, MI: University of Michigan Press.

Raheja, G. G., & A. G. Gold (1994). *Listen to the Heron's Words: Reimagining Gender and Kinship in North India*. Berkeley, CA: University of California Press.

Ramanujan, A. K. (1993). Who Needs Folklore? The Relevance of Oral Traditions to South Asian Studies. *Manushi, 532–552.*

Ramaswamy, V. (1994). Women and the Domestic in Tamil Folk Songs. *Man in India, 74*(1), 21–37.

Ramesh, R. (2006, April 4). A Tale of Two Indias. *The Guardian*. Retrieved from http://www.theguardian.com/world/2006/apr/05/india.randeepramesh2.

Rangan, H. (2000). *Of Myths and Movements: Rewriting Chipko into Himalayan History*. London: Verso.

Rao, A. (2009). *The Caste Question: Dalits and the Politics of Modern India*. Berkeley, CA: University of California Press.

Rao, B. (1992–1993). Spirit Possession in the Social Context: Gender and Social Order in Tehri Garhwal. In A. C. Fanger, M. P. Joshi, & C. W. Brown (Eds.), *Himalaya: Past and Present* (Vol. 3, pp. 181–214). Almora: Shree Almora Book Depot.

Rathore, D. (2016, October 8). Uttarakhand Shamed: Dalit Man Killed for Arguing with Upper-Caste School Teacher. *India Today* (Dehradun). Retrieved from http://indiatoday .intoday.in/story/uttarakhand-dalit-upper-caste-school-teacher-flour-mill/1/783437 .html.

Reck, D. (1972). The Music of Matha "Chhau." *Asian Music, 3*(2), 8–14.

Redfield, R. (1947). The Folk Society. *American Journal of Sociology, 52*(4), 293–308.

Redfield, R. (1955). The Social Organization of Tradition. *The Far Eastern Quarterly, 15*(1), 13–21.

Rios, F. (2012). The Andean Conjunto, Bolivian Sikureada and the Folkloric Musical Representation Continuum. *Ethnomusicology Forum, 21*(1), 5–29.

Roche, D. (2001). The Dhak: Devi Amba's Hourglass Drum in Tribal Southern Rajasthan, India. *Asian Music, 32*(1), 59–100.

Rohter, L. (2012, April 11). U.S. Visa Rules Deprive Stages of Performers. *New York Times*. Retrieved from http://www.nytimes.com/2012/04/11/arts/us-visa-rules-frustrate-foreign-performers.html?pagewanted=all.

Rose, H. A. (1894). Bihundah Fairs—Kulu. *North Indian Notes and Queries, 4*, 55–57.

Rouse, W. H. D. (1894). Folklore Items from *North Indian Notes and Queries, Vol. 3*. *Folklore, 5*(3), 344–351.

Roy, S. (2007). *Beyond Belief: India and the Politics of Postcolonial Nationalism*. Durham, NC: Duke University Press.

Russell, R. V. (1975 [1916]). *Tribes and Castes of the Central Provinces of India* (Vols. 1–4). Delhi: Cosmo.

Saklani, A. (1987). *The History of a Himalayan Princely State: Change, Conflicts, and Awakening*. Delhi: Durga.

Saklani, D. P. (1998). *Ancient Communities of the Himalaya*. New Delhi: Indus.

Saklani, S. P. (2001). *Uttarakhand ki vibhutiyam* [Great Personalities of Uttarakhand]. L. Samskarana (Ed.). Rudrapura: Uttara Prakasana.

Sanwal, R. D. (1976). *Social Stratification in Kumaon*. Delhi: Oxford University Press.

Sarkar, B. K. (1917). *The Folk-Element in Hindu Culture: A Contribution to Socio-Religious Studies in Hindu Folk-Institutions*. London: Longmans.

Sax, W. S. (1991). *Mountain Goddess: Gender and Politics in a Himalayan Pilgrimage*. New York, NY: Oxford University Press.

Sax, W. S. (2009). *God of Justice: Ritual Healing and Social Justice in the Central Himalayas*. Oxford: Oxford University Press.

Sax, W. S. (2014). Ritual Healing and Mental Health in India. *Transcultural Psychiatry, 51*(6), 829–849.

Scales, C. (2004). *Powwow Music and the Aboriginal Recording Industry on the Northern Plains: Media, Technology, and Native American Music in the Late Twentieth Century* (Doctoral dissertation). University of Illinois, Urbana-Champaign.

Scales, C. (2012). *Recording Culture: Powwow Music and the Aboriginal Recording Industry*. Durham, NC: Duke University Press.

Schafer, R. M. (1977). *The Tuning of the World*. Chicago, IL: Knopf.

Schofield, K. B. (2010). Reviving the Golden Age Again: "Classicization," Hindustani Music, and the Mughals. *Ethnomusicology, 54*(3): 484–517.

Schultz, A. 2013. *Singing a Hindu Nation: Marathi Devotional Performance and Nationalism*. New York, NY: Oxford University Press.

Sebring, J. (1972). The Formation of New Castes: A Probable Case from North India. *American Anthropologist, 74*(3): 587–600.

Sharma, N. (2015, January 22). Govt to Forge Cultural Identity of Uttarakhand. *The Tribune* (Dehradun). Retrieved from http://www.tribuneindia.com/news/uttarakhand/governance/govt-to-forge-cultural-identity-of-uttarakhand/33254.html.

Shay, A. (1999). Parallel Traditions: State Folk Dance Ensembles and Folk Dance in "The Field". *Dance Research Journal, 31*(1): 29–56.

Sherinian, Z. (2014). *Tamil Folk Music as Dalit Liberation Theology*. Bloomington, IN: Indiana University Press.

Shukla, H. K., & D. R. Purohit. (2012). Theory and Practice of Beda Theatre in Uttarakhand, India. *Language in India, 12*(5): 120–128.

Singer, M. (1972). *When a Great Tradition Modernizes: An Anthropological Approach to Indian Civilization*: New York, NY: Praeger.

Sinha, P. (1970). Folk-Classical Continuum in Indian Music, I–III. *Folklore,* 355–373.

Sinha, V. (2006). Problematizing Received Categories: Revisiting "Folk Hinduism" and "Sanskritization." *Current Sociology, 54*(1), 98–111.

Smith, F. M. (2006). *The Self Possessed: Deity and Spirit Possession in South Asian Literature and Civilization*. New York, NY: Columbia University Press.

Solis, T. (Ed.). (2004). *Performing Ethnomusicology: Teaching and Representation in World Music Ensembles*. Berkeley, CA: University of California Press.

Soneji, D. (2012). *Unfinished Gestures: Devadasis, Memory, and Modernity in South Asia*. Chicago, IL: University of Chicago Press.

Sontheimer, G. D. (1989). Hinduism: The Five Components and Their Interaction. In G. D. Sontheimer & H. Kulke (Eds.), *Hinduism Reconsidered* (pp. 197–213), no. 24. Delhi: Manohar.

Sontheimer, G. D. (1995). The Erosion of Folk Religion in Modern India: Some Points for Deliberation. In V. Dalmia & H. von Stietencron (Eds.), *Representing Hinduism: The Construction of Religious Traditions and National Identity* (pp. 389–398). New Delhi: Sage.

Srinivas, M. N. (1967). The Cohesive Role of Sanskritization. In P. Mason (Ed.), *India and Ceylon: Unity and Diversity*, 67–82. New York, NY: Oxford University Press for the Institute of Race Relations.

Srinivas, M. N. (1989). *The Cohesive Role of Sanskritization and Other Essays*. Delhi: Oxford University Press.

Srivastava, I. (1991). Woman as Portrayed in Women's Folk Songs of North India. *Asian Folklore Studies, 50,* 269–310.

Stanyek, J., & B. Piekut (2014). Deadness: Technologies of the Intermundane. *The Drama Review, 54*(1), 14–38

Strachey, R. (1851). On the Physical Geography of the Provinces of Kumaon and Garhwal in the Himalaya Mountains, and of the Adjoining Parts of Tibet. *Journal of the Royal Geographical Society of London, 21:* 57–85.

Subramanian, L. (2006). *From the Tanjore Court to the Madras Music Academy: A Social History of Music in South India*. New York, NY: Oxford University Press.

Taylor, M. (2011). Village Deity and Sacred Text: Power Relations and Cultural Synthesis at an Oral Performance of the "Bhagavatapurana" in a Garhwal Community. *Asian Ethnology, 70*(2), 197–221.

Tewari, L. G. (1974). *Folk Music of India: Uttar Pradesh*. Middletown, CT: L. G. Tewari.

Thapar, R. (1996). The Tyranny of Labels. *Social Scientist, 24*(9–10): 3–23.

Thompson, G. R. (1993). The Barots of Gujarati-Speaking Western India: Musicianship and Caste Identity. *Asian Music, 24*(1): 1–17.

Tingey, C. (1994). Auspicious Music in a Changing Society: The Damai Musicians of Nepal. *SOAS Musicology Series, 2*. London: School of Oriental and African Studies, University of London.

Toyama, K. (2012, February 20). The Two Indias: Astounding Poverty in the Backyard of Amazing Growth. *Atlantic Monthly*. Retrieved from http://www.theatlantic.com/international/archive/2012/02/the-two-indias-astounding-poverty-in-the-backyard-of-amazing-growth/253340/.

Traill, G. W. (1991–1992 [1828]). Statistical Sketch of Kamaon. In A. C. Fanger, M. P. Joshi, & C. W. Brown (Eds.), *Himalaya: Past and Present* (Vol. 2, pp. 1–97). Almora: Shree Almora Book Depot.

Tripathy, R. (2012). Music Mania in Small-town Bihar: Emergence of Verncular Identities. *Economic and Political Weekly, 47*(22), 58–66.

Tucker, Joshua. (2013). Producing the Andean Voice: Popular Music, Folkloric Performance, and the Possessive Investment in Indigeneity. *Revista de Música Latinoamericana, 34*(1), 31–70.

Turino, T. (1999). Signs of Imagination, Identity, and Experience: A Peircian Semiotic Theory for Music. *Ethnomusicology, 43*(2), 221–255.

Turino, T. (2000). *Nationalists, Cosmopolitans, and Popular Music in Zimbabwe*. Chicago, IL: University of Chicago Press.

Turino, T. (2003). Are We Global Yet? Globalist Discourse, Cultural Formations and the Study of Zimbabwean Popular Music. *British Journal of Ethnomusicology, 12*(2): 51–79.

Turino, T. (2008). *Music as Social Life*. Chicago, IL: University of Chicago Press.

Tyagi, S. (1993). *Counternarrative Strategies: An Analysis of Women's Folk Songs from Northern India* (Doctoral dissertation). Brandeis University, Waltham, MA.

Upadhyaya, K. D. (1954). A General Survey of Folklore Activities in India. *Midwest Folklore, 4*(4), 201–212.

Upreti, G. D. (2003 [1894]). *Proverbs and Folklore of Kumaun and Garhwal*. Delhi: Indira Gandhi National Centre for the Arts.

Upreti, H. C. (1981). *Social Organization of a Migrant Group: A Sociological Study of Hill Migrants from Kumaon Region in the City of Jaipur*. Bombay: Himalaya.

Upreti, K. L. (1990). Kumaoni Devi-Devtaon se sambandhit lok gathae: Jaagar [Folk Ballads Concerning Kumaoni Gods and Godesses: Jagar]. *Uttarakhand, 1*(4), 30–38.

Upreti, M. (1959). Folk-Dances of Kumaon and Garhwal. *Indian Folklore, 2*(4), 308–321.

Upreti, M. (1969). Songs of Kumaon. *Sangeet Natak, 12*, n.p.

Upreti, M. (2001). Rajula-Malushahi: The Oral Epic (Ballad) of Kumaon. In M. Kaushal (Ed.), *Chanted Narratives: The Living "Katha-Vachana" Tradition* (pp. 197–203). New Delhi: Indira Gandhi National Centre for the Arts.

Van de Port, M. (2006). Visualizing the Sacred. *American Ethnologist, 33*(3), 444–461.

Van der Linden, B. (2013). *Music and Empire in Britain and India: Identity, Internationalism, and Cross-Cultural Communication*. New York, NY: Palgrave MacMillan.

Varma, A. (1997). *The Embroidered Word: Using Traditional Songs to Educate Women in India* (Doctoral dissertation). McGill University, Montreal.

Verma, V. (1987). *The Living Music of Rajasthan: A Census of India Monograph.* New Delhi: Office of the Registrar General.

Vidyarthi, L. P. (1973). Folklore Researches in India. In L. P. Vidyarthi (Ed.), *Essays in Indian Folklore* (pp. 1–13). Calcutta: Indian Publishers.

Viyogi, N., & N. A. Ansari. (2010). *History of the Later Harappans and Shilpkara Movement.* Delhi: Kalpaz.

Wadley, S. (1976). The Spirit "Rides" or the Spirit "Comes": Possession in a North Indian Village. In S. Wadley (Ed.), *Essays on North Indian Folk Traditions* (pp. 1–21). New Delhi: D. C. Publishers.

Wadley, S., & L. Babb (Eds.). (1995). *Media and the Transformation of Religion in South Asia.* Philadelphia, PA: University of Pennsylvania Press.

Walker, M. (2014). *India's Kathak Dance in Historical Perspective.* SOAS Musicology Series. Ashgate: Ashgate University Press.

Walton, H. G. (1989 [1910]). *Gazeteer of Garhwal Himalaya* (Vol. 36). Dehradun: Natraj.

Weber, M. (1967). *The Religion of India.* (H. H. Gerth & D. Martindale, Trans. and Eds.). London: Collier-Macmillan.

Weidman, A. (2003). Gender and the Politics of Voice: Colonial Modernity and Classical Music in South India. *Cultural Anthropology, 18*(2): 194–232.

Weidman, A. (2006). *Singing the Classical, Voicing the Modern: The Postcolonial Politics of Music in South India.* Durham, NC: Duke University Press.

Wigen, K. (1999). Culture, Power, and Place: The New Landscapes of East Asian Regionalism. *The American Historical Review, 104*(4), 1183–1201.

Williams, G. R. C. (1992 [1874]). *Memoir of Dehra Doon.* Dehradun: Natraj.

Wiora, W. (1971). Reflections on the Problem: How Old Is the Concept Folksong? *Yearbook of the International Folk Music Council, 3*: 23–33.

Wolf, R. K. (2001). Three Perspectives on Music and the Idea of Tribe in India. *Asian Music, 32*(1): 5–34.

Wolf, R. K. (2014). *The Voice in the Drum: Music, Language and Emotion in Islamicate South Asia.* Urbana, IL: University of Illinois Press.

Woodruff, P. (1947). *The Wild Sweet Witch.* London: Jonathan Cape.

Zoller, C. P. (1985). Mandan in Delhi. *Mundus, 24*: 150–173.

Zoller, C. P. (2001). On the Relationship between Folk and Classical Traditions in South Asia. *European Bulletin of Himalayan Research, 20–21,* 77–104.

Index

STEFAN FIOL is an associate professor of ethnomusicology at the University of Cincinnati.

FOLKLORE STUDIES
IN A MULTICULTURAL
WORLD

The Amazing Crawfish Boat
    John Laudun
    (University Press of Mississippi)
Building New Banjos for an Old-Time World
    Richard Jones-Bamman
    (University of Illinois Press)
City of Neighborhoods: Memory, Folklore, and Ethnic Place in Boston
    Anthony Bak Buccitelli
    (University of Wisconsin Press)
Daisy Turner's Kin: An African American Family Saga
    Jane C. Beck
    (University of Illinois Press)
If You Don't Laugh You'll Cry: The Occupational Humor of White Wisconsin Prison Workers
    Claire Schmidt
    (University of Wisconsin Press)
Improvised Adolescence: Somali Bantu Teenage Refugees in America
    Sandra Grady
    (University of Wisconsin Press)
The Jumbies' Playing Ground: Old World Influence on Afro-Creole Masquerades in the Eastern Caribbean
    Robert Wyndham Nicholls
    (University Press of Mississippi)
The Last Laugh: Folk Humor, Celebrity Culture, and Mass-Mediated Disasters in the Digital Age
    Trevor J. Blank
    (University of Wisconsin Press)
The Painted Screens of Baltimore: An Urban Folk Art Revealed
    Elaine Eff
    (University Press of Mississippi)
Recasting Folk in the Himalayas: Indian Music, Media, and Social Mobility
    Stefan Fiol
    (University of Illinois Press)
Squeeze This! A Cultural History of the Accordion in American
    Marion Jacobson
    (University of Illinois Press)
Stable Views: Stories and Voices from the Thoroughbred Racetrack
    Ellen E. McHale
    (University Press of Mississippi)
Storytelling in Siberia: The Olonkho Epic in a Changing World
    Robin P. Harris
    (University of Illinois Press)

Ukrainian Otherlands: Diaspora, Homeland, and Folk Imagination in the Twentieth Century
Natalia Khanenko-Friesen
(University Press of Mississippi)
A Vulgar Art: A New Approach to Stand-Up Comedy
Ian Brodie
(University Press of Mississippi)

The University of Illinois Press
is a founding member of the
Association of American University Presses.

University of Illinois Press
1325 South Oak Street
Champaign, IL 61820-6903
www.press.uillinois.edu